ALL MY SHOWS ARE GREAT

All My Shows Are Great

THE LIFE OF LEW GRADE

Lewis Chester

First published in Great Britain
2010 by Aurum Press Ltd,
7 Greenland Street
London NW1 0ND
www.aurumpress.co.uk

A catalogue record for this book is available from
the British Library.

ISBN 978 1 84513 508 9

10 9 8 7 6 5 4 3 2 1

2014 1013 2012 2011 2010

Typeset in Garamond by SX Composing DTP, Rayleigh, Essex
Printed in Great Britain by Clays Ltd, St Ives plc

In memory of Elaine Greene and Reuben Ainsztein

Contents

Prologue

IT IS HARD TO IMAGINE, little more than a decade after his death, what Lew Grade would make of the contemporary media scene – with his beloved Independent Television (ITV) staggering on the ropes and his old, heavy-footed opponent, the British Broadcasting Corporation (BBC), punching above its light entertainment weight with, of all things, one of his very own trademark enterprises – a popular dance show. And, just to round things off, with his favourite nephew, Michael, as ITV's erstwhile executive chairman, seemingly unable to arrest the channel's decline. Well, it hardly bears thinking of.

As Britain's 'Mr Showbusiness' for a quarter of a century, Lew Grade shaped the nation's majority viewing habits through ITV and made a fortune through export sales of its programmes, before proceeding to lose another by going into movies. Still, it was difficult, in his case, to perceive any distinction between success and failure. A professional hoofer long before he donned a business suit, he was always a firm believer in keeping his sunny side up. So while Lew Grade would be distressed by the current state of ITV, it's also reasonable to conclude that his response to it would be an upbeat wisecrack, coupled most likely with a crowd-pleasing twirl designed to put *Strictly Come Dancing* utterly to shame.

No other media mogul has ever quite matched Lew Grade's capacity for smiling at grief. As plain Lew, later Sir Lew and ultimately Lord Grade of Elstree, he brought an exuberance to the making – and losing – of money and reputation that has rarely been surpassed.

When his most ambitious movie, *Raise the Titanic*, went sailing a disastrous £20 million over its original budget, Lew lightened the mood with, 'It would have been cheaper to lower the Atlantic.'[1] Later, in more analytic vein, he elaborated, 'You learn all the time in the film business. For example, you learn never to make a film using a model of ship which is bigger than any tank in the world.'[2]

He was a small man – a fraction over five foot six in his socks – who chomped and puffed his way through three yards of cigar a day in what would now be implacably non-smoking environments. It was said that on one occasion a short actor in a brown suit walked into his office and Lew absent-mindedly picked him up and lit him.

A workaholic, he habitually invited reporters to interview him in his office at 5.30 in the morning. Most found it a life-enhancing experience despite the health hazard posed by the first billowing Montecristo of the day. They came away with notebooks brimming with useful one-liners, and the feeling that they themselves were very funny fellows. Like a Jewish Falstaff, Lew was not only witty in himself but inspired wit in those he encountered. His unusual blend of humility and colourful bombast made him someone who people just loved to do business deals with, though many deemed it wise to recount their fingers after the clinching handshake.

Friends of the tycoon vied to top each other's stories of Lew's life and times. Not all of those stories were strictly true, but most were highly illustrative. Many were retold by Lew himself even when they might be construed as painting him in a less than heroic light. In an article charting his rise to international fame, *Time* magazine said, 'There are three things every Englishman seems to have, a pet, an umbrella, and a Lew Grade story.'[3] Some, by way of introduction, merit recounting here.

Chiefly famous for his sagacious advice to a child seeking guidance on what two and two made – 'Buying or selling?'[4] asked Lew – yet he could admit to not always getting the numbers right himself.

During his early business career as a theatrical agent, he went backstage at the Finsbury Park Empire to compliment a juggling act he particularly liked, and give them the big spiel. 'Fantastic, great, terrific. How much are you getting?' he asked. 'What! Only £25 a week? You're mad. I can get you £40 a week. Who's your agent?'

'You are, Mr Grade.'[5]

Lew's relationship with his less ebullient brother Leslie, his partner in the agency business, often featured in the folklore. The story is told of the time when lunching at Isow's restaurant together, Leslie jumped to his feet in a state of panic, crying out: 'Oh my God, Lew, I've just remembered something terrible. I've left the office safe unlocked.'

'Siddown, siddown,' said Lew, all reassurance. 'There's nothing to worry about. We're both here.'[6]

On another occasion, Lew was said to have experienced an acute problem of conscience when one of his clients inadvertently handed him two £5 notes instead of one in payment of his commission. Asked if he had resisted the temptation to trouser the lot, Lew stoutly responded: 'I decided honesty was the best policy. So I gave the extra fiver to Leslie.'[7] The trouble with the agency business, Lew always complained, was that 'the clients got to keep 90 per cent of my earnings'.[8]

Later on, as the double-digit deals escalated into the thousands, Lew indulged a taste for conspicuous consumption, albeit not quite so rapidly as his other brother, Bernard (later Lord Delfont of Stepney). Bernard, who was by now a leading impresario in the West End's theatreland, had acquired a Rolls-Royce with its own telephone installed. Lew, not happy at being left behind in the sibling rivalry stakes, acquired one too. He made his first call to brother Bernard's Rolls to indicate his achievement of parity, but found himself talking to the chauffeur who, after a momentary pause, came back with, 'Can you hold? Mr Delfont is on the other phone.'[9]

More often though, Lew was credited with the last word. In the early days of commercial television when his company, Associated Television (ATV), was criticised for exhibiting less than high seriousness, he found himself seated at a dinner beside a minister for education. At the time it was suggested that Lew's notion of television news was that it should ideally be presented by a line of long-legged showgirls holding up the words. Eager to dispel this impression, Lew asked the minister if he had seen ATV's recent contribution to culture – a show which featured four politicians talking about education.

'You can't call that culture,' said the minister.

'Maybe not,' countered Lew, 'but you can't say it's entertainment.'[10]

At loggerheads with Franco Zeffirelli over the casting of a suitable Jesus for the television epic *Jesus of Nazareth*, Lew broke the Italian director's resistance by brandishing his cigar and offering himself as the only feasible compromise candidate for the title role.

Lew's production of the Biblical blockbuster had some effect on his range of cultural reference. 'Cast your bread upon the waters,' he told an audience of rapt employees at a staff lunch, 'and it will come back to you as smoked salmon sandwiches.'[11] Nevertheless, he always preserved a man-of-the-people philistinism in the presence of what is defined as high culture.

'How's the Shakespeare coming along?' he enquired of Laurence Olivier on the day the great actor was appearing in a TV extract from the play, *The Master Builder*. Olivier gently explained that it was not Shakespeare, but Ibsen. 'Ah, well,' said an unfazed Lew, 'it's all costume, isn't it?'[12]

On the other hand, when TV's regulatory authorities insisted on viewers getting a diet of more highbrow entertainment, Lew bravely blew its horn. Of ATV's *Golden Hour*, a noted spectacular with classical pretensions, Lew was quoted as saying, 'Culture? I tell you this is the greatest thing that's ever happened in Culture. We have everybody: Callas, Picasso, Barenboim, Stradivarius . . .'[13]

Employees who on occasion fell foul of him were always deeply impressed by the delayed-action quality of his rebukes, which came wrapped heavily disguised in fulsome expressions of comradely warmth. They had a saying at ATV: 'You don't know you've broken a leg, until you reach the end of Lew's carpet.'[14]

But he also had the capacity to be direct. Ned Sherrin recalled a time when one of his favoured presenters was hauled up before the ATV boss to defend himself against a charge of anti-Semitism. 'Mr Grade,' pleaded the accused, 'I'm Jewish myself.'

'How much?' asked Lew.

'A quarter.'

'It's not enough.'[15]

Lew's nephew, Michael, always treasured his uncle's crisp advice when starting in the business – 'Michael, my boy, if at first you don't succeed . . . you're fired.'[16]

Lew was at his happiest, however, when singing praises, especially of his own productions. These were invariably immense, world-beating, unbelievable, wonderful, incredible and even, on occasion, titanic. As he put it: 'All my shows are great. Some of them are bad – but they are all great.'[17] Lew could occasionally be upset by the antics of his stars, but his form of censure rarely rose above 'That man must never be booked again . . . unless we really need him.'[18]

Confronted by a sharply critical reporter questioning him on the subject of the negative aspects of television, Lew responded robustly, 'I don't see nothing negative about television.' And, after a pause, 'My English isn't so good. I leave you to put in any grammar.'[19]

Lew's use of the English language had some parallels with that of the great Hollywood movie mogul, Sam Goldwyn, the only begetter of imperishable lines like 'We have all passed a lot of water since then' and 'They're always biting the hand that lays the golden egg.'[20]

Asked if he had ever met Goldwyn, Lew replied, 'Only on the telephone,'[21] which was in itself something of a Goldwynism. But there were significant differences between the two men. Goldwyn could take umbrage when his more hilarious utterances were quoted back at him. Lew, in contrast, seemed to love them all, though he did say, 'I only wish I was as sharp as the Lew Grade they tell stories about. If I could find the authors, I'd hire them.'[22]

Lew's indulgence did have some limits. He readily held his hands up to the story of how he lost a wager with scriptwriter Ted (later Lord) Willis. In response to a bet that he could not name the twelve apostles, Lew had started confidently: 'Matthew, Mark, Luke and John . . .' and then dried, with the excuse, 'Well, I haven't finished reading the script yet.'[23]

But Lew always resolutely denied the story about his trying to reduce the number of the apostles to six in *Jesus of Nazareth*, as a cost-saving measure. This denial seems to have been partly prompted by sensitivity to any suggestion of meanness on his company's part in the retelling of the Gospel story, and partly due to the cruel suggestions of rival film-makers about possible follow-ups – 'Snow White and the 4.5 Dwarfs' and 'The Two Pony-trekkers of the Apocalypse' being among them.

The mystery of Lew and the apostles was eventually clarified by Sir Ian Holm. In his book, *Acting My Life*, published after Lew's death, Holm recalled his days in the minuscule role of Zerah of the Sanheddrin in *Jesus of Nazareth*. With plenty of time on his hands, he had the opportunity to eavesdrop on the film's great movers and shakers. He remembered this conversation:

'Everything's too big,' said Lew Grade.

'Is big subject,' replied Zeffirelli, the director.

'Yes. But remember this is for television. The screen is smaller.'

'I know that. So what you suggest, eh?'

'This next scene, for example,' said Lew, fingering a script and pointing to the scene set in the Garden of Gethsemane.

'Yes. What about it?' asked Zeffirelli.

'It's got the Apostles in it.'

'Yes. They were all there. That's the point.'

'But twelve of them. Twelve Apostles!! Can't we have a few less?'[24]

ONE

Odessa

L EW GRADE WAS BORN LOVAT WINOGRADSKY in the village of
Tokmak in the Crimea close to the Black Sea, and into a world that
was no laughing matter. The nearest large town was Odessa, where Lew's
father was born and where many of the family still lived. In October 1905,
the year before Lew's arrival, the Jewish quarter in Odessa experienced the
worst of a wave of pogroms sweeping through the Russian Empire.

As Reuben Ainsztein, the eminent historian of Jewish resistance,
described it:

> Organized by the City Governor Neidhart and the Military Commander,
> Baron von Kaulbars, the looters and killers advanced behind soldiers,
> Cossacks and policemen and were followed by carts and wagons for carrying
> away the loot, which were also escorted by Cossacks or dragoons. The
> attitude of the army command to the pogrom was summed up by General
> Deryugin, the commandant of the Odessa Officers Cadet School, when he
> addressed a mob of looters and rapists in the following words: 'You, too, are
> on your way to massacre the Jews. You have my blessing for your work.
> What a pity only the plebeians are used for this job of work and we are not
> allowed to go with them.' . . . In fact, officers and soldiers not only did most
> of the killing but also openly engaged in looting. The self-defence force,
> which included a number of non-Jews, succeeded in dealing with many of
> the gangs on the first day of the pogrom, but were mercilessly shot down or
> sabred by the troops, Cossacks and dragoons, so that during the following
> three days the scum of Odessa was able to carry on looting, raping and
> murdering. Altogether 303 Jews were killed and thousands wounded.[1]

Pogroms were nothing new. Odessa 1905 was prompted by Russian defeats in the war against Japan, but almost any excuse for them would do. Whenever the troubled tsarist regime required a scapegoat, the Jews would come almost immediately to hand. The Russian masses were routinely encouraged to perceive them as responsible for all the social and political evils in the sprawling empire. Jews were deemed particularly suspect for allegedly harbouring liberal and democratic ideas which were anathema to the autocratic establishment.

Nazi Germany would later raise anti-Semitism to new heights of murderous explicitness, but the official policy of tsarist Russia towards the Jews was not vastly different in motive or intention. Konstantin Pobedonostsev, the chief ideologist of the Russian reaction, and tutor to both Alexander III and Nicholas II, envisaged that as a result of the legal, social and economic discriminations against the Jews, combined with the pogroms, 'One third will die out, one third will leave the country and one third will be completely dissolved in the surrounding population.'[2] This policy fell some way short of extermination, but obliteration of Jewishness, through terror, was certainly at its core.

The Russian minister, Count Witte, frankly told Theodor Herzl, the founder of political Zionism, 'I used to explain to our Emperor Alexander III that if it were possible to drown six or seven million Jews in the Black Sea, I would be perfectly happy to do so, but it is not possible, so we must let them live. But we encourage the Jews to emigrate: we kick them out.'[3] More than a million Jews emigrated from Russia between 1897 and 1914 with fear as their spur.

As a country boy with protective parents, Lovat, the son of Isaac and Golda Winogradsky, enjoyed some insulation from the poisonously anti-Semitic atmosphere in much of the Crimea. Indeed, Lew's conscious memories of Russia as a child had an almost bucolic charm. In his autobiography, *Still Dancing*, he wrote of the house where he lived in Tokmak, standing in its own grounds, overlooked by an orchard, and that 'there were apples everywhere'.[4] He had a sense of his parents being lively characters as they both had excellent singing voices and often appeared in amateur theatricals. His father ran a small drapery store and was said to have a financial interest in two local theatres. By the standards of the area the family was comfortable. They had a maid who came in every day and sometimes of an evening when Isaac and Golda were off entertaining another village with their lively renditions of popular folk songs. Lew remembered always being well fed and clothed. At the age of five, he had no sense of the seismic shift that was about to take place in his existence, though it must have been constantly on the minds of his parents.

After the Odessa pogrom, three of his uncles emigrated to London. One of them, Golda's brother, Herschell, wrote regularly to his sister urging her to follow 'before it was too late'.[5] From 1909, after Golda gave birth to Lovat's brother Boris (later Bernard), the letters became more insistent. In 1912 the family made its move.

It was a two-stage operation. Father Isaac went ahead, with the family's capital, to establish a base. Somewhere along the way he lost most of the money – it's assumed as a result of his passion for gambling. His natural place of refuge was London's East End, handily close to the docks, where successive waves of immigrant Jews had settled before Isaac's arrival. The Jewish quarter in Whitechapel offered much that was familiar to a new immigrant, but precious little in the way of space, and nothing resembling the rural amenity of Tokmak. With brother-in-law Herschell's assistance, Isaac managed to find new quarters for his family – a one-room flat over a shop near the brewery in Brick Lane. He also secured a job as a trouser presser, paying eight shillings a week. The second stage of the operation could take place.

Golda's trek across the continent with the two young boys had an epic quality. A seemingly endless train journey to Berlin was followed by long anxious delays in the German capital as she juggled child-minding with the need to secure a visa to enter Britain. Another wearying journey to the north German coast ended with Olga having to sell her rings to provide extra money for passage on an onion boat to Tilbury. Isaac was waiting at the dockside.

Reunited after six months, the family made its way back to Brick Lane to begin its new life. There was adequate space for a bed in the one room, but Lovat and Boris had to sleep on the floor.

Though only dimly aware of the adult forces that had propelled him into this new circumstance, the infant Lovat certainly appreciated the difference. 'After Tokmak, with our large house and orchard,' Lew recalled in *Still Dancing*, 'London looked extremely depressing.'[6]

TWO

Whitechapel

AMONG THE STORIES TOLD about the Grade brothers after their emergence as the tsars of British show business was one making mild mock of their humble origins. As it seemed impossibly difficult to imagine them ever being stumped for cash, it went: 'Lew and Bernie stepped ashore in England and were utterly skint – for about ten minutes.'[1] Unlike most of the apocrypha about them, this particular witticism contained no mitigating grain of truth. In reality, the brothers spent their entire childhood, and a good part of their adolescence, tethered close to the poverty line.

The Brick Lane to which Isaac Winogradsky introduced his family in 1912 bore no resemblance, other than geographical, to today's brilliantly lit eating-out street of that name. Then, it was dingy to a degree barely imaginable: pungent with the odours of its brewery and overcrowded humanity by day, and deeply sinister by night. On dark evenings, it was only too easy to conjure up an image of Jack the Ripper going about his business in the neighbouring alleyways. To be doomed to live in Brick Lane was to be aware of living close to the bottom of the human pile.

New immigrants to London's East End were known as 'greeners', or greenhorns, and those without family connections had a hard job locating the lowest rung of the economic ladder. The latest arrivals could be seen standing in line in what was known as the open-air *chazer markt* (pig market) in the Whitechapel Road, hoping to be recruited for the meanest unskilled work available. Kindly Uncle Herschell helped his brother-in-law to escape this humiliation. But, as a poor cabinet-maker himself, there were limits to what his patronage could do.

Although England was seen as a land not only of refuge but also of opportunity, the ability to grasp it proved beyond Isaac Winogradsky. He was, by all accounts, an attractive and sweet-natured man. Tall and fair-haired and with an easy, relaxed manner, he had time for everybody. But he was never much of a provider. In Lew's autobiography, his father was 'what you'd call a loser . . . really more of a philosopher, and just not cut out for the business world'.[2] Bernard, in his memoir, *East End, West End*, recalled his father, slightly more clemently, as 'a romantic drifter, a man of ideas without much notion of how to apply them'.[3]

One of their earliest English memories was of their mother enquiring, 'Have we come all this way to live over a shop?'[4]

The Brick Lane experience lasted for two years, before Uncle Herschell intervened again and steered the family in the direction of a relatively new local authority development over the Bethnal Green Road, to 11 Henley Buildings on the Boundary Street Estate. It was less than a mile away, and essentially part of the same neighbourhood. But its two rooms and a scullery afforded more living space for the family and more scope for addressing the problems of adjustment to a wider world.

The adjustments that had been made were already quite considerable, Christian names being among them. Lovat was now known as Louis, which was easily foreshortened to 'Lew'. Boris became Barnet, and later Bernard or Bernie. Golda decided she was more comfortable with the name Olga, though Golda resurfaced at times. However, the change of surname from Winogradsky to Grade would only come much later, after the boys began to make their way in show business. No adjustment seemed necessary at that time, as their main range of acquaintance was among people who had left or, more accurately, fled Russia. Even residents of the slightly more upmarket Boundary Street Estate were mainly recent Jewish immigrants from eastern Europe. At the Rochelle Street School, which served the estate, 90 per cent of pupils spoke Yiddish.

The Winogradskys' initial communication problem was having to bone up on their Yiddish to assist their interaction with other Jewish migrant families who were not from Russia. Thus English was essentially their third language, which Lew picked up at a good clip, faster than his parents.

There may also have been some juggling of birth dates, notoriously hard to pin down as many migrants arrived without much in the way of paperwork. Isaac, exceptionally, was reasonably secure in the knowledge of having been born in 1879, which made him thirty-five when the war with Germany broke out in 1914. Olga/Golda's age, however, was, and remained, a matter of shifting conjecture, though she was reckoned to be about five or six years younger than Isaac. Some mystery also attached to Lew's actual date of birth, which he would later flourish as being on 25 December – the same as Jesus Christ. However, in a search of old school records of the period, the writer Hunter Davies lighted upon a listing of a Louis Winogradsky, of 221 Brick Lane, being born on the more mundane date of 26 March 1906.[5] As Lew and his mother – clearly a material witness – always resolutely insisted that the event took place on Christmas Day, this intriguing fragment of evidence has never been corroborated.

Despite being considerably younger than her husband, Olga was always the family's decision-maker and, perhaps more importantly, cheerleader. Of below medium height but sturdily built, she carried the banner of family pride, refusing to accept charity even in the direst circumstances, sometimes by the time-honoured expedient of taking in other people's washing and ironing. It was said that her maiden name of Eisenstadt (meaning 'tower of iron') was more illustrative of her personality than Winogradsky (in translation, 'the town where the wine is made').

No one doubted her valour or strength of character, though she did have a tendency, detected by Lew at an early age, to exaggeration. According to his mother it was the war that put the kibosh on the family's chances of emerging from poverty, on account of her husband Isaac's best brainchild, a cinema in the Mile End Road, being obliterated by the bombing. Lew found it hard to perceive this as a major setback as he knew that the cinema, where his father had 'a general dogsbody kind of job',[6] was in fact owned by the restaurateur, Jack Isow.

Isaac and Olga still sang together but non-professionally, aside from a short appearance at the Mile End Pavilion, known locally as the Yiddisher Theatre, where they refreshed memories of old Russia with their medley of folk songs. There was not much call for the repertoire elsewhere, particularly after the Bolshevik Revolution of 1917 rendered any lingering sentiment for the old Russia largely redundant.

Most of Isaac's paid work was in the garment trade, which along with cabinet-making was the main avenue of business opportunity for Jewish immigrants. Most skilled trades, and even many unskilled occupations in the docks, were strongly unionised and not easily accessed by new arrivals. In the rag trade, Isaac's job descriptions varied widely, from 'presser' to 'mechanic' and 'button-machine operator', but all had the common denominator of being low paid. Like many in the trade, Isaac was not free of the ambition to run his own business, but found its realisation elusive. Additionally, he had a daunting habit of gambling away what he saw as any excess funds, favouring cards and wagers on the horses with the street bookies who flourished in the days before betting shops, ostensibly undercover but widely tolerated. Olga said of her husband that he was a man who 'went nowhere with his cleverness'.[7] Her ambition for her sons, who became three in number when Leslie was born in 1916, was as a result unconfined.

All the Winogradsky boys were very fair as children, though Bernard had darker eyes than the other two. Olga was pleased by this aspect of their appearance as it seemed likely to make them more assimilable with English society, albeit without compromising their heritage. The family was not given to religious fundamentalism, nor was it particularly observant, but Olga always lit the candles on Friday night. They also celebrated important events in the Jewish calendar – Passover, the New Year and the Day of Atonement – though Lew rarely saw the inside of a synagogue after his Bar Mitzvah.

Religious tolerance was perhaps the most immediately appreciated consequence of life in England. There was no pressure, as there had been in Russia, to save one's skin by making a show of conversion to Christianity. However, what is now described as the host community was not entirely hospitable. Indeed, many well-established Jewish families were alarmed by the spectacle of their co-religionists arriving en masse from Eastern Europe and creating new pressures on housing and public services in a way that is familiar with other immigrant communities today. There was little evidence of the public anti-Semitism and strife of the kind that defaced the East End with the rise of Mosleyite fascism in the 1930s, but tension was not far beneath the surface.

Dire problems of overcrowding in the Whitechapel area were to some extent compensated by the safety afforded by numbers. Most Jews who left Russia headed for New York, but a substantial minority – at least

150,000 – made London their destination. Even before the turn of the century, Charles Booth's survey of *Labour and Life of the People* in the metropolis noted of the large Jewish immigrant presence in the vicinity of Petticoat Lane: 'they live and crowd together, and work and meet their fate almost independent of the great stream of London life surging around them'.[8]

In the middle of an expanding ghetto, Jewish families could be led to believe that their land of refuge was more benevolent than was actually the case. Remarkably, both Lew and Bernard later testified that they had never experienced overt anti-Semitic aggression during their days as pupils at Rochelle Street School. There was no shortage of roughhouses in the playground involving Polish, Russian and English-born combatants, but they did not carry the freight of ethnic animosity. Relations with the neighbouring, mainly Gentile, school could also involve fisticuffs, but the battles, dividing along the lines of 'Yids' versus 'Yocks', were always reckoned, at least to their young minds, to be of the good and clean variety. To experience virulent anti-Semitism at first hand, they had to go to Reigate.

Reigate, in the leafier part of Surrey, was for a few weeks in 1917 their assigned place of safety, away from the night-time raids by Zeppelin airships on the London docklands. As two of only three Jewish boys in their new school, they found themselves the object of hostile curiosity, and sometimes worse. 'We were rather got at,' Bernard recalled, 'I got a few bloody noses. Lew tried to protect me but all he got for his trouble was a bloody nose as well.'[9] Both brothers were delighted to return to the insecurity of the war-ravaged East End.

Aside from the poverty, there was an attractive intimacy to life on the Boundary Street Estate, so named by the London County Council (LCC) because it separated the boroughs of Shoreditch and Bethnal Green. The south side of Henley Buildings, one of the twenty-two red and amber brick tenement blocks that constituted the estate, actually verged on Rochelle Street. It could not have taken Lew and Bernie much more than thirty seconds to get to school.

The physical focus of the estate was Arnold Circus, from which the tenements radiated out in all directions. In the middle of Arnold Circus there was an attractive feature, a hillock or mound, planted with gardens and topped with a bandstand. It provided a secure and creative play area for children, overlooked by the surrounding flats, and on Tuesday evenings crowds gathered to hear the bands play. It was also the outdoor social centre for Lew and Bernie, a place to meet up with mates and girlfriends before adventuring elsewhere. Arnold Circus, unlike Brick Lane, has gone down in the world, but the area retains a distinctive quality to this day. The bandstand is now dilapidated and covered with graffiti, though there is some prospect of restoration to its former glory through a recently formed local 'Friends of Arnold Circus' group.

Like most local children, the brothers were riveted by moving pictures. Lew liked Westerns and action films but affected to despise soppy love stories. He attributed his decline in synagogue attendance to having to follow the serial adventures of Pearl White in *The Perils of Pauline* at the local cinema every Saturday morning. The music hall also provided valued cultural nourishment, particularly a local haunt known as Ye Olde Paragon. Word-playing comedians were a special delight. Bernie loved to repeat the one about a boy saying to a girl, 'May I hold your Palm Olive?' and the girl replying, 'Not on your Life Boy.'

They were also able to witness an early prototype of the Two Ronnies' immortal 'fork handles/four candles' routine that went as follows: Comedian, 'It's a scandal.' Straight man, 'What is?' Comedian, extracting a candle from his pocket, 'This is.'[10]

This was excellent grounding in the world of entertainment but only as consumers of its product. Bernard later claimed that juvenile experiences at Ye Olde Paragon did kindle a feeling of wanting to 'be a part of show business'[11] one day, but the more conventionally ambitious Lew seems never to have given it a thought. He said of his attitude to show business as a boy, 'there was nothing at all in my personality to suggest I'd one day make a good living out of it'.[12]

Olga nursed ambition for all her children, but it was Lew who established himself as the one exhibiting most promise. Asked late in life to describe the nature of his relationship with his older brother, Bernard thought that it could be summed up as 'best friends and arch rivals'.[13] As children though it was no contest. Lew was the star, regarded with some awe by the rest of family. After a comparatively slow start at Rochelle Street School, due to language difficulties, he became its most illustrious pupil. A contemporary described him as being 'as quick as a lizard'.[14] His specialities were arithmetic and being able to memorise English text at high speed. Given the rudimentary nature of an East End education in those days, it was hard for a Jewish mother to glimpse the delight of being able to refer to 'my son the doctor', or 'the lawyer', but Olga certainly envisaged in Lew 'my son the accountant'.

No such maternal dream was possible in relation to Bernie, who was lackadaisical at school, played truant, and showed disquieting signs, to Olga's way of thinking, of sharing his father's addiction to gambling. 'My first truly intellectual exercise,' Bernard recalled, 'was interpreting the method used by my father marking up his racing paper to signify the strengths and weaknesses of the various runners.'[15]

Rochelle Street may have been low in the educational pecking order, but it attracted some resourceful teachers. One, a Mr Silverstein, even managed to ensure Bernie's attention in class with an instruction technique that embraced facial contortions and funny walks. Lew's academic mentor was the less flamboyant Mr Barnett. Impressed by his pupil's gift for figures, Mr Barnett steered Lew in the direction of scholarship exams that could provide him with the funds for a college education beyond the school's leaving age of fourteen. By his own account, Lew won several scholarships after each of which a half-day school holiday was announced to pay tribute to his prowess. He recalled, 'This did wonders for my popularity. It also brought a certain pride to the Winogradsky home and gave my mother something to boast about for months.'[16]

It did not, however, lead to his securing a scholarship. Like many immigrants Isaac had left Russia without a passport. And, as the Winogradsky budget had never stretched to the expense of his becoming naturalised, he and his family were still stateless. The LCC, which was the sanctioning authority for the scholarships, felt this was grounds for blocking the funds required for Lew's further academic advance.

Some months after Lew left school, Mr Barnett came round to see Isaac and Olga with the glad tidings that the LCC had decided to waive its rule about British citizenship and sanction a scholarship for their son. But by then the Winogradsky family's fragile economy dictated an urgent need for Lew's earning power. His formal education was over.

As Lew's schooling was coming to a close, the family moved again, a couple of miles further east to Grafton Street in Stepney, off the Mile End Road. It was a move more sideways than up in the world. Grafton Street, which consisted of rows of small terraced houses, had an air of being a social step up from the Boundary Street Estate, but that did not survive closer inspection. A neighbour from Henley Buildings who called on the Winogradskys at their new address, described it as 'a real dump'.[17]

Each of the tiny houses was divided into two, sometimes three, flats into which large, mainly Jewish, immigrant families were crammed. Where the Winogradskys established their home, there were other families living upstairs and down. Territorial disputes were part of life. Bernard remembered Grafton Street as being characterised by 'endless quarrelling . . . lots of shouting up and down the stairs, telling each other to keep quiet'. Though he did add, 'I'm sure my mother loved it.'[18] Despite its imperfections, 10 Grafton Street, where the Winogradskys formally established residence in January 1921, remained the family home for the next fourteen years. It's hard to imagine any circumstance, other than poverty, for the extended attachment to such a neighbourhood, though the visual evidence has now been totally destroyed. In 1960 the street was part of a development area flattened to accommodate an extension to London University's Queen Mary College.

The move to Stepney wrought some changes in the boys' lives. Bernard was enrolled at the Stepney Jewish School, where he was soon to be joined by the youngest brother, Leslie. Lew went to work, earning fifteen shillings a week, most of which he handed to his mother. There was no escaping a destiny in the rag trade, though he joined it at a more elevated level than most school-leavers. His first job was with a firm called Tew and Raymond, which manufactured stylish women's clothing, and maintained an office in Little Argyll Street in the West End close to the London Palladium.

A spell in the costing department, where Lew's arithmetic and memory skills proved invaluable, led to his rapid introduction to other areas of the business – silks, embroidery and sales – to broaden his experience. By the age of sixteen, he had established himself as Tew and Raymond's 'promising young man' and was earning close to the magic £1 a week. But discontent was setting in. Lew liked Raymond, but not Tew, who lacked a sense of humour. He also had what seemed to him a better idea.

Lew's first significant entrepreneurial move was to go into business with a man who he knew had no talent for it, namely his father. Olga's 'blessing' was crucial to this enterprise, Lew recalled, 'as she had no delusions about my father as a businessman, but she had complete confidence in me – after all, I'd won all those scholarships'.[19] In essence, it seems to have been a family scheme designed to help the teenage son improve, by force of example, the ways of a delinquent dad. It was, nonetheless, a serious commercial venture.

Winogradsky and Son established what was termed its 'factory' in one-room premises in Aldgate East in the heart of 'sweatshop' country, a short step from Lew's original home in Brick Lane. Its speciality was embroidery, then enjoying a boom time in the fashion trade. Lew was no great embroiderer himself, but he knew where to get the necessary machines at a knock-down price. And he knew the people who could work them. The firm's first two operators were embroidery specialists whose acquaintance Lew had conveniently made when they were all in the employ of Tew and Raymond.

One of the more successful lines, developed with a local milliner, involved the production of a range of King Tut hats which had their inspiration in the discovery of King Tutankhamun's tomb in 1922. The Winogradsky firm's contribution was the embroidery of King Tut's features on the crown of the hats. At its peak, Winogradsky and Son, which perhaps should have been more accurately rendered as Son and Winogradsky, had eight machines on the go.

This may have been some way from the commanding heights of the fashion industry but the business – with a modest rental overhead of £2 a week – was soon profitable. Lew showed a capacity, not only for keeping the books but for conjuring up more orders to keep the workers, and his father, hard at it. This stage in his development featured only rarely in his later reminiscence, but it does seem to have established one of the most salient features of his adult life – his liking for a early start and a late finish to the day, on the grounds that time spent working when the opposition is either sleeping or at leisure is rarely wasted.

Meanwhile, the less driven Bernard was rounding off his education in characteristic style. Asked by his class master what was the thing he had clutched in his right hand, Bernie had responded, 'Nothing, Sir.' But the hand was ordered open, revealing a sheaf of incriminating small slips of paper with the words, 'Chelsea, Tottenham Hotspur, Manchester United, Arsenal . . .'[20]

After his exposure as the betting sweepstake king of Stepney Jewish School, Bernie's attendance there was not much in demand. His formal leaving date was January 1924, but Bernard reckoned it must have been effectively at least a year earlier when his long spell of licensed truancy began. During this period he obtained some first-hand insight into the quality of sweatshop life by occasionally helping Lew and his father out at the family 'factory' in Aldgate. Not finding it to his liking, he opted for the job of office boy at Lazarus and Rosenfeld, a china and glass manu-facturing firm with offices in Houndsditch.

Not long afterwards, Olga rushed round to a neighbour in a state of alarm, shouting, 'Mrs Marks, Mrs Marks, I've got terrible pains in my stomach.'[21] Mrs Marks sensibly steered her in the direction of a doctor who diagnosed pregnancy. In January 1925, at an estimated age of thirty-seven, Olga gave birth to a girl child, Rita. This inevitably put more immediate pressure on the space in Grafton Street but with her husband and two of her sons now gainfully employed, Olga must have felt that the family was reasonably well set for the haul out of poverty.

But the new edifice of security was already showing cracks. Though loyal to his father, Lew was beginning to feel the strain of having a business partner who siphoned off much of the firm's profit to settle gambling debts. Isaac worked hard in the family business, but was never able to curb the tendency to play hard outside it.

Even more threatening to the Winogradsky economy was a new enthusiasm, indulged in by Lew and transmitted to Bernard, that riskily lifted their noses from the grindstone.

THREE

Charleston

BY PROVIDING A MODEL of how not to succeed in business, Isaac Winogradsky could be said to have sharpened the commercial acumen of his offspring; knowing what not to do often being as crucial as knowing what to do. He also, however, contributed to the family's future well-being in a more positive way, albeit inadvertently.

In his youth, Isaac had been a good dancer in the acrobatic Russian mode, and for the purposes of family entertainment, he provided repeat performances well into his middle age. Lew, who was both lightly built and extremely wiry, proved adept at picking up the more frantic Cossack-style steps.

Although there was no obvious commercial application for this talent, Lew found it blended wonderfully well with the toe-twisting routines of the Charleston, a new dance craze, imported from America, that swept into Britain in the mid-1920s. Everybody was doing it, but Lew's version of it, benefiting from the Cossack influence, had an immediately distinctive and eye-catching quality. This was further enhanced by his own invention, a spinning manoeuvre which he called 'the crossover'.

With this range of footwork Lew attracted above-average attention from the neighbourhood girls. As teenagers the one area of accomplishment in which the laid-back, near delinquent Bernard excelled Lew was in the subtle art of chatting up the opposite sex. Lew, initially at least, tended to be on the shy side where females were concerned and it seems likely that his fast-flying feet expressed a need to impress with deeds when words were not so readily available. Aged eighteen, an encounter with a young woman at the East Ham Palais enabled him to divest himself of his virginity. This was the prelude to a larger romance, with the dance floor.

Lew's prowess led him to enter what was billed as the Charleston Championship of London at the Ilford Hippodrome; which he won. Recalling this seminal moment in *Still Dancing*, Lew wrote:

> The audience went wild, and they continued to applaud and cheer for the last two minutes right until the end of my dance. Nothing like this had ever happened to me, and it was the most exciting night of my young life. To have a thousand people or more roaring their approval at me was music to my ears, and, as I walked off that stage floor, I felt that life could never be quite the same for me again. The show business blood I'd inherited from my parents suddenly came to the boil and I knew that, whatever happened, and in whatever capacity, the world of entertainment was the world for me.[1]

Isaac and Olga's enthusiasm was more confined. Despite the handsome first prize money of £25 that went with being London's Charleston champ, his parents entertained fears that their eldest son had been bitten with a bug that could seriously impair his attention to the embroidery business. Being stage-struck was, as they knew full well, a long way from actually earning a living on the stage. Fortunately for Lew there was what amounted to a halfway house between the amateur and professional world, which he was able to exploit as a sideline to the family business.

The Charleston craze became so pervasive that every dance hall in London took to running competitions, usually with cash prizes. Lew became a serial winner, sometimes with a partner but often on his own. The money was important, especially as reassurance for Olga, but as Lew later recalled, 'it was the winning that provided the real pleasure'.[2]

Dancing did wonders for Lew's self-esteem. He now appeared to be super-confident and exuberant with it. Abraham Goldmaker, a friend and dance-floor rival in those days, said of him: 'Being with Lew made you believe life was worthwhile. He enjoyed everything so much. "Isn't this meal wonderful?" he would say. He was actually very faddy about food, and wouldn't eat things like butter, but he would talk as if a snack was a feast, and believe it. "Isn't that dancer marvellous? Look at that girl, isn't she wonderful?" I never ever saw Lew depressed.'[3]

Lew's competitiveness, however, could cast a shadow. To Fay Zack, a Houndsditch shop girl who was one of his more popular partners in the dance competitions, he gave an impression of being 'ruthless and bombastic'[4] in his pursuit of success. The ruthlessness in her description seems to have derived from Lew's aversion to finishing second, which occasionally happened. When Lew and Fay were edged out of first place in the Canterbury Theatre, Catford, Lew furiously protested the injustice of the jury's decision with the theatre's manager. By way of appeasement, the manager engaged Lew for a two weeks' dancing spot with pay. Honour was satisfied. But the luckless Fay was not included in the arrangement. Even at the semi-professional level, show business had its unsentimental element along with its sunny side.

As his reputation on the dance-hall circuit rose, Lew also became aware of the need to make adjustments to his name. Winogradsky, he discerned, was too much of a mouthful now that he was operating outside refugee society. Something more punchy and anglicised seemed necessary. Lew's deft compromise was to eliminate the first and last syllables of his born name and let it be known that henceforth he would answer to Louis Grad (the final 'e' came later).

In December 1926 what was termed the World Charleston Championships was held at the Albert Hall, offering a stepping stone to glory. It was said that the winner of the amateur solo event would be guaranteed a four-week cabaret engagement at London's Piccadilly Hotel. The finest Charleston exponents from miles around showed up to be assessed by an illustrious panel of judges that included impresario Charles B. Cochran and legendary Hollywood dancing star Fred Astaire. The tension among the dancers backstage as they prepared to showcase their talents was, Lew recalled, 'almost too much to bear'.[5] But his nerve held. A few days short of his twentieth birthday – if it was indeed Christmas Day – Lew was able to bask in the title 'Charleston Champion of the World'.

The sequel was inevitable. By now Lew's sideline earnings from dance were eclipsing the dwindling profits of the embroidery business where his father, left for long periods to run the business on his own, struggled to get new orders. With his parents' approval, Lew became a full-time professional dancer, while Isaac quietly wound up the affairs of Winogradsky and Son and returned to the job market.

Bernard, meanwhile, impressed by his brother's progress in the dancing world, took to entering Charleston competitions on his own account. This was one of the few areas in which he felt able to compete with his older brother and he was resolved to give it his best shot. His motivation was heightened to some degree by going to the West End one day with a friend and seeing someone who looked like a tramp in the street. 'My companion,' Bernard recalled, 'told me that his brother was a well-known industrialist. It had an effect on me. I knew I did not want to become the brother who became a dishevelled tramp.'6

One Friday afternoon Bernard was confronted with a stark choice between going to work for his normal shift at the china and glass business or making the semi-final round of a local dance competition. He chose the competition, and Lazarus and Rosenfeld promptly chose to terminate his employment.

His parents were upset but in retrospect, after Bernard followed Lew onto the professional stage, it came to be perceived as a brilliant career move.

FOUR

Dancing Years

As professional entertainers, Lew and Bernard danced with a variety of partners, both male and female, but never together. Bernard, who grew several inches taller than his older brother, had the more elegant line and a greater range. He was also good at tap. But Lew, staying close to his Charleston roots, was the more athletic. The key prop in Lew's act was an oval-shaped table, three feet high and two feet across, with the pointed end facing the audience to create an illusion of its being even narrower than it in fact was. As a climax to his routine Lew would leap onto the table and go into a series of frenzied gyrations. 'His dexterity and speed,' wrote an early critic, 'was wondrous to behold.'[1]

Unlike crooners or comedians, dancers could not expect to top any theatre bill. On the other hand, their prospects of staying in employment were better than those of most other performers. As members of what were termed 'dumb' acts they could get work not only in Britain but all over the continent of Europe without any impediment of language. As a result, Lew and Bernard soon became widely travelled young men.

Lew's first professional break came through an advertisement in *The Stage*, which he answered citing his recently acquired credential as the amateur Charleston-dancing 'champion of the world'. Band leader Murray Pilcer was preparing a tour and wanted to feature as part of the entertainment a dancer who would initially be incognito, ostensibly wielding a saxophone as part of the band, but who could also suddenly spring forth from its ranks and dazzle the audience with his footwork. Pilcer responded to Lew's application, liked what he had to offer, and a deal was done. Heady days ensued as the band fulfilled engagements at the

Brighton Hippodrome, London's Holborn Empire and at a number of provincial venues. On £20 a week, ten times as much as the average sweat-shop worker could earn, Lew allowed himself to feel rich. Then Pilcer quite suddenly decided that his own touring days were over, and Lew found himself back in Grafton Street contemplating one of the abiding hazards of his new profession, involuntary rest without pay.

Lew decided that he had to broaden his appeal. On the band circuit his normal routine lasted for four minutes. This was too short for the music halls, where a successful spot had to be at least twelve minutes. Basic fitness was never much of a problem for Lew, who was a light eater and teetotal by choice, thankful for the experience of having been made sick by his first and last glass of champagne. But he was conscious of the need to limit the strain on his joints. To go the length of time required for a music hall engagement, Lew felt he needed a partner to diversify the act and give his knees some respite.

The one he reached for was Abraham Goldmaker, his old rival in the amateur competition days. Goldmaker had come to the East End from Russia as a child and, not unlike Lew, was eager to escape a destiny in the family business, which in his case was making beer barrels. He also had a ready-made stage name, Al Gold. Together they devised an energy-conserving act that, subject to variations, consisted of a joint soft-shoe shuffle, followed by Al doing an eccentric comedy dance as a preliminary to Lew's table routine. The finish was a high-speed Charleston featuring them both in perfect unison.

'Grad and Gold – Trick Dancers' made their first appearance at the Newcastle Empire, where they featured with a row of leggy dancing girls in a show called *Shirley's Follies*. The show ran for six weeks, with modest success, but led to greater things. It was seen by the promoter Thomas Convery, who was looking for an eccentric dancing element in *League of Neighbours*, a touring revue designed to provide a showcase for the famous northern comedian Albert Burden. Convery decided that Grad and Gold fitted the bill and offered them a year's contract.

Lew's best-remembered part of the show featured an actor saying bombastically in an American accent, 'In America everything we've got is bigger and better than you've got in England. For example, we've got the best Charleston dancers.' Two dancers from the chorus line were then deployed to demonstrate the alleged American way. 'That's nothing,'

Albert Burden would say, 'Wait until you see what we've got here in Newcastle'[2] (or wherever they happened to be performing). Then Lew and Al would take the stage as 'home-grown' talent and go into a dazzlingly superior routine to a thunder of jingoistic applause.

As most of their original engagements were in the provinces, the dancers became familiar with the niceties of how to please or appease a long succession of landladies. It was a good idea, especially if they wanted to come back, to make glowing references to their cooking in the 'Remarks' ledger. There could also be some benefit in scrutinising earlier entries in the book for hidden messages. The acronym LDOK indicated a commendation for the landlady's daughter.

In relatively steady employ, Lew was able to send more money back to Olga. Isaac did manage to find work, but with two children still of school age, his meagre pay packet did not stretch far enough. There were also clear signs that his health was failing. Despite the continuing precariousness of the family's existence, Lew had a good grasp of the psychological importance of making a bit of a splash if an opportunity arose. His young sister, Rita, recalling her infancy, said: 'I remember Lew starting to get his first bit of money. He came into Grafton Street with a car, an open yellow thing, a tourer with no hood. It had Yellow Bird written on it. I don't know what make it was. But I used to sit inside it all day long, the envy of everyone in the street. No one else had a car in those days. I was so proud of him.'[3] Rita's idolising of her oldest brother was assisted to some degree by her impression, apparently long uncorrected by Lew, that the first performer to appear on stage was the star of the whole show.

Dancing was not generally perceived as a high road out of poverty, though many male dancers in the 1920s were in fact Jewish. The female dancers were almost invariably Gentile, as even the poorest Jewish mothers were not so keen to see their daughters taking to the stage. Jewish boys who showed physical prowess were more likely to take up boxing, a hugely popular sport in the East End and one that seemed to offer better prospects of instant rewards and glory following the trail blazed by Ted 'Kid' Lewis, 'The Stepney Sphinx', and Jack 'Kid' Berg, 'The Whitechapel Whirlwind', who boxed with a Star of David embroidered on his trunks. Isaac Goldberg, a schoolboy friend of Lew and Bernard, easily outshone them in the early fame stakes as the pugilist Jack Donn.

The Grad and Gold partnership lasted for almost two years, the pair averaging around £20 a week between them – a reasonable return though well dented by the cost of lodgings and maintaining the supply of black silk shirts and red cummerbunds needed for the act. When the work dried up, as it did from time to time, they went to the Express Dairy Café in the Charing Cross Road, where many agents and some theatre managers tended to congregate. As a method of selling his act, Lew once got down on his knees on the pavement and rendered an oval the size of his dancing table with a piece of chalk. He then went into his routine within its confines, and got a booking. Sustained by such achievements, they began to make a modest name for themselves but the strain of constantly being on the road and living in digs, sometimes in the same room, began to take its toll. It got to a point where they were barely on speaking terms. One day, after making one of their better-paid appearances at the Casino in Deauville, Gold revealed that he had decided to accept an engagement without Lew. And Lew felt, as Fay Zack had done some years previously in similar circumstances, thoroughly upset.

By way of consolation, Lew took his solo act off to Paris and the Bal Tabarin night-spot, where he was obliged to share a dressing room with twenty chorus girls in a state of near or total undress. His deep embarrassment was alleviated to some extent by one of the naked girls pressing up to him and saying, 'You English boy? I like English boy. You and me, we have some fun?'[4]

It was a continental engagement that led to the final refinement of the family name. A typographical error in a Paris poster rendered Grad as Grade. Lew liked the mistake and Grade became the anglicised version of Winogradsky accepted by him and ultimately adopted by the rest of the family, except Bernard. Two Grades in the entertainment business was deemed one too many, but Bernard could not perceive any further creative plundering of the family name, as all that was left seemed to be 'Wino'. The problem was solved by his agent, Syd Burns, casting around for a catchy stage appellation for Bernard's dancing partnership with another East Ender called Albert Sutan. Burns liked the name of an American dancing duo who called themselves the Dufor Boys, but thought it needed some adjustment for the home market. Why not the Delfont Boys? Thus Lew's younger brother became, and thereafter remained, Bernard Delfont.

While Lew was in Paris, Bernard came by for a few nights of fraternal carousing, rounded off by supper-breakfasts of mussels and onion soup. The Delfont Boys, after doing the rounds of the English provinces and a rising crescendo of London spots at the Holborn Empire, the Alhambra and even briefly the Palladium, were also seeking to establish a continental foothold. They found one for a month at the Empire in Paris before proceeding on to a seedier series of engagements in the nightclubs of Marseille, where as Bernard recalled, 'The Delfont Boys were among the few performers to appear fully clothed.'[5] Marseille also lived on in his memory for the 'gloriously uninhibited' quality of the female company available to him.

Lew, billing himself as 'The Dancer with the Humorous Feet',[6] went off to strut his solo stuff in Biarritz and Nice. Both brothers applied themselves assiduously to refining their separate acts, but with an awareness that their routines had a highly perishable quality. 'No doubt in my mind,' Lew said later, 'that the same act I was doing wouldn't have earned tuppence in New York or any other American city, where the Charleston was no longer a novelty. But in Europe they lapped it up, and who was I to complain?'[7]

Jews were not so prominent in British and European show business as they had already become in the entertainment industry in the United States, but the brothers were rarely conscious of anti-Semitism impeding their continental progress. Not even in Germany where Lew and Bernard took their rival acts after their foray into France, and where Hitlerism was already on the rise. 'Anti-Semitism in Germany,' Lew recalled, 'somehow managed to pass me by . . . Politics could not have been further from my thoughts.'[8] Even early manifestations of Nazism on the streets failed to cause great alarm. The humour of the day seemed to be sufficient antidote to any excess. On the Berlin cabaret circuit, Hitler and his hooligan cohorts featured not so much as a menace but as buffoons.

While playing the Alcazar in the Reeperbahn, Hamburg's red light district, Bernard did have occasion to observe the Brown Shirts marching by, singing a lyric which he was told roughly translated as 'And when Jewish blood spurts from the knife, that will be the day.' But at the time, he thought 'it all seemed too ludicrously melodramatic to be taken seriously.'[9]

It did, however, take on a larger significance when Bernard learned that one of his presumed Aryan friends was someone in permanent denial about his Jewish background, to be on the safe side. Subsequently, when the Delfont Boys appeared at the Cazanova in the arms industry town of Essen, theirs was the only act not invited to the show's Christmas party. As the only two Jews on the bill, Bernard and Al Sutan did not have to ponder long on what that was all about.

Lew also played a number of glitzy venues in Germany including the Alcazar, the Rialto Palais in Dresden and the Barbarina ballroom in Berlin, but he was happier working on the French circuit. For two weeks in Paris he had the thrill of seeing his name in lights about the Moulin Rouge, then and for many years before and after the world's most stylish striptease establishment. They were among his happiest two weeks ever, for reasons that had little to do with the prevailing nudity: 'It didn't matter whether you were a stagehand or a headliner. No one played favourites, and this resulted in the most agreeable working atmosphere I think I've ever known. It was so different from what I experienced in England where, in most instances, the management didn't give a damn about anything – except whether or not you put bums on seats.'[10]

Even so, Lew was inexorably drawn back to England. He made good money on the continent, but only England, he felt, could make him a star. Late in 1929 he made approaches to two agents. One was Tom Rice, a representative of the Walter Bentley Agency, who had good contacts with the Moss Empire Circuit which, along with Stoll Theatres, controlled most of the major music halls in Britain. The other was Joe Collins, an experienced operator who later became the father of daughters who achieved fame in show business: Joan as a movie star, and Jackie as the author of *The Stud* and other steamy Hollywood-based novels.

With Joe Collins, Lew established an informal but highly significant relationship. Collins was the sole booker for several outlets of which Les Ambassadeurs, a cabaret club just off Regent Street, was the best known, and he was always on the look-out for new talent. Lew, in turn, had long been a keen appraiser of other people's acts, priding himself on knowing if they 'worked' within a few seconds of their opening sequence. He was able to unload his knowledge of the acts he had seen, continent-wide, and Collins tried some of them out at his venues. Impressed by the soundness of Lew's recommendations, he asked for any more the young dancer might come across in his travels. Scouting for Joe Collins would prove to be Lew's life-changing experience, eventually.

In the immediate present it was Tom Rice who most brightened Lew's horizon by booking him at the Stratford Empire, part of the Moss Empire circuit, for an eye-watering £27 10s a week. This led on to a guaranteed thirty-week arrangement for Lew, touring a mixture of music halls, cabarets and cinemas. In those days many of the bigger cinemas presented a supporting programme of live entertainment to supplement the offerings on the screen. Lew often played two cinemas on the same day, lugging his oval table between venues.

By the early 1930s, with the Depression beginning to bite, the Grade family were detectably on the rise while a high proportion of their fellow citizens were proceeding in the opposite direction. In Grafton Street the pressure eased when Leslie left school and secured what seemed like a steady job in the rag trade. Though fascinated by tales of his older brothers' picaresque adventures in show business, Leslie showed no signs of wanting to take to the boards himself. Meantime, the remittances sent by Lew and Bernard to Olga seemed to be paving the route to a better life rather than just helping to make ends meet. The only foreseeable threat to the family's more secure economy was the possibility of one of the older boys 'finding someone' and getting married. And that did not appear likely.

The life of an itinerant dancer did not lend itself to the formation of enduring relationships. Sex, however, was fairly readily available and both Lew and Bernard were keen on it, when they had the energy. Lew mournfully recalled meeting a beautiful girl after a show at Dresden's Rialto Palais, and – after his fourth performance of the day – having only the strength for 'a bit of canoodle'[11] on her doorstep before needing to make an excuse and leave. There were, nonetheless, other days with less taxing performance requirements. In Hamburg Lew fell asleep at his hotel after an evening of comparatively light duty and dreamt of being caressed by a desirable woman, only to wake up to find one in real-life attendance.

For the most part sexual opportunities were presented by touring female artistes, similarly doomed to brief encounters; a few early prototypes of what would now be called 'groupies'; and, in Bernard's case, what were then called ladies of the night. In *East End, West End*, Bernard recalled with a note of self-reproof, 'Romance had little to do with it. That I often paid for what I wanted probably suggests I still had a lot of growing up to do.'[12]

But there were also dangers in bringing a more heartfelt, grown-up approach to the enterprise. During a 'resting' period in Amsterdam, Bernard did allow himself to fall genuinely and heavily for Josette, an older woman who invited him to have dinner with her at her aunt's place in the suburbs. Once there, Bernard was surprised when Josette, apparently ignoring her aunt, led him upstairs for some vigorous love-making. On the next day Josette vanished. A baffled Bernard asked about her whereabouts when he met a man he knew had previously been acquainted with her. 'You too,'[13] said the man before patiently explaining that the upstairs room was pitted with peepholes through which paying customers enjoyed Josette's regular performances. The 'aunt' was the brothel-keeper.

For a long time Olga had no difficulty in maintaining her position as the most important woman in the lives of Lew and Bernard. But things changed, at least to some degree, when their dancing careers took off in a different direction. Around 1932, Tom Rice expressed concern about a fall-off in the bookings for Lew's act. With the Charleston no longer having significant novelty value, he felt it needed a new ingredient, and the ingredient decided upon was a young woman.

For the next year Lew went around the now familiar English circuit, with a six-week diversion into Holland, with a young dancer called Anna Roth. The partnership seemed to work well, but at the end of their run Rice thought it needed yet another new ingredient, meaning another young woman. Lew's next partner was Bobbie Medlock, aged eighteen to Lew's now seasoned twenty-seven. Bobbie, who could do acrobatics as well as dance and had a useful sideline in contortions, was more versatile than her predecessor. Together they devised a fresh-looking act – billed as 'Grade and Medlock – Those Superb Dancers' – which drew on Bobbie's range of skills, though the big finish was always provided by Lew spinning on his table. They also introduced humour into the act while still keeping it 'dumb'. Lew showed a talent for mime by losing an invisible button, finding it again, and sewing it back onto his sparkling suit with an invisible needle. Their most gruelling engagement, in October 1932, was at the London Pavilion which ran non-stop Variety starting in the early afternoon and finishing shortly before midnight. Lew sometimes had to thread the invisible needle five times a day to preserve continuity.

The partnership lasted eight months before Medlock decided she wanted to develop a different style of dance (she later toured with Vic Marlow, who became her husband, as Medlock and Marlow). Despite its short duration, her working relationship with Lew was one that engendered affection on both sides. Lew presented her with a bracelet on her nineteenth birthday but gave her no cause for alarm in other respects. Bobbie always found him kind, considerate and funny, the most perfect of gentlemen, without any detectable ulterior motives.

Lew's next partnership, however, was wholeheartedly romantic.

He spotted Marjorie Pointer when she was appearing in a show called *Bow Bells* at the London Hippodrome. She was not part of the chorus line, but featured in a solo spot doing a ballet routine in a way that exhibited both her long legs and the strict Sadlers Wells training she had undergone en route into the world of Variety. Liking what he saw, Lew invited her to fill the professional vacancy left by Bobbie Medlock. He also made no secret of the fact that he fancied her, and was pleased to find that his feeling was promptly reciprocated. As lovers and performers they toured the English Variety and cabaret venues, with a short intermission to cross the Irish Sea and play the Theatre Royal in Dublin.

Meanwhile, Bernard's career and love life was describing a not dissimilar trajectory. Despite the prediction of a *Daily Telegraph* theatre critic – 'The Delfont Boys will go far'[14] – Bernard's partnership with Al Suton was not built to last. The climax of their act was a slow-motion knife fight to the death, danced out in flickering light to emphasise the jerkiness of their movements. It was an effective routine, but one that became almost a metaphor for the partnership as Bernard became more and more irritated by his co-dancer's claims to superiority in their arrangement. When Al decided to get married, the complications became terminal and the Delfont Boys went their separate ways.

Like Lew, Bernard decided to go solo for a while. But the pickings became leaner and leaner until, again like Lew, he decided that a more assured future was likely to be in prospect with a girl partner. One evening in a Brussels night-spot he spotted a likely candidate, Toko by name, who was energetic, double-jointed and, as a solo act, displayed evidence of availability. They soon became partners, touring as 'Delfont and Toko, Syncopated-Steps Appeal'.

Toko was an unusual young woman in many respects, and, having danced professionally since the age of twelve, well steeped in show business lore. Her Scottish mother had performed on the stage as a singer, while her Japanese father, Tarro Miyake, had been a champion ju jitsu wrestler. She was just sixteen when she teamed up with Bernard in a nicely diversified act that contained elements of Charleston, eccentric dance and acrobatics before its conclusion with a romantic Ginger Rogers–Fred Astaire-style dance number. It did not take Bernard very long to fall in love with her.

In the event, the course of true love did not run smooth for either brother. Olga could not reconcile herself to any idea of having Toko as a daughter-in-law. When Bernard intimated that he wanted to marry his partner, Olga made no secret of her objection – 'You'll have Japanese children,' she said. 'That's all you should want.'[15] But the real impediment to romantic progress was Toko's mother, who travelled with the dancing duo everywhere, carefully monitoring her daughter's emotional arrangements. And Bernard, more than ten years older than Toko, was not on the maternal approved list. The act prospered but its internal love interest, for want of development, withered away.

Lew's love affair with Marjorie foundered for other reasons. Though a Gentile, Marjorie rather surprisingly managed to pass the Olga test. The two women became friendly and Olga sometimes made her approval explicit by saying to Marjorie, 'You must be Jewish somewhere.'[16] The family problems were more on the other side, with Marjorie's suburban parents indicating disapproval of their Sadlers Wells-trained daughter stooping so low as to associate with a Jewish boy from the East End. Nevertheless, the couple arrived at the stage of being what Marjorie described as 'nearly engaged'.[17]

The real problem, it turned out, was compatibility. Lew was too jealously inclined, to Marjorie's way of thinking, while Marjorie was, to Lew's mind, too outspoken in her criticisms of their act. Their altercations were almost certainly promoted by their different backgrounds in dance, but they did reach mildly epic levels. Off stage Marjorie sometimes threw her shoes at Lew and he once, in retaliation, locked her in the dressing room. It was all fairly routine show business behind-the-scenes histrionics and it never brought them to the brink of actually disliking each other, but it did help to persuade them that they might not be so well suited in the long haul of marriage.

Even with female partners, neither brother came close to the achievement of star status. Usually their acts featured as the first on the stage or, less frequently, the first after the interval. On Variety theatre bills they customarily occupied the bottom berth, which qualified them for the worst pick of the dressing rooms. They both achieved an impressive continuity of employment, but there had to be a strain in the knowledge that they only had to slip one notch to be out of the business altogether. Lew also began to experience problems with his knees, telling him his dancing days might be close to an end. And their message was reinforced by his mother. Concerned by her eldest son's seeming fragility – Lew's dancing weight rarely rose above eight stone – Olga took to counselling him on the advantages of finding a new way. 'It's no good making money mit your feet,' she would say, 'Make money mit your brains.'[18]

Nobody in the family doubted the alertness of Lew's brain, which was pressed into emergency service in 1934 when young brother Leslie got into difficulties. After a promising start in the rag trade, the teenage Leslie had decided to go into business on his own, rapidly over-extended himself by ordering too much stock and wound up saddled with debt. Taking time out from his dance schedule, Lew took over the remnants of the business and squared off the creditors himself.

Lew danced on with Marjorie into 1935 when his father, who had been ailing for some time, became seriously ill. Isaac's final diagnosis was Hodgkin's disease, cancer of the lymph glands, to which medical science then had no adequate answer. The family mustered £100 for a second opinion by a Harley Street specialist, but no hope could be offered. Lew and Bernard regularly visited their father at Hammersmith Hospital between engagements, but with the realisation that he would never return to Grafton Street. Isaac died in the hospital in October 1935, aged fifty-seven.

After their father's death, Lew and Bernard persuaded Olga to make a move out of the East End. The flat they rented for her in Pullman Court, Streatham, had a sitting room and three bedrooms, more than adequate for Olga and ten-year-old Rita, and with enough spare capacity to enable the boys to come and go as they pleased. Part of a community development, Olga's new apartment afforded a pleasant view from its balcony of the outdoor swimming pool. While the family upheaval was going on Rita was sent away to stay with friends. Of her subsequent introduction to Pullman Court, she said, 'After Grafton Street it seemed like paradise.'[19]

In the wake of this felicitous arrangement, Bernard went back to touring with Toko and Toko's mother, while Lew, finally heeding his own mother's counsel, decided to work exclusively 'mit his brains'.

FIVE

Offstage

IN HIS OLD AGE Lew Grade's most frequently recurring anxiety dreams harked back to his dancing years. The band would strike up, the lights heightening to full glare as Lew arrived centre stage. He then launched himself in the direction of his oval table only to find, while poised in mid-air, that it had disappeared. A variation on the theme was provided by the nightmare in which he could not find his music and had to plead imploringly to the band: 'Surely you know "That's My Weakness Now"!'[1]

In terms of his life story, Lew's dancing days are sometimes seen as a light, almost frivolous preamble to his career as a businessman. It did not seem that way at the time. Performance was something that engaged him heart and soul. The low position of his act on the bill never diminished his enthusiasm for actually appearing on stage or for the regular conquest of nerves that performance entails. Most Variety performers lived in a state of worry, about how their act would go over, about their position on the bill, about whether they were going up or down; if up, they worried about staying up and, if down, about their prospects of finding other work. Lew had been prey to all these concerns.

He kept a practical eye on what he might do when his anxiety-ridden dancing days were over, but he never exhibited any hurry to bring them to a close. His first dancing partner, Al Gold, remembered Lew talking about one day becoming an agent but it was mainly that, just talk. Even after Lew impressed agent Joe Collins with his talent-spotting ability, he saw the business of scouting as an adjunct to his dancing career, not as its replacement.

His father's death and his mother's imprecations were certainly among the reasons for his decision to quit the stage, but it's clear that the decisive factors were his consciousness of a physical decline, particularly around the kneecaps, and an awareness that the competition was getting ever younger and more inventive. Like many dancers approaching the age of thirty, he realised it was time to move on.

The first beneficiary of his decision was not show business so much as the family. His sister, Rita, in her memoir *My Fabulous Brothers*, recalled Lew in the Streatham phase of their existence being transmuted from a 'loved brother' into 'a father-figure, acting as my protector and giving me guidance whenever I needed it'.[2] Leslie and Bernard also bore witness to Lew's taking his position as head of the family after their father's death very seriously, and that he was perhaps even a shade over-emphatic in that role. Where Lew went, the brothers tended to follow, though not always in close harmony.

As his dancing days wound down Lew helped Joe Collins out with a problem he was having at the Alhambra Theatre, a front-line Stoll Theatre Group venue in the heart of the West End on the site now graced by the Odeon, Leicester Square. Under pressure to find a main attraction, Collins consulted Lew, who suggested that he try out an act he had shared the bill with in Hamburg, Dante and his Magical Extravaganza. Dante the magician did two solid months of good business in the West End, and Collins picked up extra pay days by arranging a successful provincial tour.

Emboldened by this, Lew proposed that Collins should do himself a big favour by taking him on as his business partner. Though evidently impressed by the young man's chutzpah, Collins was not ready to share his authority as an agent of some twenty years' standing with someone who was, for all his experience on the road, still wet behind the ears in business terms. It was agreed that they should go their separate ways, but still maintain a loose association.

For a while Lew became one of the milling crowd of agents who frequented the Express Dairy café in the Charing Cross Road, where he had previously touted his own act for hire. He also went briefly and ingloriously into business with Al Sutan, brother Bernard's old partner in his Delfont Boys dancing days, who was now performing as Eddie May. Sutan and Lew put together a band show called 'Eddie May and his

Hollywood Serenaders', which did modest business in Oldham and Belfast before an encounter with disaster in Cork where a rainstorm flooded the theatre. The enterprise ended with Lew having to go to Jersey to locate Sutan's original backer and prise loose the money needed to pay off the acts. Like Bernard before him, Lew decided to limit his exposure to Sutan's ideas, though Sutan went on to flourish, with yet another change of name, as the comedian Hal Monty.

More fruitful, from Lew's point of view, was an encounter in the Charing Cross Road with Harry Smirk, who had recently bought the Winter Gardens Theatre in the seaside town of Morecambe, aiming to diversify his basic business – a chain of sweetshops in the Lancashire area. Smirk had come south looking for new acts for his acquisition. Lew alertly made the most of their street meeting by suggesting that he go up to Morecambe and inspect the theatre's requirements on site. Apparently flattered by the readiness of a London agent to call on them in their own backyard, Smirk and his directors took a shine to a young man who clearly had an intimate working knowledge of how provincial theatres operated. But they still needed to be convinced of his usefulness. Over dinner, Lew plucked up the courage to ask:

'Why don't you let me become the exclusive agent for your theatre?'

'Because,' came the reply, 'all agents are crooks.'

'Okay,' said Lew, 'you're entitled to your opinion. But why don't you give me the chance to prove you wrong?'[3]

Becoming the exclusive booking agent for the Winter Gardens for a trial period represented Lew's first major breakthrough in the business, though it was not without its problems. The deal enabled Lew to find acts belonging to other agents, and facilitated the booking of his own few acts into the theatres they represented. However, as a tyro agent, he had virtually no contact, or clout, with the booking managers on the principal circuits. In order to book his acts and command respect at that level he needed the services of a go-between, a well-established agent. Joe Collins agreed to render this service, though a partnership was still not on offer.

In a short space of time, versions of Lew's Winter Gardens arrangement in Morecambe were replicated with the Argyll in Birkenhead, the Theatre Royal in St Helens and the Hippodrome in Wigan. In each case it appears to have been Lew's readiness to do business with theatre people on their own turf that was the decisive factor. All the deals were specifically for a limited or trial period, but they naturally enhanced Lew's faith in his personal touch. It was an excellent start, but to maintain his new client base, Lew was also aware of the need to expand his own thin catalogue of acts and reduce his dependency on the goodwill of other agents.

His next move was to go off on a three-week continental tour of the places he had known as a Charleston dancer, but this time with recruitment in mind. On his return he pointedly showed Collins a list of the beguiling new acts he had just signed up, and Collins finally gave in. Their combined strength meant that they could boast having close to a hundred acts on their books. Lew duly moved in as a full partner of the Collins and Grade agency of 41 Charing Cross Road, an address that afforded him an excellent view of the offices of Moss Empires across the street.

Despite being strategically placed, Lew was still some distance from the top of the show business pile. Agents in those days were not a highly regarded fraternity, though by no means all of them were 'crooks' as Lew's original Morecambe benefactors imagined. They were part of a lively enterprise culture that required hustling skills of a high order in order to survive. But the calling offered only slim prospects for a young Jewish boy aiming for the heights. Many of the major theatres in the country were owned by English county families who delegated the headache of actually putting on the shows. And the managements they worked with tended to be traditional in outlook. When the Collins and Grade partnership was formed the most significant figure in theatre management was Sir Oswald Stoll, the original founder of Stoll Theatres, who also played a major role in the expansion of the Moss Empires circuit.

By the outbreak of the First World War practically every large town in Britain had theatres operating under Stoll's direction. Stoll also went on to establish his name as a leading philanthropist and the Sir Oswald Stoll Foundation is active in caring for disabled and homeless ex-servicemen to this day. Back in the mid-1930s, the Moss circuit comprised most of the big theatres in the provinces, while the closely linked Stoll Theatres dominated the London scene, along with the Syndicate Theatres chain. As far as individual acts were concerned, the real thumbs-up or thumbs-down power resided with the booking managers of these chains. The business of wooing them was an agent's number one priority.

As petitioners, at the bottom of the show business spectrum, agents were not encouraged to thrust their heads too far above the parapet. At the same time, the almost insatiable appetite for Variety acts was tending to enhance their importance. They were the people most likely to discover fresh talent across the wide range of skills in demand. A conventional Variety show had to offer an extended assortment of acts, featuring dancers, magicians, acrobats, jugglers, very likely performing dogs or other animals, and, usually topping the bill, comedians and singers or singing comedians. There were suggestions, even in its early 1930s heyday, that Variety, and indeed all live theatre, would one day be wiped out by the onward march of the cinema. However, with most of the big cinemas still booking three or four live acts a week to supplement their basic fare, this prospect appeared remote. More threatening in the long term, though scarcely noted at the time, was the first live television transmission made by the BBC in 1936.

In his new capacity as Joe Collins' partner Lew was able, with Bernard's help, to lever the family's social status up another notch. The Streatham experience came to an end when Olga and Rita were relocated in a house with a proper garden of their own, in the more verdant north-west London suburb of Dollis Hill. Lew also took a creative interest in his younger brother Leslie's hitherto chequered career. Leslie operated as the agency's errand boy on fifteen shillings a week for a spell before he expressed a desire to move on to higher things, possibly with a view to escaping excessively close scrutiny by his older brother. Lew then, invoking his new-found connections, managed to get Leslie a junior post in the office of Florence Leddington, the booking manager for the Syndicate Theatres, which serviced seven London venues. One of Leslie's more educational early experiences was to go round the theatres, making enquiries about what shows they would like to see put on. Asked how *Good Night Vienna* would go down at the Walthamstow Palace, its manager had replied, 'About as well as Good Night Walthamstow would go down in Vienna.'[4]

At the Collins and Grade agency Lew was originally considered, in his own words, 'a bit of a joke',[5] due to his habit of arriving at the office at 7 a.m., an hour before the post arrived, and planning what was invariably a long day. Lew's work also led him to spend most evenings at the theatre, either watching protectively over cherished clients or attempting to seduce those of other agents into a new allegiance. There was nothing especially novel about Lew's techniques, but his level of dedication was unheard of. It certainly contrasted markedly with that of Joe Collins, who usually arrived at the office well after ten o'clock and who also paid close attention to his leisure pursuits, which included fishing, watching football and Sundays in the country with his family. Lew had no discernible hobbies, though he could occasionally be lured out to the Empire Club in Frith Street for a game of snooker or table tennis. Collins described his new partner as a 'seven-and-a-half-day a week man'.[6]

Aside from his assiduity in the office, Lew also did most of the travelling on the agency's behalf. Like all agents, Lew was constantly on the look-out for talent capable of topping the bill at the London Palladium. But the requirements of minor league theatres, operating outside the big chains, were well worthy of attention, especially when Lew could negotiate exclusive contracts to supply them with a complete programme. In those cases the agency got an extra percentage for compiling the bill, on top of its regular 10 per cent. As his original Winter Gardens arrangement in Morecambe prospered Lew added theatres in Manchester, Salford and Preston, constituent parts of the small Broadhead chain, to his agency's list of clients. In the interests of keeping in touch and sweetening relationships, Lew made a 4 a.m. start once a month and drove off for a high-speed grand tour of the agency's northern connections, taking in Preston, where the Broadhead circuit was headquartered, Manchester, Birkenhead, St Helens, Wigan and Oldham.

Between times, he was likely to surface in Stockholm, Copenhagen or Paris, or indeed any part of Europe that housed a good circus. One aspect of the business his agency was trying to develop was what were known as 'speciality acts'. This brought him into conflict with Stanley Wathon, the German-born theatrical agent who traditionally booked most of the acts for high-profile enterprises such as Bertram Mills and the Tower Circus in Blackpool. Lew's efforts managed to dent Wathon's dominance in both sectors before the opposition was finally seen off by the war, when Wathon was interned.

Lew's faith in his ability to identify continental acts that would work in Britain only faltered on one occasion, and then only briefly. Returning from one of his forays into Europe, he interested the ABC and Union cinema circuits in a 'speciality act' called Satsuma and Ona. They booked it, sight unseen, on his recommendation. Satsuma and Ona's speciality was a 'perch' routine. This involved one man lying on the floor, balancing a long pole on his feet, while his partner climbed to the top where he performed a range of gymnastic manoeuvres that caused the pole to sway dizzyingly towards the audience. The climax involved the top man hurling a large, gleaming knife down at his partner, who would nonchalantly catch it. On the day that Satsuma and Ona opened at the Carlton cinema in Islington, Lew was told by a panic-stricken Joe Collins that he had just got word that the manager had deemed the act 'horrible'. After checking out the complaint at source, Lew's confidence was restored. The failure had not been the act itself, but one of communication. The manager thought Satsuma and Ona were terrific. 'I didn't say the act was horrible,' the manager told Lew, 'I said it was horribly frightening.'[7]

Alongside 'speciality acts' the agency developed a strong line in comedians, especially ones with good singing voices which enhanced their prospects of topping the bill. Whenever its client, the popular Jewish comedian Issy Bonn, was booked the agency was usually able to make more money by insisting on supplying the rest of the programme as part of the deal.

As the agency progressed, Lew found himself making ever more impressive contacts, at home and abroad. It was the Paris connection that eventually led him to bring over the Quintet de Hot Club de France, starring the great jazz violinist, Stéphane Grappelli, and the guitarist, Django Reinhardt, and get them bookings in England. In the process Lew made his first, slightly nervous acquaintance with Val Parnell, the authoritarian figure who was then general manager of the Moss Empires circuit. It was said of Parnell that, when told there was an agent outside his office threatening to shoot him, he barked the instruction, 'Tell him to join the queue.'[8]

Collins and Grade's other popular acts included Henry Hall and his Band, the Kit-Kat Saxophone Band and trumpeter Nat Gonella. The agency also booked Flanagan and Allen, who created the famous Crazy Gang, and Max Miller, the 'Cheeky Chappie' of music hall fame. It could also claim some part in accelerating the careers of two well-known radio performers, Elsie and Doris Waters, by booking them into the music halls, where they were a huge success as the inimitable charladies, Gert and Daisy.

In addition to recruiting new talent and broadening the horizons of older clients, Lew found himself in a position to advance the careers of close earlier acquaintances of the road. His former lover Marjorie Pointer, featuring in a new dancing group called the Pointer Trio, was taken on the agency's books, as were two of his other old dancing partners, Bobbie Medlock and Al Gold. After their falling out in France, Lew and Al Gold had repaired their friendship through the emollient offices of brother Bernard. And in the spring of 1937 Bernard himself joined the agency.

Bernard's final two years as a dancer, after Lew had left the stage, had been successful and fairly profitable. Rechristened 'The Aristocrats of Dance', he and Toko had teamed up with Jack Payne, the leading dance band leader of the day, who had a huge following on BBC radio. They travelled up and down the country with the band and even to parts of the world that Lew had failed to reach. On tour in South Africa they watched and wondered at the proficiency of a group of black mine-workers performing a Zulu war dance for the visiting entertainers. Bernard, however, was also wondering how long his own skills could be maintained. Toko, still in her teens, was, he felt, deserving of accompaniment by a younger, more athletic partner. And he needed to think about the world of work beyond dance.

Lew provided the work opportunity, though, as Bernard later recalled, it was not overly generous. The original deal was that Bernard should operate without a salary but that he could keep 50 per cent of any business he brought in. Bernard calculated that if he was lucky enough to bring in five acts, maybe six if a new partner for Toko could be found quickly, and they averaged, optimistically, £20 a week, his cut would wind up in the region of £6 a week – a miserable decline from his earnings as a dancer. Still, as he said, he 'had to start somewhere'.[9] However, the terms of Bernard's engagement improved markedly after he introduced Charlie Kunz, a painfully shy musician with a magic populist touch at the keyboard, to the agency, where his career rapidly blossomed. Bernard's association with Collins and Grade lasted for a year before he got fed up with being 'a general dogsbody for Lew'.[10] He felt, as Leslie had apparently done before, that he was more likely to find himself away from his older brother's immediate day-to-day supervision.

Lew was immune to Bernard's pleas for a 'float' to furnish him with the money needed to start up his own rival operation. But he did come up with a businesslike solution to the brotherly impasse. In return for Bernard's pledge that his new business would not try to immediately 'poach' Collins and Grade's new headliner, pianist Charlie Kunz, he handed over £300. Thus financed, Bernard moved out of Charing Cross Road and into a one-room office in Leicester Square to begin his new life as an independent theatrical agent.

His most creative initiative was to persuade Carl Heinmann, who ran the Mecca dance halls, to accept his services. Bernard had played at several of the eight Mecca halls in his dancing years and had a good working knowledge of what was required for its cabaret spots. As an agent, he brought over several of the speciality acts he had worked with on the continent and their successful transfer to England soon led to his securing an exclusive contract with Mecca.

Brother Leslie, feeling that his apprenticeship with the Syndicate Theatres chain had gone on long enough, also decided to go it alone. He opened his own tiny office in Charing Cross Road, and began inviting business for a new agency called West End Varieties. Lew was openly sceptical about the prospects for this enterprise. According to their sister, Rita, Lew told Leslie, 'You! An agent! You must be *meshugga* (crazy). Who on earth is going to have confidence in you? You're only a kid.'[11]

As the youngest son, and for that reason thought to be Olga's favourite, Leslie was not deemed to be up to the speed of his older brothers. He was physically less robust, about the same height as Lew but without any of the high-voltage energy that radiated from his eldest brother. And, unlike either Lew or Bernard, whose appearance had darkened with the passing years, Leslie had preserved into manhood some of the soft fairness of his youth. He looked, as Lew asserted, like 'a kid', but one, it transpired, who had done his homework. Indeed, on the mechanics of putting together a Variety bill, the main lesson he absorbed at Syndicate Theatres, Leslie soon provided evidence of being able to emulate, or even surpass, his older siblings. A few months after opening for business, Leslie moved to more salubrious premises in Shaftesbury Avenue.

By 1939, with war clouds darkening over Europe, the Grade brothers could hardly be considered a major force in the entertainment world, but Lew, at thirty-two, Bernard, at twenty-nine, and Leslie, at twenty-two, were already rising from the serried ranks of hopeful go-getters in the agency business. They were each in their different ways gaining a reputation, and they were happy in their chosen line of work. They had also established a useful friendship with another, slightly older trio of show businessman brothers, the Hyams. Known to their employees as 'Mr Mick', 'Mr Sid' and 'Mr Phil',[12] the Hyams ran Gaumont Super Cinemas. These were emporia of rare magnificence located in some of the poorest districts of London. They included the Troxy in Stepney, the Trocadero in Elephant and Castle and, grandest of all, the Gaumont State in Kilburn, a 4,000-seater and said to be the largest cinema in Europe.

The Hyams brothers managed their circuit with an extreme attention to detail, amply testified to by Denis Norden whose first job after leaving school was assistant boilerman at the Gaumont State. In this responsible post, Norden was taught how to delicately raise the temperature in the auditorium at certain times, most notably when a feature film depicted action in the tropics or the desert, in order to maximise the sales of ice cream and cold drinks. Lew and Leslie contributed to the overall crafty design by supplying live acts for the Cine Variety spots between the movies. Soon after the outbreak of war, 'Mr Mick' left for the United States, but 'Mr Phil' and 'Mr Sid' stayed in London, keeping an avuncular eye on the Grades' progress.

As far as the Grade brothers were concerned there was no business like show business, unless it came a mite too close to home. Growing up in an entertainment-loving household, their sister Rita naturally developed a fascination with the stage. As a child she was applauded for her lively renditions of songs like 'Easter Parade' and 'Keep Your Sunny Side Up'. She had good pitch and, like her brother Bernard, was a capable tap dancer. Aged fourteen, she slipped away from school one day to see the Canadian band leader, Teddy Joyce, who was then performing at the Kilburn Empire. After his show, Rita persuaded Joyce to audition her, mentioning, as a credential, that she was the sister of the notable young theatrical agent, Lew Grade. Joyce liked what he heard and offered Rita a job singing with the band, starting the following week.

Agog with excitement, Rita rushed home to impart the good news to Lew and Bernard, who received it with utter horror. They made it clear that they did not think show business was a proper calling for a nice Jewish girl who had experienced a sheltered upbringing. Their combined censoriousness persuaded Rita to abandon any plans for a stage career, at least until her schooling had finished. It was Lew's job, as head of the family, to get on the phone to Teddy Joyce and tell him in no uncertain terms: 'How dare you encourage fourteen-year-olds to go on the stage.'[13] Not long afterwards Lew encountered the love of his life, who had, as it happened, been singing professionally on stage since the age of twelve.

Lew's romance with Kathleen Sheila Moody began shortly after Hitler's army invaded Poland. He was taking a break at the Quality Inn in Leicester Square when he spotted Kathie, blonde and petite, sitting talking to another girl. Lew recalled: 'I thought "Dare I ask?" So I said, "Do you mind if I sit and have a cup of coffee with you?" She looked at me as if she could have killed me, but I was an agent, so she agreed. I started going out with her and, gradually I assume, she got to like me. I was mad about her instantly.'[14]

Though technically a wartime romance, their acquaintance had peacetime roots. Kathie, the eighth of nine children born to an Irish father and an English mother in Manchester, had been a performer in the first act Lew had booked into the Winter Gardens Theatre in Morecambe. It was called 'Beams' Breezy Babes' and Lew watched it at the time, but saw nothing that particularly differentiated Kathie from the twenty-three other little girls, aged twelve to fourteen, doing their thing on stage.

Recognition would come three years later when the seventeen-year-old Kathie, who had a beautiful coloratura voice, was offered the role of leading lady in *Running Wild*, a new revue featuring a comedy team called the Diamond Brothers. Or so she thought. As part of the deal she had to be vetted by Lew Grade, whose agency was involved in putting on the show. Lew vetoed her for the role, telling her she was too young. Recalling this rejection, Kathie said, 'I was furious. I really disliked him.'[15]

However, the real reason for the rejection, subsequently revealed to Kathie at the Quality Inn and later divulged in Lew's autobiography, was, 'I was secretly very attracted to her and didn't like the idea of her being exposed to smutty jokes and suggestive routines.'[16]

Kathie was apparently mollified by this explanation, but assured Lew that she really could look after herself. This, along with Kathie's favourable impression of Lew's 'beautiful, sincere, blue eyes',[17] proved to be a solid foundation for lasting affection.

SIX

Wartime

THE WAR YEARS WERE bad for the organised delivery of Variety shows, but not altogether destructive. Theatres closed when the bombs started falling, and some went dark for the duration. Yet in spite of the hazards, many opened again and flourished in the intermissions between the more devastating bombardments. Similarly, many of the people with peacetime occupations in the entertainment business opted, or were conscripted, out of it. But many others – like the Grade brothers – hung in.

For the first time in decades, the disruption of the old tightly controlled theatrical hierarchies created something like an open market, and a relatively buoyant one at that. The one aspect of Variety that escaped serious war damage was the public's appetite for it. And the showmen and entertainers who provided the fare were often seen as making a vital contribution to the nation's morale.

All three brothers emerged from the conflict with their theatrical careers and status mightily enhanced, though Lew and Leslie also saw service in uniform. British-born Leslie served in the Royal Air Force for five years, while Lew was a highly implausible soldier for eighteen months before being invalided out. Bernard tried to enlist, but was rejected. Unlike Lew, he had never got around to completing the legal technicalities of becoming naturalised. He had travelled the world on a Nissen passport, a document introduced by the League of Nations which gave refugees a recognised status, but one that fell short of full citizenship. He was therefore in 1940 still stateless, classified as an alien, and not qualified for military service.

With the outbreak of war the Grade family lost some of its hitherto remarkable cohesion. Up to that point Olga had always been at the centre of its concerns. In return for her sons' generosity in supplying her needs, she provided the touchstone for their achievements. Olga was not a matriarch in the domineering sense that implied her children went in absolute fear of her, but she had her say on anything of importance that related to them. And her forcibly expressed approbation, or censure, tended to be what counted most in the family. It revolved around her. Her home in Dollis Hill was still, for much of the time, the boys' home, even after they moved out into flats of their own shortly before the war.

Suddenly that home seemed an unsafe place to be. Lew's original idea was that Olga and Rita should be relocated in the United States as a suitable place of refuge. His second thought was to see merits in Australia, but Rita, still secretly hankering after a singing career on the English stage, would have none of it. They compromised on Bognor Regis.

Lew's mother and sister went to live there as evacuees in two small rooms of a council flat with Joe Collins's two young daughters, Joan and Jackie, as company. Then a bomb fell on Bognor. Lew went down again in his car from London to drive them to Bournemouth, and later, for a more extended stay, on to Lynton in North Devon. Later still, they moved on to Blackpool.

Brother Leslie, meanwhile, proceeded to complicate family matters no end by marrying secretly shortly before he was called up. Leslie's nerve had failed at the prospect of telling Olga that his new wife, Winifred Smith, the daughter of a business associate, was not only not Jewish, a shiksa, but heavily pregnant before the knot was tied. For the first year of their marriage, Leslie lived a double life between being a family man in and around London and paying dutiful visits to Olga, wherever she happened to be evacuated, as a loyal unmarried son.

When the secret inevitably came out, there was a new source of friction. Olga found her late-discovered granddaughter, Lynda, irresistible, but never accepted Winifred as part of the family. All this would give Lew and his new love, Kathie Moody, another shiksa, more than the war to worry about.

In one respect, however, Leslie provided a beacon of hope for the future by demonstrating that King and Country and the interests of the agency business could be served at the same time. Posted to Enfield in north London, Leslie was able to run his business practically unfettered, a privileged position that was connected to his persuading superstar 'Ukulele' George Formby to give a free performance for a RAF charity show. This, in turn, gave rise to other charity events, 'Presented by Leading Aircraftman Grade, by kind permission of the Air Ministry'.[1] Concurrently, Leslie was given time off to drive into the West End each day, where he would meet up with his business partner, Albert Knight, in the agency's Shaftesbury Avenue office and devise his own personal shows.

With Knight, who had production experience, Leslie was able to extend the role of the agent, taking it closer to impresario status. This was a stage beyond the type of exclusive booking arrangements Lew had developed in the north of England. Instead of simply providing all the acts, for a modest extra percentage, Leslie's agency put together the entire entertainment 'package' and went to a theatre's management with an offer to share the proceeds of the show, usually on the basis of 60 per cent to the agent and 40 per cent to the management. This could be appealing to managements who, in deeply troubled times, were trying to minimise their financial risks. It was of course riskier for the agent, who stood to lose most and could wind up with disgruntled clients if the deal came unstuck, or if a bomb suddenly plunged a theatre into darkness. But Leslie's luck held up well and most of his deals worked out efficiently.

When Lew enlisted he did not expect to be able to fully replicate Leslie's good fortune, but he did feel assured that he would be deployed on the entertainment side of the army's activities. His card had been marked, or so he thought, by Colonel Hodgkinson, an ex-army officer who was the musical director at the Morecambe Winter Gardens. Hodgkinson had told Lew that his entry into the army would lead to his prompt attachment to the Pioneering Corps, which badly needed an entertainments officer to cheer up the troops before going overseas.

In the event, Lew found himself sent for training to a unit of the Royal Signals Corps near Preston, and no call to entertainment service in the Pioneering Corps ever came. The army proved immune to Colonel Hodgkinson's pleadings for Lew's transfer. With his squeaky knees playing up on parade and his stomach revolting at the intake of army food, Lew began to feel thoroughly sorry for himself. He recalled, 'I felt suicidal. I honestly didn't know how I was going to survive in that atmosphere. I was having to sleep and eat alongside boys who were half my age – and I needn't have been there in the first place!'[2]

Matters were made worse by Lew's relations with one of the officers. The adjutant had asked Lew why he was not sending his mother any money out of his army pay, as many other enlisted men were doing. Lew replied with complete honesty, 'I don't have to. I still get my salary from my company, Collins and Grade, and she gets her money out of that.'[3] To the adjutant's ears this had the ring of an uppity response, which guaranteed Lew's acquaintance with the more disagreeable duties around the barracks.

To ease the awfulness of it all, Lew responded with characteristic invention by having his car sent up from London and garaged nearby. Every evening one of the garage hands parked the car outside the entrance to the barracks and Lew drove it into downtown Preston. Once there, he would park himself in the Bull and Royal Hotel's comfortable restaurant and tuck into a large evening meal. This solved the problem of how to survive on army food, essentially by avoiding it. But it only served to aggravate his problems with the adjutant, who, it transpired, had his lodgings outside the barracks – in the Bull and Royal Hotel. Outraged to discover that Lew was eating under the same roof, the adjutant demanded that 'Gunner Grade' be denied admission to the hotel. When that failed, he checked out of the hotel himself as an expression of his profound disgust.

The festering animosity between the two men endured until Lew had his accident. Instructed to ride a motorcycle for the first time in his life, Lew came close to ending it by steering the machine straight into a tree. When he recovered consciousness in Preston Hospital, he was encouraged to hear the magic word 'discharge' being bandied about in relation to his case. On returning to his unit Lew felt confident that his discharge papers would come through any day. But what came instead was another two months of purgatory in the Preston barracks before his unit was given instructions to move on to Harrogate.

The move to Harrogate, made in full kit, began and ended with a long route march which caused Lew's knees to swell up to a frightening size. He was sent to York Military Hospital and this time there was no question about his qualification for an immediate discharge. Thereupon, Lew, weak in limb but suddenly strong in bargaining power, did an unusual deal with the British army, with advantageous consequences on both sides.

The Harrogate Training Centre actually did need an entertainments specialist, and urgently. The base provided an intensive six-week training course for soldiers about to be posted overseas, and the War Office had recently given instructions that the men should be provided with some light relief prior to their leaving. As things stood, the base was equipped with a large barn-like hall, but without any entertainment to put in it. The colonel in charge of the centre asked Lew if he would do the necessary, and agree to put his discharge, to which he was now fully entitled, on hold. The word 'please' figured in the request. The terms agreed were that the colonel should keep Lew's discharge papers all completed save for the date, to be added at Lew's discretion.

For the next nine months, as the centre's voluntary in-house impresario, Lew led a charmed military life. He was free from dress restrictions and provided with his own private room. Though given the rank of lance-bombardier, he was called 'Lew' by all and sundry, as he operated outside any formal service hierarchy. He was welcomed in the officers' mess and enjoyed the dream-like experience of having the regimental sergeant major knock on his door every morning with the enquiry, 'Lew, what would you like for breakfast?'[4] Awareness of his special status, however, was not universal. Stopped by military police in the town one day, ostensibly for being incorrectly dressed, he was advised, 'You think you Jew bastards can do what you like.'[5] He was given a thumping before a cohort of Lew's mates from the base arrived and saw the policemen off.

Inside the base, Lew could do no wrong after he kitted out the hall with curtains, lighting and basic scenery from London to create the desired theatrical effects. And his productions for the outgoing troops, staged every Sunday evening with artistes imported through his connections, were all reckoned to be massive hits.

With the freedom to come and go where he pleased to recruit talent, Lew made several visits to London, where he was able to pick up the threads of his Collins and Grade agency career and fine-tune his romance with Kathie in hope of an early wedding date. By now Lew was well acquainted with several of Kathie's sisters and had earned good marks with her mother by presciently advising her to move out of her Primrose

Hill home, located near a gun battery in Regent's Park, shortly before it was obliterated in a bombing raid. Kathie, meanwhile, had become a successful singer, much in demand and earning over £100 a week, more than Lew's army and agency pay combined. At this stage Lew acquired the one item of jewellery that he wore every day: a gold bracelet inscribed '1123014 Lance Bombardier Grade L. With all my love darling. Kathie.'[6]

Kathie also often starred on BBC radio's popular *Variety Bandbox* show and, in June 1942, she sang at a special 'Aid to Russia' show at the London Coliseum, which was staged by Lew as an extension of his military duties. Immediately after the Coliseum show, Lew told his colonel that he would be filling in the date on his discharge documents, on grounds of his imminently impending marriage.

Lew and Kathie were married at Caxton Hall Registry Office on 23 June 1942, Kathie's twenty-first birthday. Photographs of the wedding establish that she was a genuinely beautiful bride. Lew, at thirty-five, presented a dapper figure, only slightly thickened since his dancing days. His hair was stylishly slicked back and, aside from mild recession at the temples, largely intact. Among those wishing the couple well on the day were representatives of the War Office and several senior officers from the Harrogate Centre, who came bearing a tea and dinner service as a wedding gift. Joe Collins, as best man, headed a strong show business contingent. Olga, however, was conspicuous by her absence, unable to witness the spectacle of a second son marrying 'out'.

Lew's marriage to Kathie was rapidly followed by a business divorce. On his return to the agency full time, Lew's relationship with Joe Collins took a sharp turn for the worse. It is possible, after the respite afforded by his partner's military career, that the senior man was suddenly made to feel yet older by Lew's renewed hyper-energetic presence. But for whatever reason, tempers grew drastically short on both sides, with Joe concluding one office row by throwing his telephone on the floor and bawling, 'Right. You run the business.'[7]

The upshot was to be that Lew disentangled himself from Collins and Grade and went into partnership with his brother Leslie, whose relaxed arrangement at RAF Hendon was beginning to look less secure. They negotiated a favourable loan of £10,000 from Sid and Phil Hyams, whose cinema circuit was still highly profitable, and set up the Lew and Leslie

Grade agency. The time Lew and Leslie actually spent working together during the war was nonetheless limited. In early 1943 Leslie became a father for the second time when Lynda's brother, Michael, was born, but his family and business life was soon dislocated when the RAF posted him to North Africa.

Lew took sole charge of an agency with five show 'packages' touring the country, a useful list of top-liners on the books headed by the Billy Cotton Band, a broad range of middling attractions, and money in the bank. These responsibilities required high-level negotiating skills, but there was still time for the occasional lingering vigil outside Cranbourne Mansions where the Moss Empires headquarters was located, in order to keep a look-out for cheerful-looking artistes emerging from the building. Reasoning that their good spirits were proof of their having just found work, Lew offered them a cup of coffee and his services as a good agent. And if they already had a good agent, they might conceivably be interested in getting a better one.

It was all part of his aim, avowed from the beginning, to make the Lew and Leslie Grade agency the greatest ever. In 1943 he had some way to go, but he did achieve early mastery of how to look like a tycoon.

The first person to equip him with a seven-inch cigar was his new wife. Soon after their marriage, Kathie astutely realised that her husband was not quite as super confident as he liked to appear. Indeed, when dealing with the major circuits and some of the bigger stars, he could experience anxieties that made him almost tongue-tied. In pursuit of a remedy, Kathie took a box of cigars into Lew's office with the suggestion, 'Why don't you offer these to some of your stars when they come in to see you. Perhaps it'll put you at your ease with them.'[8] The box lay unopened for several weeks, until one day Lew decided to dip into it and light one of its contents. As he was taking his first puffs, Val Parnell, the Moss Empires executive who ranked as Lew's most intimidating business contact, came on the line.

'Yes, Val,' said Lew, leaning back and waving the cigar expansively, 'what can I do for you?'[9]

Having discovered the confidence-enhancing qualities of a good smoke, Lew became an addict and an evangelist. Eventually his consumption of Montecristo cigars rose to sixteen a day, and he gave away almost as many as he smoked. 'Have one,' he would say. 'They give you energy.'[10]

Bernard was an interested observer of Lew and Leslie's business arrangements, though not an envious one. 'There was never any question of my going in with them,' he recalled in *East End, West End*, offering a snapshot of the brothers' relationship at that time. 'Lew and I were too much alike to spend long in each other's company. Both outward-going personalities who enjoyed the limelight, we were natural competitors. Leslie, on the other hand, was more the backroom boy who was happiest when he had his head down in the account books or was negotiating on the telephone . . . They made a perfect couple. Three would have been a crowd.'[11]

Bernard was not the most motivated agent in the business, but he sensibly recruited as an associate someone who was. Billy Marsh, a one-time farmer's boy from Kent with an obsessive attention to detail, provided the necessary TLC for the performers represented by the Bernard Delfont Agency. This freed Bernard for the contemplation of grander designs. After ten years footing the bill as a dancer, he had a keen desire to see his name at the very top in the form of 'Bernard Delfont presents'.

Bernard wanted to have the hands-on experience of putting on his own productions, including musicals and straight plays as well as Variety bills. His hero was the great impresario Charles B. Cochran, who produced more than a hundred West End shows, promoted the occasional world championship boxing match, and twice went spectacularly bankrupt. Of the three Grade brothers, Bernard was the one most addicted to risk, albeit of the calculated variety. 'I believe in pushing my luck,' he would say, 'but not in giving it an almighty shove.'[12]

To those who knew him in the war years, Bernard always seemed to be on the verge of insolvency as he juggled his projects, constantly robbing Peter to pay Paul, though he always repaid Peter eventually. His first initiative on the production side was *Hello America*, which was based on the simple idea of bringing all the main American acts available in Britain together in one programme. Revivals of old favourites, such as *The Admirable Crichton* and *Rose Marie* and *The Student Prince*, followed in its wake. With the cash flow from these enterprises he bought up the leases of any London theatres that were going cheap, as many were after the

Blitz. By 1945, 'without investing a fortune'[13] as he recalled, Bernard controlled seven West End theatres – The Whitehall, St Martins, Garrick, Saville, Comedy, Winter Gardens and Duke of York's.

But finance of a high order was required to stage Bernard's shows as they became increasingly ambitious. The start-up money needed for *Old Chelsea*, an extravagant musical production starring Richard Tauber, the most famous tenor of the day, and Carole Lynne, was a then prodigious £30,000, way beyond Bernard's means. Fortunately, Sid and Phil Hyams, the cash-heavy cinema owners who had previously extended a favourable loan to Lew and Leslie, were also inclined to smile on the efforts of their brother. They came through with most of the money. Though blessed with 'My Heart and I', a song that made hoarse-voiced tenors of half the nation, *Old Chelsea* had rotten luck, with its run being seriously curtailed by the bombing. But an opportunity to recoup was achieved with *Gay Rosalinda*, based on the Johann Strauss operetta *Die Fledermaus*, which deployed the versatile Tauber, by his own choice, as the man wielding the baton in the orchestra pit.

Through much of the war, Bernard and Lew kept in close touch, especially after Bernard moved his office into Astoria House in Shaftesbury Avenue, one floor above the Lew and Leslie Grade agency. But the two brothers kept their business dealings strictly separate. Lew's enterprise was unquestionably the more successful in the art of recruiting or, when necessary, poaching new talent. Nonetheless, Bernard was disinclined to see this as much of a threat as long as his impresario activities were going well. The only point on which the brothers seriously combined their forces was in their efforts to scupper the stage career of the young woman billed as 'Rita Grey, Sweet Sophistication', London's newest singing sensation.

Grey was the stage name of their sister Rita, who had slipped away from her last place of evacuation with her mother, in Blackpool. She resurfaced in London, where, aged eighteen, she landed a job singing in a touring show called *See Such Fun*. Lew and Bernard repeated the mantra about show business being no place for 'a nice Jewish girl' but this time it cut no ice. Indeed, Rita insisted that Bernard put her in one of his musicals. Deeming it wise to placate his sister, Bernard gave her a part in his revival of *No, No, Nanette*. She played Betty from Bath and sang 'I

Want to Be Happy'. After her first night Bernard sent her a telegram, which she cherished – 'Even if you weren't my sister, I'd still use you.'[14]

But Bernard had only given ground in order to regroup. At the war's end he and Lew weighed in heavily with another argument: it's all very well for a nice Jewish girl to boost the nation's morale by singing in time of war, but in peacetime . . . Having had her modest taste of fame, Rita viewed this as a clincher and eventually went back to living with Olga in Bournemouth, her mother's ultimate address after going almost full circle round the country as an evacuee.

In one sense the Grades could be said to have had a lucky war in that all the family's members emerged from it alive. The closest call was experienced by Kathie's sister, Norah, while appearing in pantomime at the Ilford Hippodrome, the venue where Lew had won his first Charleston competition. During a performance in January 1945 the theatre sustained a direct hit by a V2 rocket, though the injuries Norah sustained were, thankfully, minor.

Even so, the outbreak of peace was almost as traumatic for the Grade family as the onset of war had been. Leslie, who had gone down with typhoid fever while serving with the RAF in Cairo, was still in a weak condition when he came home to England to find that his wife had fallen for another man. Winifred, never comfortable as a Grade family member, had taken up with Kenneth Walton Beckett, who was serving as radio operator and front gunner in Bomber Command. And it seemed to be a serious arrangement. At one stage Lew and Kathie moved out of their Cavendish Square flat, off Regent Street, hoping to provide a comfortable ambience for reconciliation between Leslie and Winifred. To no avail. Leslie filed a divorce petition in February 1946, on the grounds of his wife's adultery, and was eventually granted custody of Lynda and Michael. The actual rearing of the children, however, was entrusted to Olga. They would remain with her even after Leslie's second marriage to Audrey Smith, a dancer, who was also not Jewish.

Divorce also featured, rather more flagrantly, in Bernard's immediate post-war odyssey. He had fallen in love with Carole Lynne, who starred in two of his wartime productions, *Old Chelsea* and *The Student Prince*, and who was already married to a war hero. Her husband was the film actor Derek Farr, who had served in the army with distinction through the El

Alamein campaign and in the invasion of Normandy. The hearing of Farr's divorce petition, on 14 June 1945, was a rugged day for Bernard, made worse by the press picking up on an exchange that clearly showed the judge's antipathy. Told in evidence that Farr had on one occasion been summoned to Bernard's room to discuss his wife's affair, the judge inferred that this was an example of Bernard pulling show business rank on the betrayed husband. When asked if the venue was dictated by Farr's being 'only an actor' while Bernard was 'a producer', Farr replied, 'I don't know.' 'Neither do I,' said the judge, 'but it seems monstrous.'[15]

In fact, the location of the meeting had been agreed by the two men, but the sting in the judge's remark lingered on in the Grade family for a very long time, though without deflecting the romance from its course. Bernard and Carole were married quietly at Caxton Hall on 22 January 1946, with Lew and Leslie in close attendance. Richard Tauber was the best man. As Carole was not Jewish, Olga completed a hat-trick of non-attendances at her sons' nuptials.

Despite her failure to show up on their wedding days, Olga went on to establish relations of great warmth with all her Gentile daughters-in-law (aside from Winifred). This was no doubt partly due to the full re-establishment of her matriarchal importance in the family. As the person with direct responsibility for the nurture and raising of the first Grade grandchildren, she could allow herself to be generous. But it seems to have been more closely connected to a strain of fatalistic acceptance in her nature that almost certainly derived from the privation of her early years as a refugee.

As a young boy, Leslie's son, Michael, was fascinated by a conversation on Bournemouth beach that seemed to provide an insight into the complexities of his grandmother's thought processes. Surrounded by an audience of elderly ladies, Olga launched into an emphatic discourse on the evils of Jewish boys marrying outside their faith. Eventually one of the old ladies summoned up the courage to interrupt her flow by saying, 'But, Olga, your three sons married four shiksas.'

'That was different,' replied Olga, quite uncorrected, 'it was *beshect*.'[16] Fate.

SEVEN

Taking Planes

IT SOON BECAME CLEAR that the war years had trained up some wonderful comic talent. Harry Secombe, Spike Milligan, Tony Hancock, Jimmy Edwards, Frank Muir and Denis Norden were among the many who entertained their fellow troops in time of war, earning themselves the title of 'NAAFI entertainers'. Even so, the first stage of their post-war careers was often fraught with difficulty. Experience in raising a laugh from captive audiences of soldiers en route for the front line was not, they discovered, quite the same thing as enlivening admission-paying, civilian theatregoers.

Harry Secombe, in the first flush of peace, refined what he thought was a hilarious routine demonstrating how different characters went about the business of shaving while singing an aria from *The Barber of Seville*. It always got a laugh with the troops. After it had played in Bolton to a hushed peacetime audience, the theatre manager paid him off with the comment, 'In future he can shave on his own bloody time.' Peter Sellers, despairing of a mirthful response in Coventry, came on stage one night and solemnly played a record of Jimmy Shand's eightsome reels instead of his regular act. He then bowed and walked off to the realisation that he was getting 'more applause than I usually did'.[1]

Denis Norden recalled a nervous atmosphere being engendered by post-war theatre managements, empowered to remove an act from the line-up after the first house on Monday. Hence the ominous backstage sign: 'Do not send out your laundry until the manager has seen your act.'[2]

These were uncertain times, not only for artistes but for the agencies who represented them. But the Lew and Leslie Grade agency, allied with

Albert Knight who had rejoined the operation as general manager after a spell in the RAF, seemed to have a better idea than most of the way ahead. It could soon boast of having twelve different Variety shows on the road, with a full complement of nine acts in each show, along with some special productions. One special, based on a popular newspaper cartoon, was called *Jane of the Daily Mirror* and featured showgirls in advancing stages of undress. In those days the law, expressed by the rubric 'If you move, it's rude',[3] dictated that nudes could only appear on stage striking static attitudes. So the action was essentially restricted to a series of tableaux representing the seasons of the year, with autumn – when the leaves fell – ranking as the most risqué.

The imaginative flights in these productions were primarily those of Bert Knight, while Lew and Leslie directed their main energies to building up the muscle of the agency. The method chosen was to acquaint their contemporaries with the safety offered by numbers. By the end of 1946, they had recruited some twenty other agents into their operation, each paid a modest salary and incentivised with a small percentage. In the process the operation grew to a point where it had to take over two floors of a large building in Regent Street to provide extra leg-room. Lew was particularly adept at persuading his peers that life under the wing of the Grades could be more profitable than independence in a declining market. With the resumption of the BBC's television transmissions, which had been suspended during the war, and Hollywood gearing up its peacetime assault on the cinema circuits, it was evident that Variety could not achieve pre-war levels of popularity. And those delivering the goods had to become better organised to survive.

Some of those recruited were novice agents, but the Grade bandwagon was also joined by many with good client lists of their own, people such as Dennis Selinger, who represented Peter Sellers, and Solly Black, an ex-boxer and Lew's personal favourite among the new recruits, who had a young comedian called Spike Milligan heading his list of clients. Within the business the Grade expansion programme caused some surprise, but it seems to have excited little resentment. Indeed, it was seen as having some benevolent features in that it offered a refuge for smaller agents, naturally nervous in a predatory world of having their acts 'poached', very possibly of course by the Grades.

Both brothers were already reckoned to be past masters of what was known in the business as 'schmooze', the winning flattery and attention that kept clients loyal. They also had some competence in the administration of what were called 'unhappiness pills', doom-laden prophecies that could when, all else failed, be slipped to the clients of rival agents to assist them in a change of allegiance. Small agents confronted with the choice of being in a hired situation, which still allowed them to maintain contact with the clients they had developed, or an uncertain independence that entailed losing all control of their precious human assets, were disposed to look favourably on what Lew and Leslie had to offer.

One of the things specifically not on offer was a quiet life. According to Bert Knight, high-decibel argument was very much part of the office routine: 'Lew and Leslie shouted at each other, constant rows about one of them paying too much, why did you book so and so. You would have thought they were deadly rivals at certain times when you heard them discussing business.'[4] Both were obsessed with work, abjuring holidays and taking only short breaks during a working day that began at the crack of dawn, although Lew would occasionally sneak out for a game of snooker with Solly Black.

While similar in some respects, there was a manifest contrast in their styles of operation. Dena Waldman, who worked as a secretary to both brothers at different times, saw Leslie as perhaps being the more hard-headed in business terms, but Lew had the more emollient technique. She said, 'Lew might have the same object, in fixing a deal, or trying to book someone, or taking an act from another agent, but he would do it in a nicer way, using charm. Lew was very good at buttering people up, doing little favours for them. He had more finesse when dealing with people.'[5]

What was most evident was the degree to which their talents complemented each other. Leslie was the master organiser, keeping track of the agency's rapidly expanding interests and monitoring the day-to-day activities of its artistes; Lew was the outfit's peripatetic super salesman. Leslie lived on the telephone, while Lew spent much of his time on the road. Their epic office rows, though widely celebrated and thoroughly enjoyed by the agency's staff, were limited by Lew being so often up, up and away. It was soon apparent that one aspect of Lew's genius was an infinite capacity for taking planes.

Initially, most of his travelling would focus on the continent of Europe, where Lew went about the business of resuscitating his pre-war circus contacts. At the Knie Circus in Switzerland he encountered the Pierre Elysée Trio, whose trapeze act featured a man doing a triple somersault. Deeply impressed, Lew promptly signed them up for a full season at Blackpool's Tower Circus. Further bookings would arise from his visits to the Schumann Circus in Copenhagen, the Circus Togni in Italy, and Cirque Medrano and Circus Bougliani in Paris. Along the way, Lew assiduously beefed up the Variety side of his enterprise with deals designed to introduce new performers, like the young singer Edith Piaf, to Britain. Although the agency had no contact with America at that stage, Lew alertly signed up any continental stars who took his fancy for America as well. Just in case.

Within the space of two peacetime years the Lew and Leslie Grade operation established itself as the second largest theatrical agency in Britain, but it was a distant second. The number one berth was occupied, as had been the case before the war, by Harry Foster's agency, which still maintained a long lead. Fosters had the precious advantage of being linked with the powerful William Morris agency in New York. This provided a conduit for many of the American stars who were popular in British venues after the war, the London Palladium being their prime showcase. However, Val Parnell, who had assumed full responsibility for bookings at the Palladium after the death of George Black in 1945, began to feel that Harry Foster was too conservative in his approach, and let it be known that he was considering other options. This was Lew's window of opportunity.

In January 1947 Lew arrived in New York, accompanied by George Le Roy, his agency's long-time representative in Paris, and equipped with letters of introduction supplied by Val Parnell. Lew later recalled his first attempt at beguiling the movers and shakers of the American entertainment world as being a less than spectacular success. Accustomed to experiencing the warmest of welcomes on his European tours, Lew found the brusqueness of New York off-putting. At Lindy's, the famous delicatessen near Times Square, he and Le Roy incautiously asked another diner for help in getting a table. 'Sure,' was the man's response, gesticulating randomly to a waiter. 'Get these bums a table.'[6] And as they went round the agencies, endeavouring to talk up the mutual benefits of a tie-in with the Grade operation, the responses they received often seemed to be on a similar level of impoliteness. After two weeks in the city, Lew said, 'I couldn't wait to get home. The number of rejections we were getting really undermined my confidence.'[7]

But Lew had left his calling card much more efficiently than he had originally imagined. On a second visit to the United States a few months later, taking in Hollywood this time, he reaped the benefits of the first miserable trip by shaking hands on a deal with the mighty Music Corporation of America (MCA) which firmly established his credibility on the American scene. Under the terms of the deal Lew became the exclusive representative in Europe for personal appearances of all the corporation's talent, while MCA undertook to represent and book in the United States any suitable talent provided by the Lew and Leslie Grade agency. As the appetite for US stars in Britain was comfortably in excess of the demand for British acts in the United States, Lew saw himself as being on the more favourable end of the deal.

The MCA arrangement was the decisive factor that persuaded Lew to concentrate his best energies on the American market. Within the Grade agency his responsibilities for finding new acts on the continent were delegated to Solly Black and Brian Roxbury, another of the outfit's bright young men. Freed for more transatlantic travel, Lew took care to develop a wide range of contacts, particularly with the American TV networks, which were then seen as the breeding ground for upcoming talent. His lucrative relationship with MCA lasted almost two years before the corporation, evidently tiring of an arrangement that seemed be enriching its British friend without offering sufficient compensating advantages to MCA, made Lew an offer – to buy Lew and Leslie Grade Ltd outright.

Lew was tempted. The money was good, and the offer came with a pledge of guaranteed continued employment for Lew and Leslie. When acquainted with the offer Leslie said he would go along with whatever Lew decided. Kathie, however, unusually, did state a strong preference. On a conducted tour of MCA's smart New York office in the company of her husband, she happened to notice one executive being ticked off for spending too long on a long-distance call. At the end of the tour, she turned to Lew and apparently crystallised his thoughts by saying: 'I'm sorry darling, but I don't think you should accept their offer. You won't be happy working for a huge corporation like MCA. If you have to account for every telephone call you make – and you know how much time you spend on the phone – it'll drive you crazy.'[8]

Lew rejected the offer, and when MCA predictably declined to continue with the old arrangement, he had a response ready to slot into place. Within a week of the termination of the MCA agreement, Lew and Leslie Grade Inc. opened its first American office on West 57th Street in New York, and set about establishing alternative pathways to the American stars. Lew was its chairman, and the knowledgeable Eddie Elkort, formerly of MCA, became its president. Soon afterwards they established another branch office of the business, on Hollywood's Sunset Strip.

Lew's success in establishing an American beachhead automatically warmed his relationship with the autocratic Val Parnell. With Lew's help Parnell managed to provide the Palladium with a range of American pop stars who had gone undetected on Harry Foster's more old-fashioned show business radar. However, Lew's eagerness to overtake the Fosters agency caused an embarrassing rupture in relations with his brother Bernard, whose prime ambition after the war came to focus on the London Casino, a musical theatre off Cambridge Circus.

In 1947 Bernard acquired its lease and set about mounting the most ambitious undertaking of his career thus far. His idea was to make it an upmarket Variety theatre with international headliners, which he saw as being complementary to the shows being put on at the Palladium. His first major attraction was Laurel and Hardy, past their peak in Hollywood but still well loved in Britain. They went down so well that Bernard, after putting out feelers in the United States, was able to bring over further crowd-pleasers of the calibre of Sophie 'The Red Hot Mamma' Tucker, the melodious Ink Spots and Chico Marx. This was an expensive under-taking, as the main act rarely cost less than £1,000 a week, though in Chico Marx's case Bernard was able to mitigate the expense by organising a short provincial tour for him after his Casino engagement, taking in Hull, Dudley and Coventry. 'Eternal Gratitude', Chico cabled Bernard after his return to America, 'for sending me to Hell, Deadly and Cemetery.'[9]

Despite the expense, Bernard was close to ecstatic at the good houses he was getting at the Casino. Unfortunately, Val Parnell also noticed they were good, indeed too good. Bernard was summoned into Parnell's presence and told, 'You must stop this nonsense. You're hurting the Palladium and I won't have that.' When Bernard advanced the argument that the West End was surely big enough for both of them, Parnell responded, 'I give you fair warning. If you go on, I'll break you.'[10]

And he very nearly did. In the wake of the Parnell interview Bernard rapidly discovered that in any showdown with the Palladium's boss, he was pretty much on his own. And this applied to his own family as much as anybody else in the business. In a rueful passage in *East End, West End,* Bernard recalled going to see his brother Lew and asking if he could exercise his American contacts and come up with some stars for the Casino. Lew shook his head, before indicating where his business loyalties had to lie: 'Not a chance of booking them. Val Parnell comes first.'[11]

'I pleaded family loyalty,' Bernard related, 'I pleaded wife and daughter, I pleaded a lot of things but Lew was adamant. I couldn't blame him. The interests of the Grade Agency dictated a good working relationship with Val Parnell who had not only the Palladium at his command but all the best provincial theatres. Still, I can't say I was not hurt.'[12]

Parnell showed he meant business by hiring American acts that Bernard was targeting at prices the Casino could not hope to compete with. He also banned the acts on Bernard's books from further appearances on the Moss Empires circuit. According to Billy Marsh, who ran the agency side of the Delfont operation, 'Bernie never did mean to take on Parnell. But that was the way it seemed. Val's tactics brought us a crisis.'[13]

Realising that he could not match Parnell in a bidding war, Bernard hung in for a while with some of the more talented British performers his own agency had helped to develop, most notably the comedian Norman Wisdom and a black pianist, then resident in Brixton, called Winifred Atwell. But it was a rearguard action. Parnell's money power allied with Lew's new-found American connections could only lead to one outcome. Eventually, the Grade agency combined forces with the Fosters agency to bring over the American comedian, Danny Kaye, who was an absolute smash hit at the Palladium. Parnell was jubilant. Soon afterwards Bernard gave up the Casino's unequal struggle, and retired from the field to contemplate his losses.

Despite their rivalry, Lew derived no pleasure from his brother's discomfiture. It was their different relationships with Parnell that had set them, inadvertently, on a collision course. There was no lasting bitterness between them, but some lasting wariness in that they always thereafter tried to avoid head-to-head business conflicts, though not always successfully. In the short term, however, any problems were smoothed out through the emollient effects of the Folies Bergère.

In the spring of 1949 an unrepentant Bernard resurfaced with the idea of giving the famous Parisian entertainment a British airing. Lew had the fonder memories of France's stylish striptease culture, but it was Bernard who developed the contacts that made it possible, under strict Gallic supervision, to create a cross-Channel version of the show. Bernard let it be known that he envisaged putting it on at the Saville, one of the theatres acquired in his wartime lease-buying spree that he had managed to hang on to. He also envisaged, correctly, that Val Parnell would be unable to resist taking an interest in the enterprise. Eventually, on cue, Parnell approached Bernard with the suggestion that the Folies Bergère could be better presented at one of his Moss Empire theatres, namely the Hippodrome off Leicester Square. Bernard was happy to accept this arrangement, though less thrilled when Parnell insisted that his name should appear as co-presenter of the show. But at least it ensured they could all again be the very best of pals.

The good vibes engendered by the Folies Bergère ensured that all three Grade brothers were in an upbeat frame of mind in the run-up to the major family event of the year – their sister Rita's marriage to Joe Freeman, who was not only Jewish but a doctor into the bargain, with his own practice in Twickenham. After the experience of having three of her children marry 'out', Olga was about to enjoy the wedding of her dreams. And her sons exuberantly planned to give it the works. Rita remembered Bernard introducing her around as 'the sister who was soon to make the family respectable'.[14] While Lew, whose job it was to give her away, enlivened Rita's pre-nuptial experience by rendering a mock wedding speech attired in his pyjamas and a top hat.

On the appointed day in September, the bridal party proceeded from

Lew and Kathie's Cavendish Square home in a black Rolls-Royce to the New West End Synagogue in St Petersburgh Place, which had to be cordoned off by the police to hold back the crowd of well-wishers.

At the reception in the Park Lane Hotel there were more than three hundred guests, drawn from every echelon of show business. Maurice Chevalier fronted a continental contingent, saying he would not have missed the event 'for zee world'. The ample Sophie Tucker weighed in from America, exciting comparison with another guest, the home-grown 'Two Ton' Tessie O'Shea. George Formby was there, as was band leader Billy Cotton, and a buzzing 'Big Hearted' Arthur Askey who greeted all and sundry with his famous catchphrase, 'Hello playmates'. Lew did a demonstration Charleston, while brother Leslie's new dancer wife, Audrey, contributed an exuberant can-can.

It was perhaps all a bit over the top for the union of a suburban general practitioner and his young bride, but thoroughly in keeping for what Olga termed 'the first real wedding in the family'.[15]

EIGHT

Up with the Stars

L EW GRADE WAS FOND of saying that without Kathie Moody he would only ever have been known as an ex-world champion Charleston dancer. A typical hymn in praise of his wife ran as follows: 'Kathie gives me tremendous support. She has tremendous belief in me, a greater belief than she should have. She helps me. She supports me. She answers the telephone for me. She gets the same excitement out of the business as I do. People don't realise that without my wife I might have been nothing.'[1]

However, Lew's gain had to be considered, to some extent, a show business loss. From the beginning of their marriage it was evident that Kathie had a talent that transcended that required by any domestic environment. Cecil Madden, the BBC's first Head of Programmes, said of her, 'I could have made her a very big star. But she decided instead to devote herself to being Lew's wife.'[2]

It was nonetheless a decision that was made by degrees. As a young wife Kathie cut back severely on touring engagements, though she was among those who starred in the first post-war TV Variety show broadcast from Alexandra Palace, along with the Beverley Sisters and a ten-year-old Petula Clark. She later featured in several television shows, culminating in her appearance as the principal boy, Prince Charming, in a Boxing Day production of *Cinderella* as late as 1950. But emotional support for Lew in his drive to build the world's best theatrical agency always came first, and eventually Kathie would turn down all offers of work. She never became an anonymous 'Her Indoors', but most of her public appearances were in a supporting role to her husband.

Although they had no children of their own, Lew and Kathie presided over a lively domestic situation, particularly after Olga, with Lynda and Michael still in her charge, moved back from the coast to live near them in an apartment off the Edgware Road, and later even closer in Wimpole Street. In his autobiography, Michael Grade wrote of how much he enjoyed the visits to see Kathie and Lew at Cavendish Square as a child, not least because 'we got plenty of treats'.[3] Lynda also appreciated the opportunity for extended stays with her aunt Kathie when she found life under Olga's guardianship too overpowering.

Nevertheless, Kathie did not immerse herself in family life without some sense of sacrifice, and of deferment to her husband's wishes. Looking back, she would say, apparently without resentment, 'It was obvious he didn't want me to be a success [on the stage]. He didn't encourage me, and I realised that if I was a success, he couldn't be. Anyway, it was obvious he was the brainy one and needed taking care of.' Her compensation was their closeness as a couple. 'I see him a lot,' she said. 'Usually with a telephone glued to his ear, but I see him. Probably more than most wives.'[4]

By the early 1950s Lew could certainly be rated a success, as was illustrated by the 'Knock, knock' story that was going the rounds of the theatrical community at the time. To the opening 'Who's there?' the responses progressed:

'Lew and Leslie.'

'Lew and Leslie who?'

'Lew and Leslie who! No wonder you've got no work.'[5]

The agency Lew and Leslie had built up now employed more than a hundred people occupying five floors of Regent House in neighbourly proximity to the London Palladium. It had edged ahead of Fosters as the most important British agency operating in the United States. And it was still setting a frantic pace. Peter Pritchard, one of the young agents lured from Fosters to work with the Grades at that time, always remembered an exchange with Leslie Grade about his starting time for work the next day.

'Is it OK for seven?' asked Leslie.

'Won't you be shut by then?' asked Pritchard, puzzled.

'Seven in the morning, you berk,' said Leslie.[6]

With the expansion of the business, Lew's own energies would be increasingly directed to securing the big stars for the flagship London theatres like the Palladium and the Hippodrome. And his confidence was high. 'By now,' he recalled in *Still Dancing*, 'there was no star in the world I was afraid to approach. With my cigar to give me Dutch courage, and my excellent track record to stand surety for me, I usually got who, and what, I wanted.'[7]

What was most wanted was a flow of top-flight American entertainers to meet Val Parnell's requirements. To ensure this, Parnell sometimes accompanied Lew on his trips to the United States. They must have seemed an odd couple to their transatlantic cousins. With Parnell, an aloof 6ft 3in, towering over his fast-talking, pocket-sized, smoke-wreathed companion, it would be hard to imagine more contrasting British types. But they were highly effective, and apparently lucky with it.

On one Stratocruiser flight back to England, Lew was seized with severe stomach pains. Concerned about his welfare, Parnell asked the passenger in one of the lower sleeping bunks if he could change places with Lew, who could not manage the ascent into the upper bunk assigned to him. The request was graciously acceded to by a man who turned out to be General Sarnoff, owner of the National Broadcasting Company (NBC) and later a pioneer of colour on American TV. Another great show business relationship was established, while Lew's stomach pain, caused by a cyst in the groin, was alleviated by a simple operation back in England.

Relationship was at the heart of Lew's method. Having had what he regarded as a poor experience by virtually going in cold on his first New York visit, he was a firm apostle of the need to know somebody, or know somebody who knew somebody, as the crucial preliminary to any deal. And if one of the chain of known somebodies was high up in the business, so much the better. Thus, as a result of his stomach complaint, he could now claim to be on high-flying terms with the heads of all three American TV networks, the others being Leonard Goldenson of the American Broadcasting Corporation (ABC) Network and William Paley of the Columbia Broadcasting Company (CBS). Their names might not mean much to the average TV viewer or theatregoer, but they were wonderfully useful to drop into any business context.

The names that did mean something to British theatregoers were those of the actual American stars, and Lew ensured they got plenty of them.

Among the male entertainers who owed their British appearances to Lew's efforts were Bob Hope, Jack Benny, Nat King Cole, Cab Calloway, Harry Belafonte, Louis Armstrong, Johnnie Ray and Mario Lanza; the female list was headed by Judy Garland, Jo Stafford and the sarong girl, Dorothy Lamour. Lew's services to these performers did not end with their arrival in London, as he and Kathie were often intensively involved in providing the off-stage therapy that their star status required during their stay in England. Though disinclined to tell tales, Lew did confide to his autobiography something of the special problems of dealing with the emotionally fluctuating Judy Garland and the barrel-chested tenor Mario Lanza, and the abiding worries about getting them to the theatre on time:

> Some nights it was really touch and go, and Kathie and I found ourselves having to be psychiatrist, wet-nurse, wife and father-confessor all rolled up into one. Handling temperamental stars, I discovered early on, was an art in itself, and if you didn't learn the art quickly, you could be in big trouble. With Lanza it was a case of pandering to an inflated ego all the time; with Garland it was just the reverse. You had to keep building up her confidence and reassuring her how good she was. Either way, though, it didn't make life easy.[8]

The importance of ego massage was also drilled into the Grade staffers when, as frequently happened, they were enlisted in the cause of entertaining the American stars in their leisure moments. One young agent, assigned to the job of providing a superstar singer with a relaxing day's golf, was seriously reprimanded for incautiously outplaying his opponent on the links. 'You obviously haven't got the bloody idea,' Lew told him, on learning of this outrageous breach of protocol, 'You always let clients win.'[9]

Lew's cosseting of the stars, though no doubt born of a generous sympathy for all great entertainers, was also an integral part of the agency's sales effort. He had his personal favourites like the comedians Jack Benny and Bob Hope, whose wit was constantly refreshed by a peripatetic platoon of gag writers, but no visiting star was allowed to return home feeling other than deeply loved and cherished. As Lew saw it, their reporting of a wonderful experience in London would encourage others to follow, and very likely at more favourable rates, as entertainers who were actually keen to come over to England tended to cost a lot less. He was proved right to the extent that an appearance at the London Palladium did come to be regarded as an important item on the CV of many American performers.

Lew's confidence in his star-spotting ability never seriously wavered, but he did learn to think of himself as less than infallible. On one trip with Parnell, taking in the Latin Quarter in Miami, their attention was directed to a dishevelled singer with an ill-fitting toupée, and who went by the name of Frankie Laine. Both were impressed with his total unsuitability for the Palladium, until they returned home to find Leslie insisting that Laine should be booked on account of his hit record 'Jealousy', which was then zooming up the charts. The booking was duly made and, with a more precisely fitting toupée, Laine was a big success at the Palladium. This enabled the deskbound Leslie to crow to the two globetrotting talent-spotters, 'The trouble with you chaps is that you don't listen to the radio as much as I do.'[10]

On some occasions the talent sought out the Grade brothers. One day Lew received a call from Frank Sinatra, who was passing through London and urgently required $12,000 in cash to pick up on his arrival in Rome the next day. Lew rapidly transformed the favour into a relationship by ensuring delivery of the money, and Sinatra called from Rome to ask what Lew would like in return. Lew specified ten concerts in Italy on dates he could arrange, and Sinatra was happy to agree. Lew was later asked by a show business writer whether he had ever got the actual money back. 'Ask for $12,000 back when I've got ten Sinatra concerts?' said Lew. 'I'm a lot of things. One of them isn't crazy.'[11]

Along with the flow of incoming Americans, the Grade agency was able to ensure a counter-flow of British artistes into the United States. Particular use was made of the close connections Lew had developed with Ed Sullivan, who hosted a TV Variety show broadcast every week on the CBS network, and with Lou Walters, who ran the Latin Quarter nightclub in New York. Although these arrangements featured stars of a less luminous quality, they gave an even brighter sheen to Lew's repu-tation as a super salesman. Indeed, he surprised himself on occasion. Not least when he managed to persuade the Latin Quarter nightclub to book an English act consisting of demurely kilted girls playing the bagpipes and wholesomely called the Dagenham Girl Pipers. In the event, they went down superbly well and made several return engagements. Others who achieved American exposure through the Grade agency included Norman Wisdom, Tommy Cooper, Tommy Trinder, Richard 'Mr Pastry' Hearne, Alma Cogan and Petula Clark. Lew was also instrumental in providing an American experience for some the agency's more favoured continental clients, like Edith Piaf and the Parisian heart-throb Jean Sablon.

Between his transatlantic travels and occasional side trips to Paris, Rome, Milan and Sydney to keep old relationships in good repair and consecrate new ones, Lew put in long days at the London office where his man-management skills were much admired. Staff members whose productivity was not up to requirements, were taken aside with the ominous avuncular preliminary, 'Exactly how long have we known each other?' When young Peter Pritchard asked for a raise in salary, cheekily suggesting an amount equivalent to that spent by the boss on his cigars each week, Lew responded: 'My boy, if you give me as much satisfaction as these cigars, you can have your raise. Now get out.'[12]

There seemed to be no limit to Lew's energy level and his appetite for the business. Even a short intermission at the St John and Elizabeth Hospital in north London, caused by the need to remove a grumbling appendix, scarcely provided an opportunity to switch off. In the interests of assisting his speedy recovery, Kathie and Val Parnell arranged for six of the Palladium chorus girls to visit him at the hospital. There, after divesting themselves of their overcoats, they revealed themselves in sequinned simplicity, and did an impromptu high-kick routine at Lew's bedside.

Lew was immune to the suggestion that all work and no play was a recipe for dullness, on the tenable grounds that his work was in fact his play. On the other hand, he was not insensitive to the notion of having a leisure pursuit. All the Grades were gripped by a powerful work ethic, but could also see that recreation had its place. Even Leslie had a passion outside the office as a keen supporter of Leyton Orient Football Club, of which he became a director. He later roped his brother Bernard into similar service. Inside the family, and indeed the agency, some entertained hopes that Lew had found a similar opportunity for outdoor relaxation when he expressed a keenness to play golf.

Lew's initial enthusiasm seems to have been sparked partly by its being the preferred game of many of the agency's clients, and partly by the fact that golf balls bore a close resemblance to the ping-pong balls to which he had often applied an adept top-spin in his youth. He therefore approached his initiation into the game with supreme confidence. The task of acquainting him with the rudiments was assigned to Johnny Riscoe, a family friend who was on the agency staff and a keen golfer. Lew was less than appreciative of Riscoe's suggestion that he should first take some lessons – 'I was the world Charleston champion dancer and never had a lesson'[13] – but he did exhibit genuine commitment by kitting himself out with the best bag of golf clubs and golfing accessories that money could buy. Riscoe's recollection of their first and last game, played on a course in Finchley, was of Lew taking approximately one hundred swipes to get to the first hole. He also remembered Lew creatively cutting his losses back at the office with a phone call to Val Parnell – 'Val, I'm sending you around a new set of golf clubs as a present. And a golf umbrella . . .'[14]

No more was heard about this particular leisure activity, and Lew was probably right in thinking that his working life yielded a better class of fun. Unlike Bernard, Lew had never appeared on the stage of the Palladium during his professional dancing years. But his friend Bob Hope would put this to rights. Taking Lew by the hand during one evening performance, he led him out in front of the audience with the introduction, 'This is Lew Grade. He's my agent, and he used to be the world's champion Charleston dancer. Tonight, he's going to do the Charleston for us.'[15] And the audience was well entertained by their joint performance of the dance, though most of them must have wondered – Lew Who?

Despite his increasing eminence on the financial side of British show business, Lew Grade was still an unknown quantity as far as the rest of the nation was concerned. Theatrical agents were not deemed sufficiently interesting to be written up in the popular press in those days and the rectitude of Lew's personal life ensured that he was of scant interest to gossip columnists. The family did garner a measure of press attention but most of it was directed to the exploits of Bernard, who of course was not a Grade but a Delfont in terms of public report. Many people, including a substantial number inside the newspaper business, had not cottoned on to the fact that Bernard was a sibling of the two brothers who ran the country's most enterprising theatrical agency.

Bernard's fame was to some extent due to the reflected glory provided by his marriage to Carole Lynne, who became one of the leading musical comedy actresses of the post-war period. Unlike Kathie Grade, Carole Delfont showed no inclination to decelerate her stage career in the interests of a greater domestic rapport with her husband. She returned to the boards after the birth of each of her two daughters, Susan and Jennifer, though she did finally retire when pregnant with her third child, David. Her last stage appearance was in 1952 at the Palladium as Principal Girl in a pantomime version of *Robin Hood*, along with the comedians Jimmy Jewel and Ben Warriss.

Bernard's own career, meanwhile, had both prospered and faltered. The prosperous aspect derived from his exploitation of the Folies Bergère asset, which had lifted him out of the pit of the London Casino disaster. The British run of the Folies Bergère inspired him to mount another show, *Encore des Folies*; this, Bernard immodestly told the press, featured 'A thousand yards of gold braid and a quarter of a billion sequins, not to mention feathered head dresses, white fox fur and enough jewellery to stock a fair-sized emporium.'[16] *Encore des Folies* ran along these sumptuous lines for a while, to be followed by *Folies Bergère Revue* and other spin-offs, *Plaisir de Paris* and, later, *Pardon My French*, which deployed the fast-budding talent of comedian Frankie Howerd. 'Bernard Delfont was very kind,' Howerd later said of the impresario in what was dubbed his 'French period'. 'He never shouted or screamed or ran down the aisle. Oh no, he sent other people to do that. No, he was never grand or snobbish. He just treated you like a fellow worker. He knew the artistes' problems.'[17]

Bernard was indeed refreshingly free of snobbery and pretension, but he was not without aspiration. He did not want to be forever regarded as the supreme provider of multi-sequinned showgirls and knockabout Variety acts. Accordingly, he used the revenue from the successful Folies operations to finance an incursion into what was regarded as more serious theatre. His most ambitious effort in this direction was the presentation of *First Drama Quartet*, which featured the talents of some very big names indeed – Charles Laughton, Sir Cedric Hardwicke, Agnes Moorehead and Charles Boyer – in a reading of 'Don Juan in Hell' from Bernard Shaw's *Man and Superman*. The show had played to packed audiences in New York, giving Bernard the confidence to lure it to England.

Unfortunately his timing was awry. A version of *Man and Superman* was already being staged in the West End and was deemed to have exclusive rights to the territory. As a consequence, the star-studded cast of *First Drama Quartet* found themselves obliged to take their high-minded offering to the provinces, where its level of sophistication kept audiences away in droves. After the stars had been paid off, Bernard calculated that he had lost £12,000 on the whole venture, though he always treasured the message sent to him by Charles Laughton after a performance delivered to an infinitesimally small house in Manchester – 'Compliments to Mr Delfont. Should we not forget the theatre and perform our little show in the street?'[18]

Despite this setback, Bernard was able to achieve a domestic ambition, moving further out of central London to a new family home in the leafy environs of Hampstead, an area which he ironically described as representing for an upwardly mobile Jewish immigrant the 'pinnacle of respectability and foretaste of heaven'.[19]

Meantime, Lew also showed some signs of a willingness to steady down and seek consolation outside his immediate working existence. In August 1952, he and Kathie started their own family by adopting a six-week-old baby boy, whom they named Paul. However, the new business of fatherhood soon found itself in competition with the birth of something called commercial television, and with it Lew's dawning realisation that his hour had come.

NINE

Television

TELEVISION ULTIMATELY ELEVATED Lew Grade to superstar status, but his brother Bernard could claim a much older connection with the new medium. Back in the late 1920s, for a fee of £2, Bernard had danced in front of a camera trained on him by John Logie Baird, then bent on demonstrating the moving image-transmitting capacity of his novel device to an audience of potential backers located in front of a large screen a couple of hundred yards down the street. Baird's invention was adopted by the BBC Television Service when it first opened for business in November 1936, though it was soon superseded by the more highly defined, American-originated, Marconi-EMI system.

Despite this early connection and the spicing of the first week's transmission with a demonstration of tap dancing, Lew and Bernard were not overly excited by the actual birth of television. With receivers retailing at up to £100, equivalent to the price of a small motor car, it seemed like an expensive toy, available only to the few. During the three years before the war, which signalled the end of all transmissions for the duration of hostilities, it was estimated that fewer than 20,000 television sets had been sold, mainly to affluent families in London and the Home Counties. And, from a performer's perspective, there was precious little money in it.

Cecil Madden, the BBC's first Head of Programmes, had £1,000 a week at his disposal to finance three and a half hours of programmes a day. In consequence the pre-war fees on offer were less than alluring to most leading agents, though Lew Grade was among the first to exhibit genuine interest. Madden would say later, 'Lew was a wonderful man, he never sent us a dud . . . always reasonable and never overcharged.'[1]

Even so, Lew's eyes were rarely glued to a screen. When Kathie was scheduled to appear in the first Variety show on resumption of the BBC Television Service after the war, it precipitated a minor crisis in the Grade household. In common with most of those in the country, it was not equipped with a television. Eventually, Lew was able to beg and borrow a set from the rehearsal room that Kathie had used. Just for the day. The extended family assembled in Cavendish Square to witness the telecast. 'It was,' Lew recalled, 'a thrilling and proud moment for us,'[2] but it had been a close run thing.

With the rapid expansion of television ownership, all the brothers did business with the BBC, but it was a minor area of their overall activity. They valued BBC TV for the exposure it gave to their British clients, but economically it still represented something of a loss leader. In 1950 Bernard staged one of the first Variety shows broadcast from the Lime Grove studio, featuring eight performers supported by a sixteen-piece orchestra. Including wardrobe, scenery and make-up, the budget for the whole show was £300. And Bernard got ticked off for going £12 over the limit. This was at a time when a big star at the Palladium could earn £2,500 for a week's work. Despite the BBC's much improved output, the theatre was still where the money was as far as the Grades were concerned.

Because of his American experience, Lew realised much earlier than most of his contemporaries just how much money could be made by the adoption of a television system financed by advertising revenue. But he took no part in the great, vituperative public debate that raged through Britain on the subject through the early 1950s. Even those who favoured the introduction of some form of commercial television tended to deplore the American sponsorship arrangements that could transform even the most serious programmes into advertising vehicles. Hostility on this score became even more intense in 1953 when the BBC won enormous praise for its dignified coverage of the coronation of Elizabeth II.

As part of the enterprise, the event was recorded as it was televised, and the film was flown over for rapid re-broadcasting in the United States. This achievement was soured when an American screening of the holy communion service was interrupted halfway through by an advertisement for tea featuring the channel's resident chimpanzee, J. Fred Muggs. The chimp was asked: does the monkey world have queens and coronations?

Outrage at the prospect of such techniques being allowed to deface British television screens knew no bounds. Christopher Mayhew, a Labour MP and broadcaster, efficiently conveyed the puritan distrust of many in his party for free enterprise in television. In a pamphlet entitled *Dear Viewer*, Mayhew wrote: 'I ask you to exercise all the influence you have, as a free citizen of the most democratic country in the world, to prevent this barbarous idea being realised.'[3] Among those who lent support to his campaign were the distinguished philosopher, Bertrand Russell, and the novelist, E.M. Forster.

Mayhew's pungent sentiments were echoed on the right by Lord Hailsham, who likened commercial television to Caliban emerging from his 'slimy cavern', while Lord Esher viewed it as a 'planned and premeditated orgy of vulgarity'.[4] Lord Reith, the acclaimed architect of the BBC, detected in the commercialisation of the medium a distinct resemblance to the onset of 'small pox, bubonic plague and the Black Death'.[5]

All the Grade brothers kept their heads down while this kind of rhetoric was flying about, but preserved a keen interest in what the outcome might be. They privately favoured the commercial lobby, but no immediate benefit could be achieved by their adoption of a public posture upsetting to their contacts at the BBC when the Corporation's monopoly was under direct threat. And there was even less point to their alienating the ranks of theatre managers who, worried about the potential competition, had fearfully aligned themselves with those vociferously campaigning against advertising on television. As it was by no means certain which way the argument would go, wait and see had to be their best policy.

As recently as 1951, Lord Beveridge had produced an official report for the Labour government rejecting the idea of setting up a commercial rival to the BBC. However, proponents of a new way derived encouragement from the attitude of the incoming Conservative Prime Minister, Winston Churchill.

In truth, Churchill had little time for television in any shape or form, characterising it as 'a peepshow' or 'that tuppenny Punch and Judy Show'.[6] But he did positively dislike Lord Reith and the BBC, which he felt had been insufficiently supportive of his 1930s campaign against the appeasement of Nazi Germany. He also, like many Tory MPs, held the BBC partly responsible for his party losing office in the Labour landslide of 1945. According to Professor H.H. Wilson, whose book *Pressure Group* ranks as the standard text on the campaign for commercial television, Churchill could have squashed the Tory backbench cheerleaders for the project, if he had wanted to. But he evidently did not. The patrician wing of the party, which detested the whole commercial concept, found itself increasingly isolated and out on a limb, while the younger, business-orientated element gathered in strength.

Professor Wilson wrote severely, 'Britain was given commercial television against the advice of almost all the nominal leaders of society in education, religion and culture, as well as significant sections of the business community.'[7]

The opposition did, however, exert a high degree of influence. The Television Bill which became law in July 1954 was a victory for the commercial lobbyists, but a qualified one. There would be no American-style free-for-all. British commercial television was to operate under the direction of a statutory body called the Independent Television Authority (ITA), of which the first chairman would be the renowned aesthete, Sir Kenneth Clark, then head of the Arts Council and a former Director of the National Gallery. Advertisers could only buy time within 'slots' in or between programmes. Programme-making and advertising had to be rigidly segregated. Sponsorship was totally forbidden. There was also a specific requirement that programmes about royalty should not be interrupted by a commercial break.

The ITA was to own and operate the transmitters, and it was given powers of control over advertising content and the direction of programme-making. However, it was not designed to make actual programmes. Its first major responsibility therefore was to allocate a number of regional franchises on a fixed-term basis, originally nine years, to programme-making consortia, known as the contractors. At the outset there were three regions – London, Midlands and the North – to be followed by more later. To supply the three regions and, hopefully, provide a degree of internal competition between contractors, four main contenders were required. It was accepted, as viewers could only watch the one ITV channel, that there would have to be some negotiation between the different consortia in producing the fully networked programmes. But it was hoped that the regional structure would ensure a healthy quantity of material tailored to local needs.

Those applying for the franchises needed to show some evidence of programme-making competence and financial credibility. Despite all the hedging about with statutory restrictions, becoming a contractor was clearly a glittering business prize.

Although Lew put together a contractor's bid that outshone those of all other contenders, he was by no means the first out of the blocks. Having read that the capital requirement for each franchise application could be in the region of £3 million, he initially thought that he had been priced out of the marketplace.

The unlikely person who allayed these fears was a flame-haired, California-born press agent called Suzanne Warner who, according to Clifford Davis, the *Daily Mirror*'s observant show business correspondent, was equipped with 'a pair of the most stunning breasts post-war London had ever seen'.[8] Suzanne had come to London as the publicist for the film *The Outlaw*, which starred Jane Russell in a cantilevered bra invented for her by the film's eccentric producer, billionaire Howard Hughes. Suzanne had devised the line that dominated British advertising hoardings, which in homage to Miss Russell's smouldering charms described her as being 'Mean, Moody and Magnificent'. After the experience of *The Outlaw* Suzanne stayed on to work in a freelance capacity for the Lew and Leslie Grade agency. Her speciality, at which she excelled, was arranging press interviews and photo sessions for the acts Lew brought over from the United States. She was married for a while to a London-based journalist and developed a wide acquaintance in Fleet Street, where she became known as 'The Princess'.

The crucial connection at this stage of her career, however, was a medical one. Suzanne was a patient of Dr Nathaniel Mayer Green, who had a fashionable practice in Mayfair. Among Dr Green's other patients was a Mr H. Grunfield, who happened to be a senior partner in Warburg and Company, the merchant bankers. Shortly after the ITA was established, Dr Green fostered communication between these two patients, who proceeded to discuss an interesting theoretical business proposition relating to the new TV franchises on offer. The first to learn of its import were the American singer Jo Stafford, for whom Suzanne was organising publicity at the time, and Mike Nidorf, Stafford's manager and a man firmly of the opinion that commercial television had as much chance of losing money as a Las Vegas fruit machine. On hearing what Suzanne had to say, Nidorf promptly commandeered her telephone to call Lew Grade. Lew later recalled initially giving a blank response when Nidorf urged him to apply for a franchise.

'I said, "Mike, I know all about it. Where am I going to get £3 million?"

'He said, "Suzanne says that provided you have a sufficiently distinguished board to make the application, plus £1 million, she has somebody who will put up the other £2 million."

'I said, "Put her on the telephone."'[9]

Lew still experienced some hesitation, even after Suzanne imparted the intelligence that Warburgs were, in principle, ready to come up with the money if a suitable cast of high-profile business characters could be assembled. Not being a close student of the City pages, Lew was not sure who Warburgs were, though he thought they might perhaps be chocolate manufacturers. However, he promptly rang a man who knew about such things, Sid Hyams, one of the cinema-owning brothers who had originally invested in the Grade agency. To his urgent question, 'Sid, are Warburgs good for £2 million?', Hyams came back with the sweetest of replies. 'Lew, they're good for £50 million.'[10]

With this reassurance, Lew rapidly went about the business of consortium-building. He had no problem interesting the Palladium's Val Parnell, but it seemed as if a serious obstacle might be presented by Prince Littler, Parnell's ultimate boss. Littler had successfully bought control of the Stoll Moss and General Theatres Corporation of which the Palladium was a part, along with eight other leading London theatres and many more in the provinces. He had also been a determined critic of commercial television and had given money to the campaign against its introduction, on the grounds that it would inevitably lead to theatre closures. It took two hours of Lew's fast-talking time to persuade Littler that the new style of television entertainment could not be beaten. It just had to be joined.

Among others who surrendered to a similar logic were Stuart Cruickshank of the Howard and Wyndham Theatres, which put on musicals, operas and even ballet in a string of provincial theatres, and 'Binkie' Beaumont, the head of H.M. Tennant, noted for its production of plays in London. These were all good names to put on headed notepaper – as indeed was that of Lew and Leslie Grade Ltd, which was in the process of raising its tone by merging with London Artists, a company that represented serious actors of the stature of Laurence Olivier, Ralph Richardson and John Gielgud.

All these interests would coalesce and be gift-wrapped into an enterprise called the Incorporated Television Programme Company for presentation to the ITA's adjudicators, along with the information that it already had £500,000 in the bank as well as substantial guarantees from Warburgs. Lew's personal contribution to the pool of money was £15,000. This was less than immense, given the leading role he was assuming in a multi-million pound operation, though he would later claim that at that time it was 'all I had in the world'.[11] Leslie put in the same amount. Despite the comparative frugality of their investment, both brothers were entirely confident of the application's success.

It was certainly by far the most eye-catching as far as the national press was concerned. After her achievement as a behind-the-scenes go-between, Suzanne Warner was let loose as the project's press officer, and was triumphantly successful in attracting positive news coverage. One of the stories that had most impact, published in the *Daily Mirror* on 27 September 1954, ran under the headline 'Top Stars in TV Sensation'. In an appraisal of Lew's consortium, the *Mirror*'s showbiz writer, Clifford Davis, described it as 'the first big broadside in the battle to win viewers away from the BBC'. He went on to comment: 'If the Independent Television Authority approves the application, it means that commercial television will be able to take nearly every star name away from the BBC studios – leaving the BBC more star starved than it is today.'[12]

Shortly after this magnificent build-up, the ITA revealed the identity of the four successful consortia, out of twenty-five original applications, and allocated their franchise areas. Associated Rediffusion, which featured Associated Press in its line-up, was assigned London weekdays; Granada, the vehicle of brothers Sidney and Cecil Bernstein, who had a close friendship with Lew dating back to the days when he danced on their cinema circuit, was allocated the North weekdays; the ABC cinema circuit was assigned North and Midlands weekends; while the group headed by Norman Collins, the former director of BBC Television who had defected to campaign for its commercial alternative, was earmarked for London week-ends and Midlands weekdays. Lew Grade's highly trumpeted Incorporated Television Programme Company was not among the chosen few.

In the sad aftermath Lew learned that his application had been too impressive for its own good. The ITA's new hierarchy had been scared off by what seemed like its monopolistic aspect. While the intention was to compete vigorously with the BBC, they were frankly nervous about an enterprise that seemed designed to deny the Corporation all access to the best available talent in the sphere of entertainment. They did not want to be seen to be combating one monopoly by apparently replacing it with another. By way of appeasement, chairman Kenneth Clark and the authority's newly appointed director general, Robert Fraser, suggested that Lew's group could perhaps find a niche in the new scheme of things by acting as a 'sub-contractor', supplying programmes to those who had actually been awarded the franchises. This consolation prize was not gratefully received.

At this point an ill wind blowing across the ranks of one of Lew's erstwhile competitors changed everything. The successful consortium headed by Norman Collins and Sir Robert Renwick, the electrical industry magnate, ran into problems with its original financial backers and seemed to be on the verge of having to pull out. Under pressure of time, the ITA came back to Lew's men with the proposal that they should combine forces with the Collins/Renwick group and form a joint enterprise to fulfil the needs of the new franchise. This was finally agreed, and by the spring of 1955 Lew was in the television business, though not without causing a few social tensions along the way.

During the complicated negotiations with the ITA, Kenneth Clark invited Prince Littler, Val Parnell and Lew Grade to come and meet some of the other members of his board on an informal basis. Littler and Parnell apparently impressed these establishment figures with their poise and demeanour. But Lew aroused their social snobbery to the point where they protested to Clark about his inclusion in the project. However, Clark, who by this time had come to appreciate something of Lew's extraordinary abilities, closed off further discussion by curtly saying, 'He's the best of the bunch.'[13]

With the rejigging of the two consortia into Associated Television (ATV), it became a very large bunch indeed. ATV's unwieldy original board consisted of eleven directors, necessarily including the bigwigs from both groups along with the resourceful Suzanne Warner as its most decorative member. Most of those involved had little experience of working together. And most were new to television. But they struggled up to the starting line with the help of some technical support, mainly enticed from the BBC.

On 22 September 1955 the nation, or more precisely that tiny fraction of the nation that was equipped to receive the transmission, braced itself for the novel impact of Independent Television (ITV) on its screens. 'It's tingly fresh. It's fresh as ice. It's Gibbs SR toothpaste', jingled Britain's first ever TV commercial over the image of a toothbrush embedded in a block of ice. This unexciting visual event was supplemented by a classical interlude with the Hallé Orchestra, conducted by Sir John Barbirolli, which some thought, correctly as it turned out, was evidence of the new enterprise starting as it did not seriously mean to go on.

Viewers were also treated to a speech delivered by Dr Charles (later Lord) Hill, the Paymaster-General, explaining how very unlike American television British commercial television was going to be. 'We shall not,' he declaimed, 'be bothered by a violinist stopping in the middle of his solo to advise us of his brand of cigarettes, nor will Hamlet halt his soliloquy to tell us what toothpaste they are using at Elsinore.'[14]

This much was true, but accidents could happen. Some years later a crisis occurred when the commercial channel, making one of its rare incursions into culture, screened an uninterruptible live production of *Hamlet*. There was a time overrun. The emergency was dealt with on the spot by fading the action halfway through the duelling scene between Hamlet and Laertes, and inserting an advertisement for Kia-Ora orange drink. Outraged at this flagrant defilement of the independent network's high purpose, Lew promptly rang the control room and demanded of the technician who answered the phone, 'What happened? What the devil happened to *Hamlet*?'

'Oh,' came the reply, 'they all died in the end.'[15]

TEN

Showtime

BOTH LEW AND BERNARD had a favourite brother, and in each case, perhaps unsurprisingly, their preference was for the overtly less competitive Leslie. The rivalry between the two older brothers was not something that could be allowed to deface any family gathering; at such times, as their long-time associate Albert Knight bore witness, 'they all stood strong together'.[1] Nor did it involve their putting each other down, much less plotting each other's downfall. But it did sometimes involve one not giving the other a leg up.

Commercial television was a clear case in point. Bernard was left out of the loop as Lew's consortium was being assembled. Given Lew's tunnel vision in pursuit of any specific objective, this might conceivably have been an accident, but Bernard could not be blamed for taking it personally. He would later say, 'I could hardly complain when Lew took the leap into television without thinking to involve me. Yet I had to confess to feeling a little hurt that, unlike Leslie, I had not been given an opportunity to buy shares in ATV. As a producer I was naturally attracted to the medium everyone spoke of as the future.'[2]

Although Roy (later Lord) Thomson had yet to mint his famous observation about commercial television being 'a licence to print your own money',[3] it is fair to say that most of those who obtained the original franchises expected to be able to recoup their investment rapidly as a preliminary to making large profits. In the event, the start-up costs were higher than expected, and the initial advertising revenue was much more disappointing. Lew's ATV, along with all the rest of the companies, lost money at breakneck speed. For a year at least Bernard could have considered himself lucky *not* to have any shares in ATV.

The reasons for ITV's shaky start were in part technological. When it was first transmitted in September 1955 only 188,000 homes in the London area were equipped for its reception. Would-be viewers had to fit a special aerial or, in some cases, buy a new television set. Only a third of households in the franchise areas had taken these measures. As a direct result the medium was markedly less attractive to advertisers than had been anticipated.

A year later the numbers equipped to receive ITV had risen to 1.5 million and thereafter continued rising fast, but it had been a harrowing twelve months for the contractors and a deeply confusing one for communications experts at all levels. Indeed, none seemed more confused by the prospects of the new venture than the great press lords of the day.

Lord Rothermere of the *Daily Mail,* whose Associated Newspapers Group was one of the original key shareholders in Associated-Rediffusion (A-R), holder of the London weekday franchise, lost his nerve and decided to cut his company's losses by bailing out. Cecil King of the *Daily Mirror* proceeded in the opposite direction by taking a risk, and providing a fresh capital injection of £400,000 that calmed seriously frayed nerves at ATV at a critical juncture. While Lord Beaverbrook, the most illustrious press baron of them all, used his *Express* newspapers to rage against the whole idea of commercial television and issue dire predictions of its early well-merited demise.

The year of confusion was Lew's year of opportunity, though his realisation of it dawned relatively slowly. Even after he negotiated a successful outcome for his consortium's bid, Lew had no intention of making television his prime occupation. He foresaw that he and Parnell would probably have some involvement in assembling Variety programmes which might take a couple of half-days a week, but his principal wish was just to serve as a director of ATV, and get back to proper business as usual at the Lew and Leslie Grade agency. ITV's disastrous start would put paid to that notion. Although there was a prospect of advertising revenue picking up once transmission started in the Midlands and North, scheduled in the summer and autumn of 1956, there was real anxiety on the ATV board about their money actually running out before these opportunities knocked.

What was instantly required was more popularity in the programming. This was accepted as being of the essence by the more conventional members of the Norman Collins group on the ATV board, as well as by the showmen Lew had brought in. In a swift series of moves, orchestrated by the board's chairman, Prince Littler, the existing programme chief, Harry Towers, a veteran of commercial radio, found himself looking for another job while Val Parnell and Lew Grade were given executive status as managing director and deputy managing director. Their mandate was to power the operation in a new direction towards what became known as 'people's television'[4], a mix of home-grown quiz and game shows, Variety and quick-fire comedy programmes. These elements were combined in the schedule with significant input from America which included series such as *Dragnet* (cops and robbers with Jack Webb as the gruff – 'Just the facts, ma'am' – Sergeant Joe Friday of the Los Angeles Police Department) and *I Love Lucy* (dizzy domestic comedy with Lucille Ball and Desi Arnaz), a type of entertainment that had not been seen on British screens before.

Under Lew's guidance ITV also followed the American practice of screening programmes with mass appeal at peak times while relegating those of less appeal to earlier or later slots. The idea was that this should wrong-foot a BBC still inclined to transmit serious and minority-interest programmes, like an opera, a highbrow play or even an educational visit to a glassworks, in the middle of the evening. Lew's other early scheduling contribution was to insist that the most popular shows had to broadcast punctiliously at the same time every week, to assist the viewing habit.

From December 1955 Lew was allocating one early morning hour to the affairs of his theatrical agency and spending the entire rest of the day at Television House in Kingsway. He was now thoroughly and inextricably in television.

It took a few weeks for Lew to make his mark, and then mainly by inadvertently raising a laugh. Ned Sherrin, recalling his early days as one of ATV's first trainee producers, wrote in his autobiography:

> We were aware of the showman Val Parnell, of the impresario Prince Littler and dimly of Little Lew Grade, the agent, though no one thought of tipping him as the ultimate survivor in the ATV power struggle. We laughed condescendingly when we heard his response to a deal for the coverage of athletics meetings which Keith Rogers (the head of outside broadcasts) had proudly negotiated with 'the three As'.

'What's the three As?'

'The Amateur Athletics Association, Mr Grade.'

'I don't want any amateurs – get me professionals.'[5]

Sport never did become one of Lew's stronger suits, but those parts of the operation that were capable of responding to his instinct for getting the best professional help did rapidly feel the benefit.

Nevertheless, the early months of 1956 were an uphill struggle for the commercial companies, and reassuring for the BBC. There was modest consolation for ITV in that its output could demonstrably be said to outshine the efforts of politicians making party political broadcasts. When Sir Anthony Eden was screened doing his party political for the Tories on the BBC, four out of five viewers promptly switched to ATV's offering of *People Are Funny*, which specialised in playing daft practical jokes on ordinary members of the public; and Hugh Gaitskell, speaking up for Labour a few days later, lost out in much the same way to the new channel's *Jack Solomon's Scrap-book*, featuring the reminiscences of the boxing promoter. However, this embarrassing disparity was exceptionally short-lived. In March 1956, both the BBC and ITV were obliged to announce that henceforth party political broadcasts had to be aired on both channels simultaneously.

Early audience research clearly showed that ITV was least popular when it was trying to ape the BBC in areas where the BBC had always been strong, particularly in sport, documentaries, news magazines and classical theatre and music. On the other hand, the same research showed ITV as being much stronger in the areas where the BBC had traditionally underperformed, most notably in the sphere of popular entertainment and Variety. Necessity dictated that the schedules should be adjusted to exploit this perceived weakness in the opposition. What was called 'serious' programming was cut by a third to accommodate much less serious output. In consequence, Lew never had to use his elbows to extend his bailiwick at ATV. His company, and indeed the entire network, was desperate for expansion in his particular area of expertise.

ATV's most popular show was undoubtedly *Sunday Night at the London Palladium*. It ran for an hour and was almost unvarying in its format. Viewers were welcomed into the action by the Tiller Girls performing a high-kick routine before a series of Variety acts took the stage. There was then an interlude for a game show (usually *Beat the Clock*, which Lew imported from America), prior to the appearance of the big star. The British comedy songstress Gracie Fields was the first to command this spot, but American headliners (again imported by Lew) were often deployed. The show always closed with the entire cast waving fond farewells as they moved around in formation on the venue's revolving stage.

Credit for the success of the Palladium show had to be shared with Parnell, but Lew was acknowledged to have no equals in the arcane sphere of networking, which would soon become crucial to the success of the whole enterprise. Despite the appearance that the original franchise-holders were in competition with one another, it was soon clear – as long as viewers could only actually watch one ITV channel – that there would have to be a large measure of commercial understanding between them. If they actually tried to produce programmes that competed for the same time spots costs could be driven up to impossibly high levels. So there had to be some mechanism for eradicating duplication of effort as far as humanly possible. The answer to the problem was what the television companies called network arrangements, and what critics would later dub 'the carve up'.[6]

The companies negotiated between themselves, sometimes bilaterally but later more often in committee, which of them would fill the programme requirements of the service at any given time. This was a complicated procedure taking into account programme costs, scheduling, peak time considerations, the different advertising markets and necessarily the overall impact of the programme mix on the viewers. They were, in essence, constantly doing horse-trading deals with each other, with an eye to manoeuvring their own pet programmes into the most favoured slots. And dealing was what Lew was supremely good at, with the added bonus of his being entertaining with it.

Howard Thomas, managing director of ABC Television and a broadcaster of long experience who devised the famous wartime *Brains Trust* radio series, later recalled having many epic networking jousts with Lew as the independent service progressed. He wrote of his ATV adversary, 'His repertoire was as varied as a cinema organist's. He could pull out all the stops – sentimental, threatening, pleading, admiring. His best act was when he would go down on his knees and fling out his arms, one hand still gripping the cigar.'[7]

Beaten down in one encounter, Lew signed a cheque to ABC Television for one penny and presented it to Thomas to establish that he had been completely cleaned out. All this of course was good clean fun, but it also usefully helped to sweeten the pill for the other three main contractors, who had to digest the fact that ATV, as a consequence of providing more days than anyone else along with access to the richest advertising area, almost automatically had the most clout in any networking discussion. Thomas also noted that while big arguments about programme arrangements and exchanges might begin with Val Parnell, when it came to the actual discussion of money changing hands ATV's managing director would shrug his shoulders and leave 'all that'[8] to his supercharged deputy.

In the earliest days, however, with only the two London franchise holders, ATV and A-R, actually being able to transmit their programmes, Lew's budding networking talent had limited room for exercise. At one fraught stage, his boss Prince Littler even allowed his competitive juices to get the better of himself, to the point of advocating that ATV should go it alone in scheduling terms. This was accurately defined as being akin to a drowning man throwing away a lifebelt. Much to Lew's relief, Littler was hauled back by the ITA from the brink of abandoning the rudimentary networking arrangements that already existed, and order was restored.

Even so, the rate of switchover from the BBC to ITV remained perilously low right through the spring of 1956. The ITA later claimed that by the summer the television companies were 'on the brink of complete collapse'.[9] This was probably an exaggeration, but in March ATV did get to the point of using up all its Warburgs money, and its directors were obliged to conduct a whip-round from their resources to keep the show on the road. Lew and Leslie Grade came up with another £10,000 between them.

'You look worried,' Prince Littler said to Lew, who acknowledged that he was, as a consequence of the refinancing, running his first four-figure bank overdraft. 'You're crazy,' said Littler by way of reassurance, 'I have plenty of money but I always keep a £2 million overdraft. The manager is always ringing me up, asking after my health, being nice to me.'[10]

Of more practical comfort to Lew was the entry of Cecil King into the consortium, by invitation, with the life-preserving £400,000 of *Daily Mirror* money. The connection with the Mirror Group also brought Lew into constructively close contact with its charismatic editor-in-chief, Hugh Cudlipp, who became an ardent fan. 'It's true to say of Lew,' Cudlipp once remarked, 'that he's missed wherever he isn't.'[11]

By the autumn an upturn in ITV's prospects was becoming distinctly perceptible, mainly because more people were actually able to receive its transmissions. This automatically triggered enhanced attention among advertisers, especially when it became evident that the 'people's television' was providing fare that the nation's working class wanted to see.

Suddenly, the rise in the fortunes of the TV companies became almost as dizzying as their earlier financial nosedive had been. By July 1957 the BBC was obliged to acknowledge that in homes able to make a choice three adults watched ITV for every two that stayed with its own service. Soon afterwards, the ITA's Sir Kenneth Clark asserted an even more devastating ratio of 79:21 in favour of the commercial channel. In December the Television Audience Measurement (TAM) ratings figures conveyed a yet more remarkable disparity. In the London area, of the 539 programmes listed in the Top Ten since ITV started only three were broadcast by the BBC. In the Midlands the BBC's score was two out of 556, and in the North two out of 544. For a while it appeared not merely as if ITV was beating the BBC in terms of popularity, but that it was turning into a rout.

As part of its expansion and diversification strategy, the ITA issued additional franchises until there were no less than fourteen in operation. However, these satellite manifestations had little effect on the dominance of what was now known as 'The Big Four' (ATV, A-R, ABC and Granada). The new regional companies' efforts at programming were mainly confined to inexpensive shows with a local flavour and, as long as they were profitable, they were not overly distressed at effectively being excluded from creative participation in the national network, though they would pay part of its programme costs. Indeed, Roy Thomson, the Canadian businessman whose Scottish Television was the biggest contractor north of the border, thrived on a version of this arrangement.

Back in January 1956, when ATV was desperate for funds, Thomson had done an astute deal with Lew Grade, obtaining all the programming needs for his upcoming operation, long term, for £1 million a year. The arrangement gave Thomson access to all ATV's own programmes along with all those they had acquired from other companies. Later on, when it was realised that programme costs were much higher than was first thought, other regional operations like Anglia, Southern and Harlech had to pay £5 million and more for essentially the same service. Thomson also struck a highly advantageous long-term deal with Independent Television News (ITN) which, combined with his original programming bargain, equipped him with a licence to print more money than most. As a mark of appreciation, Thomson, who went on to buy *The Times* and *Sunday Times* newspapers, sent his ATV benefactor an annual Christmas box of glacé fruits. Lew was not partial to these, but it was the thought that counted.

Apart from his brilliance as a talent-spotter, Lew brought one powerful insight into commercial television that would profoundly influence its output, namely that it should not be too taxing. This was not through any 'dumbing down' instinct. It proceeded directly from his insight into what the average working-class family's evening would be like with a television set for company. In the early days of BBC Television, when possession of a set was a highly significant status symbol, there were authenticated reports of viewers changing into dinner jackets to watch the presentation of its plays. As Lew saw it, there was no possibility of the medium being accorded anything remotely resembling this level of respect on becoming widely available in poor households. People would be fatigued after a day's work, their ability to concentrate limited by having to prepare the supper, take in the washing, do the ironing, feed the budgie, put the cat out and the children to bed, and be on constant alert for their unscheduled returns. The chances of action on a television screen being watched with the absorption that might be possible in a cinema or a theatre were, in Lew's judgement, virtually nil. And due allowance for that fact had to be made.

Thus, while the BBC, by virtue of attitudes formed in its elitist Reithian upbringing, felt it had to command viewers' attention, Lew went into action accepting as a given that there was likely to be a high degree of attention deficit among those catching his programmes. This would be defined, sometimes sneeringly by critics, as 'giving the public what it wants'. However, it was as much a case of giving people what it was thought they could handle, which often amounted to entertainment that could comfortably bear interruption, quite apart from the advertisements. Although the concept of television as moving wallpaper had yet to be adumbrated, Lew had an instinctive grasp of its essence.

It was no accident that the first drama series Lew promoted on ATV should be *The Adventures of Robin Hood*. It would be hard to imagine a more predictable offering for English viewers, most of whom could recite the plot-line in their sleep. Yet Lew contrived a circumstance that spun it out through 165 lightly entertaining episodes over a period of four years and, by way of an added bonus, sold it on to the CBS Network in America. Each episode – starring former Hollywood idol Richard Greene alongside a range of upcoming actors that included Donald Pleasance and Paul Eddington – was produced swiftly and cheaply using mobile sets, yet the bold opening titles and a memorable theme song swiftly captured viewers' attention.

Nobody could accuse Lew of having avant garde notions in terms of entertainment, but he was capable of propelling the medium in directions it had not been before, if he sensed a populist angle. When he devoted his energies to promoting a hospital drama series, there were critics who deplored the grisly morbidity of the whole notion. But ATV's *Emergency Ward 10*, which kicked off in 1957, ran high in the ratings. Set in the fictional Oxbridge General Hospital, the first twice-weekly drama series to be broadcast in Britain ran for ten years. In keeping with Lew's general approach, however, the scriptwriters were permitted a maximum of five patient deaths per year.

Lew's ready access to so much show business talent gave ATV an undoubted edge in terms of comedy shows, assisted, to some extent, by the restraint exercised by the opposition. While not especially innovative, comedy on the commercial channel could at least express itself with more freedom than was possible on a BBC still under the lingering influence of the notorious 'Green Book' that provided guidance for its producers and writers.

'Green Book' restrictions included an 'absolute ban' on jokes about 'lavatories, effeminacy in men, immorality of any kind, suggestive reference to honeymoon couples, chambermaids, fig leaves, prostitution, ladies' underwear (e.g. winter draws on), animal habits (e.g. rabbits), lodgers, commercial travellers'. It also recommended that 'extreme care' should be exercised when dealing with 'jokes about pre-natal influences (e.g. his mother was frightened by a donkey)' and advised that 'Well-known vulgar jokes (e.g. The Brass Monkey) "cleaned up" are not normally admissible since the humour in such cases is almost invariably evident only if the vulgar version is known.'[12]

Comedians were counselled to steer clear of religion altogether and comedy scripts had to be scrutinised with a view to deleting such words as 'God, Good God, My God, Blast, Hell, Damn, Bloody, Gorblimey etc etc.' Impersonators were subject to the serious inhibition of requiring the permission of the people being impersonated, though exceptions could be allowed if the impersonated persons were dead. Additionally, there had to be avoidance of derogatory references to 'professions, trades, and "classes", e.g. solicitors, commercial travellers, miners, "the working class", coloured races'. Overseas broadcasters had to be aware that jokes about 'harems' or the 'Chinese laundry' could be offensive in other parts of the world. By the same token, 'enough to make a Maltese Cross' had to be considered a joke 'of doubtful value'.

In general, the 'Green Book' advised, 'There can be no compromise with doubtful material. It must be cut . . . Music hall, stage and, to a lesser degree, screen standards are not suitable for broadcasting.' With fewer constraints on how a laugh could be raised, the new commercial companies operated at an advantage, particularly in Lew's area of light entertainment, and it was one they naturally exploited. Even so, the BBC, despite its reticence, managed to produce what was probably the funniest show on either channel, *Hancock's Half Hour*.

Much of ITV's 'non-serious' early output was pronounced vulgar by its critics, though none of it plumbed the depths of the 'Big Brother'-style programmes that many viewers found so appealing at a later stage of the medium's development. It could be argued that the first boreholes were sunk by Lew's ATV series, *People Are Funny*. But the humiliations heaped on that show's participants were feeble in comparison to those so eagerly embraced in more recent reality TV offerings. And *People Are Funny*, after meeting with ITA disapproval, was soon taken off air.

Lew was not an outright enemy of serious subject matter. He could take on board programme ideas with pretensions to cultural or intellectual uplift, provided they could be presented in an accessible and entertaining way. His fellow ATV director, Norman Collins, said of him, meaning it as a compliment, 'Lew's greatest talent is responding with enthusiasm to things he can't understand.'[13]

When Sir Kenneth Clark stepped down as chairman of the ITA in August 1957 he was promptly waylaid by Lew and Parnell and presented with a contract offering him the chance of a new career, as a performer. Clark in 1969 presented for the BBC a famous series entitled *Civilisation*, which still ranks as one of the finest ever made for television. Less well known is the fact that this achievement was preceded by Clark honing his skills with forty-eight programmes on cultural subjects for ATV. His first show did not encourage great expectations. It emerged as a rather shambolic examination of the word 'beautiful' with an assessment of whether a pig could be beautiful, or perhaps a crocodile; Clark himself subsequently deemed it 'one of the worst programmes ever put on'.[14] But he soon exhibited a more crowd-pleasing ability by making programmes about individual artists. His early *Five Revolutionary Painters* series was reckoned a success in reaching parts of the nation thought to be immune to high culture. A sophisticated friend of Clark told him that he had just had the experience of overhearing two market porters in a pub discussing Caravaggio; he thought he must be having an hallucination.

Lew could also claim direct responsibility for lifting the Oxford historian A.J.P. Taylor out of the ranks of talk show regulars and promoting him as a lone lecturer, giving his talks unscripted and straight to camera. In an informal audition, Lew had asked Taylor to tell him about Russian history, a subject with which he had some personal acquaintance, and discovered, 'I learnt things I had never known, and it was put so simply, and so easily understandable . . . You knew that here was a star, an unusual type of star.'[15] The first of many televised Taylor lectures, delivered in ATV's Wood Green studio on 12 August 1957, had as its main theme 'The End of the Tsars'.

However, there was no way in its infancy that ITV could compete with the BBC in terms of high-mindedness, and for the most part it did not even try. As Peter Black, the *Daily Mail*'s talented TV critic, saw it, ITV gained its advantage over the BBC through its presentational skill and the avoidance of straight programme comparisons. In *The Mirror in the*

Corner, his book about the early battle to establish commercial television, Black wrote:

> What the companies took the audience with were a more entertaining time schedule, friendlier and unpatronising presentation, particularly of news, Sunday Variety, half-hour drama and comedy series, and the giveaway show. Until ITV arrived the public had never seen a newsreader who exploited his personality instead of carefully neutralising it. They had never seen Sunday night Variety, or an American drama series: most important, they had never seen anyone earn a pound note for correctly distinguishing his left foot from his right, or a wife win a refrigerator for whitewashing her husband in thirty seconds starting NOW. And if any single programme innovation can be said to have won the mass audience it was the giveaway shows . . . Nothing else ITV did announced more clearly that the BBC's concept of the audience as middle class, or lower class that would be middle if it could, was to be challenged head on.'[16]

Lew was not a deviser of giveaway shows, but he was certainly among those most responsible for their prominence in the schedule, to the point where by May 1957 eight such shows were running every week. In essence, they were the primitive ancestors of today's carefully crafted enterprises like *Who Wants to be a Millionaire*, *The Weakest Link* and *Golden Balls*. For inducements in cash or kind, ordinary people were invited to display their talents or, in some eyes, make fools of themselves, in front of the cameras, usually with a quiz element involved. Aside from being enormously popular in an area where the BBC at that time felt too fastidious to tread, these productions were appreciated by the commercial companies for being outstandingly cheap. A-R led the field with Hughie Green's *Double Your Money* and Michael Miles's *Take Your Pick*, but ATV was not far behind with *Beat the Clock*, the segment in Lew's cherished Palladium show in which first Tommy Trinder and later Bruce Forsyth encouraged couples, preferably honeymooning ones, to partici-pate in elaborate games. These were commonly of an acrobatic, sometimes highly slapstick nature, involving bouncing balls, bursting balloons and contestants prepared to get very wet on occasions, and had to be completed against the background of a large, relentlessly ticking clock.

Success for those surviving the fun-loving ordeal could win them up to £1,000.

The winnings for the commercial companies after their original ordeal were of a somewhat higher order. By 1958 the number of homes in the country able to receive ITV had risen to three-quarters and all of the 'Big Four' were well down the road to recovering their original investment, and blissfully contemplating massive clear profits during the rest of their franchise years. Meanwhile, with their original one shilling shares being traded for £11 and more, the pioneer investors in ATV were in the process of becoming seriously rich. The value of Lew and Leslie Grade's original modest stake was estimated at £615,000 and deemed likely to pass the million-pound mark very soon. In the following year A-R and ATV, the first two companies to go on air, each racked up a profit of close to £3 million (around £45 million in today's money).

In accordance with its new-found wealth ATV moved to imposing new headquarters in Great Cumberland Place with the Marble Arch as its near neighbour. On the top floor there was a huge room shared by Val Parnell and Lew Grade, who would occasionally reminisce sentimentally, between contented puffs on his cigar, 'These days they call us tycoons. But if it hadn't been for that turnaround in 1956, we'd have all been called martyrs.'[17]

ELEVEN

'Mr ATV'

IN THE HEADY PERIOD WHEN commercial television seemed to have beaten the BBC out of sight, the name of Lew Grade featured prominently in the newspapers, occasionally with the prefix 'Mr ATV'. At the age of fifty-two, with a previous career spent outside the glare of national press attention, there had to be some concern about the possibility of Lew's natural confidence shading into conceit. Fortunately, there were countervailing pressures to keep his egotism within bounds.

There was always Kathie of course to provide stability, and her grounding efforts were now supplemented by those of their adopted son, Paul. Enrolled at the Kensington Lycée Français, Paul, aged seven, had usefully taken his father down a peg by correcting his French grammar and pronunciation. And then there was Bernard, still reliably dedicated to demonstrating that anything Lew could do he could do as well, or better.

Far from licking his wounds after Lew had neglected to accord him a stake in ATV, Bernard had responded by raising his game to a much higher level. In November 1958, he could even be said to have inched ahead in the sibling contest, at least in social terms, when he played host to the Queen and Duke of Edinburgh at the Coliseum Theatre on the occasion of the most glittering charity event of the year, the Royal Variety Performance. Concurrently, his position as Britain's leading impresario was being confirmed by the appearance of his name on showbills all around the country: five in London and a string of others in the provinces, from Blackpool to Brighton.

In parallel with his own theatrical ventures, Bernard had also developed his relationship with Val Parnell to the point where he was invited to produce Palladium shows. It was his readiness to serve an apprenticeship as Parnell's organising understudy on the Royal Variety show that led, ultimately, to his being asked to take over as its front man. This promotion was apparently welcomed by most performers, though it rendered obsolete the backstage joke – 'At a Royal Variety Performance you should bow to the Queen – and kneel to Parnell.'[1]

Along the way, Bernard's exposure was enhanced by the *People* newspaper, which commissioned him to contribute a major series of articles under the heading 'Backstage Secrets'. Some of these had more than a little charm. Readers learned from Bernard that Norman Wisdom was not nearly as daft as he looked on stage. When Billy Marsh, Bernard's top agency man, first schmoozed Wisdom by telling him, 'One day you're going to be a big star,' the pint-sized comedian responded, 'Never mind about that. How about Monday week?'[2] Bernard also recalled being bamboozled when Billy Marsh played him a record of what he thought was a top-line American singer. Bernard asked excitedly, 'When is that boy coming to Britain?' Whereupon Marsh responded 'Right now,' and produced a young north country hopeful called Frankie Vaughan, subsequently of 'Give Me the Moonlight' fame, who had been lurking in the next room.[3]

Another of Bernard's accomplishments, again in 1958, was to establish a long-term London home for international top-class Variety, realising an ambition that had been previously thwarted by his unhappy London Casino experience. In partnership with the catering magnate, Charles Forte, he opened a new venture in what had been the premises of the London Hippodrome. It was called the Talk of the Town and provided 'dinner-dancing two act revue' all in, originally for £2 2s. It started uncertainly, as it was discovered that comedians did not blend too well with the dining arrangements. But singers went over fabulously, particularly when they were of the star quality of Lena Horne, Ethel Merman, Judy Garland and, later, the Supremes.

Bernard's initiatives as a showman and Lew's high profile in television ensured their frequent appearance in press photographs – though rarely together. Had they been submitted for entry in a beauty contest, there can be little doubt which brother would have been selected. With a full head of hair that still retained its generous bounce, an easy informality of style and a generally smiling demeanour, Bernard seemed to embody amiability. He looked like a man who both liked people and liked to be liked, an image not far divorced from reality.

Lew was less well served by the lens. Invariably dark-suited, with a hairline in deep recession, a fleshy nose, a thickening jowl and a cigar rarely more than a few inches from thickly protruding lips, he looked the epitome of a bloated capitalist, and not a particularly friendly one at that. As part of its campaign against what Lord Beaverbrook saw as the evils of commercial television, the *Daily Express* published a mugshot of Lew over a caption asking its readers: 'Is this the Man you want to choose the programmes for your children?'[4]

In one respect the pictures told a true story. They conveyed Lew's authority. But one-dimensional images failed to capture two of his other most important characteristics – his playfulness and his eagerness to please – which could make real-life encounters with him such an agreeable surprise. 'The endearing thing about him,' according to Nancy Banks-Smith, the *Guardian*'s normally severe TV critic, 'was his friendliness. The small, circular body seemed to radiate warmth',[5] though it would also lead another of her journalistic colleagues to suggest that Lew, in live close-up, resembled 'a pin-striped budgerigar'.[6] According to Clifford Davis of the *Daily Mirror*, Lew originally tried to avoid press photographers altogether because, as Lew had told him, 'I look so ugly.' But Davis felt able to reassure him, 'Nonsense. Don't worry about it. Just hold the cigar and no one will notice how you look. Anyway, you don't look *that* bad.'[7]

What was missing from the public image was the twinkle behind the tycoon's mask. However, this deficiency was remedied in July 1959 by James Green of the *Evening News*, who penned what seems to have been the first public appraisal of Lew's unusual qualities as a businessman. Appearing under the heading 'The funny stories they tell about Lew Grade', it began: 'Look out Sam Goldwyn. You have a rival for the title of the most colourful character in show business. LEW GRADE is the name. Find any two entertainers with their heads together and chances are that another Lew yarn is on its way. Suddenly everybody is telling these jokes.'

Green detailed several instances of Lew being very funny indeed, though the stories told about him were less interesting, at least in biographical terms, than the one Lew had told Green himself. Other sources would later confirm it as being Lew's all-time favourite anecdote, presumably because it struck some personal chord. There were some variations in how it was told, and retold, but it went something like this:

Mr and Mrs Cohen were walking round a large department store when Mrs Cohen said how much she admired it.

'If you like it – I'll buy it,' said her husband. So he told the general manager, 'I've just called in with a takeover bid.'

The manager choked. 'You're mad,' he said. 'This store is worth about £20 million – cash.'

'Why all the fuss?' said Mr Cohen. 'Sadie, take the front door key. You know the small bedroom – go there and lift up the third floor-plank. You'll find two bags there. Bring back the small one.'[8]

Aside from glancing references to him in articles lauding one or other of his famous brothers, Leslie Grade was barely known to newspaper readers. He was nonetheless a very busy man. With Lew out of the picture working full time in television, Leslie assumed full charge of the agency and, if anything, upped its already prodigious rate of expansion. By taking over the London Management agency, he was able to add stars of the order of Dirk Bogarde, Robert Helpmann, Ian Carmichael and Margaret Leighton to his own client list.

In 1960 Lew and Leslie Grade Ltd changed its name to the Grade Organisation, seemingly to emphasise the fact that Lew no longer had any hands-on role in its affairs. Through the late 1950s, Leslie and Audrey also became busier on the domestic front with the arrival of their own two children, Anita and Anthony, though Leslie's two children by his first marriage were still being brought up by the formidable Olga.

Leslie never seems to have resented his absence from the spotlight trained on his brothers. In fact, reporters who had to contact him about the arrangements being made for his starry clients found him reluctant to be quoted directly about anything, unless it concerned the prospects of the Leyton Orient football team. It was therefore something of a surprise, and not an agreeable one, when he made the front pages of the tabloid newspapers in the autumn of 1959.

The occasion was a developing romance between his daughter, Lynda, aged nineteen, and Arthur Davidson, aged twenty-four. Davidson was of impeccable East End Jewish lineage, coming from a family who owned a cream cheese and bagel factory in Stepney. His own curriculum vitae included a spell as sales rep for the Percy Dalton peanut company. For reasons that were not entirely clear but seem to have been connected with a presumption that Lynda's beau had gold-digging intentions, Olga, and subsequently Rita, took against Davidson as a prospective member of the family. Olga's principal objection seemed to be – 'A peanut salesman, I ask you!'[9] Thereafter, things in the family rapidly became polarised, with Lew and Kathie emerging in what proved to be the minority 'give the boy a chance' party.

At first, Lynda and Arthur considered going the route of Gretna Green, the popular destination for runaway couples determined to get wed while still under the age of consent, which was then twenty-one. However, they decided that Arthur should formally approach Lynda's father and ask for her hand. Leslie, apparently taking his cue from Olga and Rita, said 'No.'

Shortly afterwards Leslie was served with a writ, Grade v. Grade, indicating that his daughter was applying to the courts to rule that he had unreasonably withheld his consent to her marriage. The newspapers loved it, dragging in references to Lew and Bernard to spice up the tasty ingredients of the story. It was said to be the first time a Jewish couple had ever taken a father to court. The case was heard at Westminster County Court in January 1960 before a judge who proved sympathetic to Lynda's complaint. He observed that the Grade family was commendably hoping for the best suitor that Lynda could find, possibly a Jewish Duke. 'Unfortunately,' he added, 'Jewish Dukes are a bit thin on the ground.'[10]

Lynda won the case, partly it seems because Leslie was too thoroughly distressed to give his own evidence in the courtroom. And there were ripples of further distress after the case closed, with Lynda finding herself 'suddenly cut off'[11] by a swathe of erstwhile Jewish friends. Lew and Kathie were among the few who remained supportive throughout. Lew gave Lynda away at her wedding and let the couple have the small flat above his garage as a makeshift first residence in what proved a long and successful union.

Despite the intensity of the family rift, the business relationship between Lew and Leslie showed no evidence of ever being in any way impaired. And Lynda herself did eventually manage to re-establish a relationship with her father, though it always seems to have been rather tentative. The breach with Olga, her surrogate mother, was never healed.

Bernard escaped much of the Grade family flak surrounding Lynda's courtship and marriage by having a heart attack. The relentless pace of his existence caught up with him shortly after his fiftieth birthday. He experienced acute chest pains and was prescribed complete rest. His illness was kept very much in the family, Bernard's immediate medical care being provided by his sister Rita's husband, Dr Joe Freeman. At the Delfont Agency, an appearance of upbeat business-as-usual was preserved by Billy Marsh along with his co-director, Keith Devon, another boy dancer turned agent, whose close connection with the Grade family went back to its pre-war Streatham period when Olga had provided him with shelter during an extended period of unemployment. Bernard's absence from front-line duties was subsequently described by the *Daily Mail* as 'one of the best-kept secrets in show business'.[12]

After three months in bed at his Hampstead home and another month, on Dr Freeman's orders, in Monte Carlo, Bernard returned to action in the early spring of 1960 with some imaginative new ideas. One would be, somewhat belatedly, to regularise his citizenship status by completing the process of naturalisation, thus ending his long run as Britain's most successful stateless person. Another, which caused no end of bother, involved a plan that could have had the consequence of placing him alongside Lew as a senior director of ATV; there is little doubt that such a consummation was devoutly not wished by his older brother.

The prize that Bernard had in mind was the Moss portion of the Moss Empires and Stoll Theatres operation. At that time the two companies were linked by complicated interlocking share ownerships under the joint chairmanship of Prince Littler, who was also, in another capacity, one of the 'three musketeers'[13] of ATV alongside Lew and Val Parnell. Moss Empires, which included the Palladium and the Victoria Palace among its nationwide theatre interests, also owned a substantial proportion of the voting shares in ATV.

Believing that Prince Littler had grown weary of the theatres and convinced that he could run them with much greater élan, Bernard put together the elements of a takeover bid with two of the leading property developers of the day, Charles Clore and Jack Cotton. They were prepared to back the idea to the tune of £5.7 million. Bernard's hand was further strengthened, or so he thought, by Val Parnell, who was also a director of Moss Empires. Parnell publicly indicated his readiness to go along with the scheme and Bernard bullishly told the press, 'The theatre business needs to be more virile and competitive – and that means more diversity of control is required.'[14]

It all seemed to be going rather well until Jack Cotton emerged from his background role and incautiously expressed the view that some of the Moss theatres could provide wonderful sites for brand new office blocks. Aghast at this disclosure, Bernard assured the press that this was never the intention behind the bid. But the damage done proved to be irreparable.

From a position of wavering uncertainty, Prince Littler moved sharply to one of outright hostility to any takeover, and to Val Parnell in particular for having publicly broken the Moss ranks. In what was seen as a blocking move Littler used his position as chairman of Stoll to buy all the preference shares in Moss. As part of the operation Parnell's own 1,300 preference shares in Moss were also voted over to Stoll by his fellow directors without his knowledge. In the face of Littler's determined stand, the threat of takeover melted away, but the bitterness endured.

Littler made it clear that Parnell was no longer welcome on the Moss board and he was out by Christmas, thus dissolving one of the oldest alliances in show business. Parnell was too powerful to be dislodged from his position as managing director of ATV but a deep frost descended on relations between two of its three musketeers. Throughout these troubled times, Lew, without being lured into taking sides on the takeover issue, remained publicly loyal to Parnell personally, at one stage declaring him to be 'a genius'.[15]

He was certainly exceptional. The ratings showed that Val Parnell's *Sunday Night at the London Palladium* was now effectively shaping the Sunday evening habits of half the nation. In January 1960 Cliff Richard sang on the show to a television audience of 19.5 million. Max Bygraves drew 21 million a few months later, and both would be eclipsed by the year's end by Harry Secombe with 22 million. 'It's no use hiding the fact that *Sunday Night at the London Palladium* is more popular than going to church on a cold winter's night,'[16] said a Woking vicar who adjusted to the problem by asking worshippers to come to evensong half an hour earlier.

Yet Lew's protestations of fealty to his ATV superior were not wholly convincing. Tensions between the two men, previously latent, were becoming more apparent. Lew was emerging as the company's great all-rounder, with an across-the-board competence that encompassed networking, finance, promotion and showfinding, and he was often portrayed in the press as being the most important figure in ATV. Parnell did not much care for that. There was also a tricky undercurrent caused by their contrasting attitudes to the opposite sex, Parnell being an assiduous womaniser while Lew held firm to a belief in the benefits of monogamy. Such a divergence of outlooks might not be particularly disruptive in a big organisation, but it was capable of creating difficulties between two individuals working in the same room, even a large one.

It was, therefore, no great surprise to insiders when Parnell resigned his post as managing director in September 1962, with almost two years of his contract still to run. The full reason for Parnell's departure was never publicly divulged, but it was thought to be connected with the embarrassing circumstance whereby his second wife was on the brink of suing him for restitution of her conjugal rights. In his resignation statement, Parnell, who was then sixty-eight, said, 'I thought it about time I should be relieved of some of the arduous tasks that go with the managing directorship and give the younger men a chance in this very modern field.'[17] Lew, younger by twelve years, promptly became Parnell's successor in the top job, assuming an open appearance of the power that many thought had long since been his in reality. Parnell's services were retained on a limited basis, specifically for presenting the Palladium show.

Not long after his assumption of full authority, Lew did an interesting deal. In pursuit of ATV's diversification programme into other business areas, he allocated £6 million of the company's swollen profits to the outright purchase of the whole Stoll Moss theatre operation. When confronted with his brother's success in an area where he had previously come unstuck, Bernard looked determinedly on the bright side. 'Though naturally disappointed at the failure of my bid,' he said, 'I was pleased the theatres were in the family.'[18]

TWELVE

Pilkington

Sir Robert Fraser, the long serving, deeply forbearing director general of the ITA, was often obliged to tell ATV that the level of frivolity in its programming was too high. His guidance was customarily deft, but sometimes he had to tell Lew bluntly, 'You know very well you can't get away with a schedule like this.' Lew's unblushing rejoinder on such occasions was, 'Well, you tell me what I can get away with.'[1]

If Lew had a blind spot, it was an inability to see grounds for commercial television being anything other than popular. To him the equation was quite simple: ITV, unlike the BBC, well provided for by its licence fee, needed viewers to survive, and viewers could only be recruited by giving them what they most seemed to want.

However, it became apparent that what most people were adjudged to want was anathema to a large number of those who did not share, or claimed not to share, majority viewing habits. And those who dissented from Lew's perspective included some who routinely dipped their pens in vitriol. The young Bernard Levin, writing in the *Manchester Guardian*, six months into the commercial television era, made this assessment of its programming content: 160 minutes to Category X – neutral ('for example, weather forecasts and the national anthem'), 320 minutes to Category A ('programmes which people of intelligence and taste might be able to watch for two hours a week without actually feeling ill'), 345 minutes to Category B ('ordinary trash'), and 1,195 minutes to Category C ('not fit to be fed to the cat').[2] Warming to his theme, in another article Levin lambasted ITV in general, and ATV in particular, for its output of an 'incessant cataract of drivel'.[3]

This may have represented a minority opinion, but it was not a tiny one, nor was it uninfluential. As the pattern of competition between the BBC and ITV developed, it became clear that two separate viewing nations were in a process of emerging. There were those, primarily the middle and upper classes, who watched the BBC, only tuning into ITV very occasionally, and those, members of what used to be known as the working class, who watched ITV almost exclusively and the BBC only rarely (usually for the sports). This divide would provide a rich loam for those commentators rooted to the idea that commercial television was somehow damaging to the country's cohesion and moral discipline.

In the early days of transmission, Sir Kenneth Clark had, by way of reassurance, told his more conservative colleagues on the ITA that they could expect ITV to be much like the press, the only serious difference being that it would be aiming at the *Daily Mirror*'s readership, not the *Daily Telegraph*'s. There was something in this. But now that Britain's traditional 'two nations' were able to become more thoroughly acquainted with each other by the simple flicking of a switch, they were less able to go their separate ways untroubled by each other's social and cultural aroma. Much criticism of the Levin variety seemed to have a large element of fastidious nostril-pinching, brought on by a sudden and unexpected encounter with a bad smell wafting up from the lower orders.

Lew's ATV, and indeed all the franchise holders, were fortunate in having at the helm of the ITA a tough-minded character who was prepared to take such criticisms on the chin, and at times come back aggressively. Sir Robert Fraser was never a conventional establishment figure. Born in Australia, educated at the London School of Economics, and a left-inclined journalist in his youth, Fraser owed his elevation to television's commanding heights almost entirely to Sir Kenneth Clark, who had formed a high regard for him when they worked closely together at the Ministry of Information during the war. As the post-war director of the Central Office of Information, Fraser had considerable experience in the communications field. Even so, at the outset of his long reign at ITV, which lasted until 1970, he was a virtual beginner in television terms.

Despite their differences of background and their not infrequent contretemps over programming emphasis, Lew and Fraser were very much on the same wavelength. To the Bernard Levin-style school of criticism of

ITV, Fraser made this rejoinder in an address to the Manchester Luncheon Club in May 1960:

> If you decide to have a system of people's television, then people's television you must expect it to be. It will reflect their likes and dislikes, their tastes and aversions, what they can comprehend and what is beyond them. Every person of common sense knows that people of superior mental constitution are bound to find much of television intellectually beneath them. If such innately fortunate people cannot realise this gently and considerately and with good manners, then of course they will be angrily dissatisfied with television. But it is not really television with which they are dissatisfied. It is with people.[4]

Fighting words, but ones that cut no ice with the august committee appointed by the Conservative government to report on the impact of commercial television on the nation. Published in June 1962, shortly before Lew ascended to ATV's top post, the Pilkington Committee Report found Fraser's ITV wanting in almost every respect, while according high praise to the BBC. In its opening essay on 'the purposes of broadcasting', it found that these were not 'to give the public what it wants' but to 'broaden and deepen public taste'.[5]

With this purpose in mind, the report noted: 'The disquiet about, and dissatisfaction with, television are, in our view, justly attributed very largely to the service of independent television. This is so despite the popularity of the service, and the well-known fact that many of its programmes command the largest audiences.'[6]

Unfairly, some felt, the Pilkington Report did not deign to distinguish between the differing outputs of the 'Big Four'. Thus, Granada, run by Denis Forman and two of Lew's oldest chums, the Bernstein brothers, got no credit for its notable coverage of political and social issues. Similarly, Howard Thomas's ABC received no plaudits for its ground-breaking contemporary dramas in *Armchair Theatre*, which were subsequently complimented by the BBC when it 'poached' Sydney Newman, ABC's controller of drama. Instead, the report dealt in general impressions of the overall quality of the new service provided by the commercial companies. In doing so it found virtually no evidence that public taste was being either broadened or deepened. Its trenchant criticisms homed in most directly on ITV's light entertainment, 'game shows', 'American imports' and the like, all areas undeniably in Lew's sphere of maximum influence.

On the publication of the report, Lew's chairman, Sir Robert Renwick, who had recently taken over from Prince Littler, sent a message to all ATV shareholders: 'The Pilkington Committee has tabled a biased report which has one objective – to destroy in one vicious blow the whole structure which has given the public the programmes they enjoy . . . This is Lord Reith all over again.'[7] Peter Cadbury, chief executive of the regional Westward Television operation, expressed the industry's indignation more graphically by ceremonially burning the report to which Sir Harry Pilkington, the glass-making industrialist, had given his name. In retrospect, this incineration seemed a bit hard on Sir Harry, whose hand in drafting the report had, it later emerged, been heavily guided by the committee's most resolute member: Richard Hoggart, an academic sociologist and the author of *The Uses of Literacy*, who had stern views on workers' education and an abiding distrust of mass culture.

Outside the columns of Lord Beaverbrook's partisan *Daily Express*, the Pilkington Report had a generally rough ride in the national press, largely because it seemed close to despising all that was popular or entertaining; praise was reserved only for the rigorous and the demanding. The notion that many people might want to switch on their television sets in order to switch off from everyday concerns and anxieties never seems to have entered the committee's calculations. However, it had to form part of any politician's assessment.

The report's central recommendation, that the whole apparatus of the ITA be dismantled and replaced by a stronger state authority, with more precise powers to control programming and advertising content, never found favour. Even politicians who approved of the report's tone and general line of argument saw this as being too large an upheaval in a service that had clearly won over much of the electorate. But 'people's television' was dealt a severe body blow by Pilkington, and it would never recover. The prime consequence was a marked change in the operating environment of the 'Big Four'.

Granada's Denis Forman wrote in his memoirs, 'I used to call the pre-Pilkington years the Age of Innocence. Froth, fun and profit had been the order of the day – Lew Grade could go to the limit with quiz shows, Variety and comedy without let or hindrance.'[8] Post-Pilkington, Forman became aware of a huge difference. There was suddenly an acute awareness that 'brownie points' for more high-minded programmes could be just as important as ratings, at least for those who wanted their franchises renewed. And this very much included all of those concerned, even after the government skimmed off some of the industry's cream by imposing a levy on advertising revenues.

Sir Robert Fraser still robustly defended his enterprise in public but became more severe in his background dealings with companies, ruthlessly cutting back ITV's populist output and upping its 'serious' content. The new puritanism was further entrenched by the appointment of a new ITA chairman, Charles Hill, a pugnacious political heavyweight with broadcasting experience that went back to his wartime days as 'the Radio Doctor' on the BBC. Hill's firmly stated mission was to give ITV 'balance'.[9]

Alert to the new shift in ethos, Lew invited Hill, soon to be ennobled as Baron Hill of Luton, to a slap-up lunch in Cumberland House, and was at his beguiling best. The subject of the war years came up and Lew described his army days in a way which, Hill himself later fondly recalled, 'had us all in convulsions'.[10] No serious business was discussed, but Lew established what he always regarded as its most important preliminary, a relationship. But he also realised that more than force of personality would be required to navigate the way ahead.

In *Still Dancing*, Lew could not bring himself to mention the dire word 'Pilkington'. He did, however, devote a large section to his most conspicuous response to the report's impact – a show called *The Golden Hour*, self-vaunted as 'an undoubted highlight'[11] of his career. It displaced the mighty *Sunday Night at the London Palladium* for an evening, and actually ran for two hours, fully networked. It featured Rudolf Nureyev, recently defected from the Kirov ballet, as well as the opera immortals, Tito Gobbi and Maria Callas, along with a large cast of other artistic notables. To allay the ratings fears of the other contractors, Lew personally guaranteed all the advertising slots, and then went round the leading agencies and convinced them of the need to take air time during 'such a prestigious programme'. Lew's emergence as a late-running friend of high culture naturally merited a huge stack of 'brownie points' with the ITA, though without seriously impairing his reputation for low cunning in Great Cumberland Place.

In the run-up to *The Golden Hour* ATV's press officer, David Stevens, had occasion to express a concern about advance publicity for the great event. Stevens recalled:

> At the rehearsal at Covent Garden Opera House, knowing how difficult Maria Callas was with the photographers and what terrible scenes there could be, I warned Lew Grade.
>
> He said, 'I don't care. Get the boys in.' So I got the boys in and there they all were in the front row of the stalls with their Hasselblads, and three rows back was Lew. Gobbi and Callas came on with the opening music of Act Three, for the scene where she stabs Scarpia, and she starts to sing. She couldn't see all that clearly from the stage, but she felt there was some movement down there, and suddenly she raised an arm and said, 'Stop! Either they go, or I go.'
>
> And Lew looked astonished and shouted to me, 'Get those photographers out of here!' So I did. But they'd got all the shots they wanted for some super spreads in the next day's tabloids.[12]

Aside from having to wrap his mind around the need for enhanced cultural and serious documentary coverage to appease Charles Hill and the newly vigilant ITA, Lew also had to contend with the problem of a resurgent BBC under the leadership of an opponent well worthy of his mettle.

Hugh Carleton Greene, brother of the novelist, Graham, became director general of the BBC in January 1960, bringing to the job a wealth of broadcasting experience in troubled times. He had been instrumental in the re-creation of broadcasting in the British zone of war-devastated Germany, and, as leader of the BBC's East European service, had been closely involved with the propaganda campaign launched against the Soviet bloc at the onset of the Cold War. Though a seasoned BBC veteran, he had managed to progress through the Corporation's ranks without being infected by its deferential attitudes. As Head of Television News and Current Affairs, his last post before his ultimate promotion, he had efficiently terminated the tradition of leading off the news, whenever possible, with an item about the royal family. The witticism about the ideal BBC news lead item being, 'Yesterday, the Queen Mother did something or other'[13] ceased to have any basis in reality.

Greene was an exceptionally large man, about a foot taller than Lew, but deft with it. While the commercial companies had blundered in their presentations to Pilkington, exhibiting an over-confidence that verged on bombast, Hugh Greene had enchanted the committee with his deeply respectful submissions. He had also steered the BBC out of its trough by a combination of shrewd rescheduling and selective larceny of some of ITV's more populist clothes. The BBC now unashamedly competed for the better American sitcoms to bolster its viewing figures. But the main accomplishment of Greene's BBC was the introduction of a new informality into its domestic output, particularly in the area of current affairs. This new ethos led to the creation of programmes that attracted major public attention, and had the useful by-product of demolishing the Corporations' old 'Auntie' image.

In 1963 the most talked about television programme in Britain was the BBC's *That Was the Week that Was* (TW3), a topical satire, anchored by a fresh-faced David Frost, which relentlessly mocked establishment figures of the day and, to some people's way of thinking, paved the way for Labour's victory in the 1964 general election.

High excitement was also generated on another level by *Steptoe and Son,* the BBC comedy series starring Wilfrid Brambell and Harry H. Corbett as the eternally-at-odds father and son making a dodgy living in the rag and bone business. Among those moved to public protest at its colourful language was none other than the new managing director of ATV. In February 1963, Lew exposed the – hitherto largely unrecognised – strait-laced side to his nature by denouncing *Steptoe,* citing its unsuitability for the ears of his ten-year-old son, Paul. 'I will not,' he told the *Daily Mail,* 'allow my boy to hear such things as "Where the bleeding hell have you been?" and "Cobblers to you". There's no need to use this sort of language in a so-called comedy series. It's just filth, sheer vulgarity.'[14]

Unsurprisingly, Lew also took a dim view of the BBC's *Till Death Do Us Part* comedy series in which the central character, the cantankerous Alf Garnett, regularly turned the air blue with a stream of 'bloodies'. Lew's hurt, in this instance, was compounded by the fact that the show's talented writer, Johnny Speight, had once been an integral part of the ATV team, churning out most of the material for its popular comedian, Arthur Haynes. One of Speight's more hilarious character inventions for Haynes was of a belligerent tramp with a chestful of medals. But when Speight tried to expand the concept by introducing another tramp into the action, Lew always blocked the idea, saying, 'Why change a successful format?'[15] Frustrated by this, Speight had moved on.

Lew was no slouch in the comedy department, but his response to *Steptoe* and *Till Death* indicated why those who liked their humour to have a cutting edge were more likely to find satisfaction by tuning into the BBC. ATV's comedy successes tended to be in the homely tradition that raised laughs through inspired daftness, but rarely caused offence, let alone drew blood. With brother Bernard's help, Lew lured Tony Hancock, formerly a BBC star turn, into the ATV schedule. Even more to his credit, Lew resuscitated the on-screen careers of Eric Morecambe and Ernie Wise. The pair had bombed on BBC Television back in 1954 in a show called *Running Wild* which earned the Corporation two of its all-time worst reviews – 'Definition of television set: the box in which they buried Morecambe and Wise yesterday', coupled with, 'How dare they put such mediocre talent on television.'[16]

Six years later Eric and Ernie summoned up the courage to have another go at television, and asked Billy Marsh for advice on how to go about it. Marsh thought something could be arranged if they supplied their own material. Ernie remembered a nicely graduated response to their efforts that allowed them to rebuild their confidence:

> We sat down and wrote the judo sketch and a lot of other spots were adapted from radio. The judo sketch is the one where Eric knows all about judo and wants to demonstrate it to me but he's the one that keeps getting hurt and he can't understand it. We did a *Sunday Night at the London Palladium* and some *Saturday Night Spectaculars*. We used to get £100 for them. They began to take notice. Lew Grade asked us if we'd like to do a series and we agreed . . .[17]

Lew could also claim credit for ensuring the popularity of Gerry Anderson, British television's original puppet-master. Having invented the technique known as Supermarionation, whereby the mouth movements of his puppets could be synchronised electronically with the words spoken by the actors, Anderson entered his sci-fi phase in 1962 with the creation of *Supercar*, a vehicle that could go anywhere and do the most extraordinary things on land or sea or in the air. When the concept proved too expensive for Anderson's original backer, Granada Television, Lew stepped into the breach. With ATV as its outlet, Anderson's output took off with titles like *Stingray, Captain Scarlet and the Mysterons* and the classic *Thunderbirds*, which featured the fearless agents of International Rescue in a fleet of futuristic aircraft protecting our fragile planet from evil intent in outer space. Lew rendered consistent support for Anderson's projects, while bargaining tough over their cost. At one negotiating session, Lew broke off suddenly and walked out of the side door. Anderson then heard the murmur of high-powered money talk through the door, before Lew came back with a hardened business stance. Anderson later discovered that the door led into Lew's clothes cupboard.

Back in the pre-Pilkington 'Age of Innocence', Lew showed no interest in current affairs programmes. He confessed to having trouble with documentaries because viewers were inclined to switch off their sets if they did not like the subject matter. This, to his way of thinking, contrasted unfavourably with Variety shows, which were more likely to keep people with their sets in a switched-on condition, if only in hope of catching something they might like. No more analysis of this kind was heard, at least in public, with the dawning of the new era of responsibility and respectability. Lew dutifully ensured that ATV buckled down and did its worthy bit in this area, though not to any great effect. Its efforts were reckoned to be poor in comparison with BBC programmes such as *Panorama*, and not impressive in relation to the productions of the other commercial companies.

In *The Mirror in the Corner*, Peter Black compared ATV's efforts in the sphere of documentaries and current affairs highly unfavourably with those made by Granada and Rediffusion, companies which backed the independence of their programme-makers against interference by Lord Hill's ITA. Lew, in contrast, was inclined to order cuts if the material was controversial, or advise producers to phone the ITA for prior clearance if anything looked sensitive. Despite his protestation that his documentaries were, like all his other programmes, 'just great', Lew's heart was not in this aspect of television; and it showed, though he got points for making an effort. In Peter Black's view, 'Lew Grade and ATV wanted no trouble with the ITA and tried to see to it that they found none.'[18] Lew nonetheless had to be allocated some merit marks for introducing the first serious consumer guidance segment on television as part of the Saturday night current affairs and light entertainment show *On the Braden Beat*. The fact that this pill could be sugared not only by sketches and music but by using as presenters two breezy Canadian entertainers, Bernard Braden and his wife Barbara Kelly, obviously helped.

Lew's unsureness of touch in current affairs contrasted with his huge confidence in the entertainment sphere. Jeremy Potter wrote of him in ITV's official history, *Independent Television in Britain*:

> As a manager Grade was inspirational. He was a delegator who left his staff alone, but in case of need backed them to the hilt. He personally set up and clinched all his deals with the star performers and marketed the programmes with panache and hyperboles as soon as they were made, but apart from appointing those responsible he took no part whatever in the making of them.[19]

This was not entirely true. Lew did occasionally interfere. After watching a few episodes of *The Plane Makers*, a drama which depicted the shop-floor machinations of management and workers in a noisy aerospace factory, Lew persuaded Bill Ward, his long-time programme controller, to translate the action to a quieter environment with more dramatic potential. The series returned, with most of the action taking place in the boardroom, as the immensely popular *The Power Game*. Portraying the wheeling and dealings of businessman John Wilder (Patrick Wymark), and his subsequent political manoeuvring as he obtains first a knighthood and then a diplomatic post in the Foreign Office, it was later seen by many as the forerunner to the hit American series, *Dallas*.

Lew also took a creative interest in the origination and development of *Police Five*, a tiny five-minute slot presented by Shaw Taylor and produced with the cooperation of Scotland Yard, in which the public's assistance was sought in helping solve crimes. Some merriment was caused by Taylor's parting advice at the closure of each programme – 'Keep 'em peeled' – but the show did provide the pathway to the huge *Crimewatch* enterprises of later years. Still, aside from a few instances, it is true to say that Lew was always more interested in responding to other people's ideas than coming up with his own. 'I'm a visualiser,' he would claim, 'not a creator. People bring in the ideas and I say I like it or I don't like it.'[20]

For the most part, he did see his job as carefully selecting and setting up the shows – assembling what he called 'the package' – and then leaving well alone. But he also, as importantly, used his networking skills to ensure that ATV's output got the lion's share of screen exposure. Bernard Sendall, Robert Fraser's deputy at the ITA, said of Lew's talent in this regard:

> Such was the force of his personality that whatever he chose to offer, the rest of ITV did not usually think twice about taking – and even taking twice! There were, however, occasions when ABC or Granada or Rediffusion or even a regional company would steel themselves to the exhausting process of deviating from his wishes. Those were truly titanic battles.[21]

Given his range of output, Lew encountered less trouble than might have been expected with the nation's moral watchdogs. The most pugnacious of these were organised into what was called the Clean-Up TV Campaign, which became in the mid-1960s the even more aggressive National Viewers and Listeners Association. Under the leadership of Mary Whitehouse, an ex-teacher and campaigner of rare tenacity, the NVLA railed against anything seen to be a violation of Christian or what it regarded as traditional British moral values. Its particular targets were what were deemed to be excesses of violence, sex and bad language in television programmes. Mrs Whitehouse's efforts contributed to the introduction of a nine o'clock television 'watershed', aimed at protecting the innocence of young viewers.

On the score of bad language, Lew and Mrs Whitehouse could be said to be at one, but ATV could hardly be held blameless in other areas. There was simulated violence aplenty in *The Saint* and *Danger Man* and the company's other dramas, though its victims tended to die abruptly or gracefully, with a bare minimum of gore. Sex was also widely hinted at, though seldom made explicit much beyond the first clinch. Still, it's probable that Lew would have encountered more difficulty with the NVLA on the sex-and-violence score, had it not been for the fact that Mrs Whitehouse perceived the BBC as being the more flagrant transgressor in all departments. 'If you ask me', she wrote, looking back on her long crusade, 'who, above all, was responsible for the moral collapse which characterized the sixties and seventies, I would unhesitatingly name Sir Hugh Carleton Greene.'[22]

Lew was not a great writer, understandably perhaps given the necessity of having to juggle a telephone and a cigar, and always needing a hand free to extend for shaking purposes – his preferred method of closure to any deal. He also had scant faith in letters as a method of communication – 'You get much better results phoning people. I love phones! I don't believe in writing letters.'[23] But he did manage to dash off the occasional crisp memorandum when necessary. One of the most significant of this period, sent out to a number of writers, ran as follows:

> What is needed is a soap opera, five days a week across the board, to go out at 4.30 for twenty-five minutes. A programme that would appeal in the main to the housewife – a kind of Mrs Dale's Diary – but one that would reflect the Midland life and could at the same time be acceptable in the rest of the country. Not as broad as Coronation Street, realizing that it is in the afternoon. The sets could not be large, nor moved about too much. The cast would be small and, of course, new characters could be introduced now and again and we could use a number of extras . . .[24]

The consequence was *Crossroads*. The series, devised by Reg Watson and written by Peter Ling and Hazel Adair, detailed the comings and goings, and goings-on, in a small motel somewhere in the West Midlands. It was first transmitted in November 1964 and no show on television more successfully divided the nation. After watching the early episodes, the distinguished television critic, Philip Purser, was moved to write: 'It seems to me to be the lowest, feeblest and laziest form of drama ever invented, as if they'd simply gone home and left the tap running.'[25] Other critics were not so kind.

The daily schedule ensured that the actors were routinely under-rehearsed, while the set-ups in the Birmingham studio could only be described as rudimentary at best. There were clearly no ITA 'brownie points' to be earned by maintaining such a show and even Bill Ward began to feel that ATV might be better off without it. However, it became apparent that it had audience appeal. This was due in no small measure to its unconventional star, Noele Gordon, coupled with the compelling nature of Tony Hatch's signature tune, which adamantly refused to leave a viewer's head.

After a long apprenticeship on the stage, Gordon had joined ATV as a producer, where her concentration was to some extent impaired by an ill-starred secret romance with Val Parnell. Her first television appearance involved hosting a talk show before moving on to front *Lunchbox*, an advertising magazine vehicle of the type that disappeared from ITV screens after meeting with Pilkington's disapproval of their blatantly commercial formula. Subsequently, as Meg Richardson, the widowed owner of the Crossroads Motel, she built up a fan base of rare fervour. When it was publicly rumoured that she might be written out of the show because of a pay dispute, Cumberland House and the Birmingham studios were both inundated with letters of piteous complaint. 'Don't let Meg die,' wrote one woman. 'If you do I'll kill myself.'[26]

At this point, Lew knew that he had got what he had set out to achieve, a credible soap to rival Granada's *Coronation Street* in terms of loyal attachment, if not esteem. Gordon was given her pay rise and the show marched on. Rarely out of the ratings and with an audience averaging more than fourteen million, *Crossroads* survived, and generally flourished, for twenty-four years usually as a Top Twenty rated show, and as a constant butt for the critics. It was a neat demonstration of the point made by one commentator – 'the only people who seem to like Lew Grade's shows seem to be people'.[27]

Outside Variety and the protection of *Crossroads*, the area that engaged Lew's passionate attention was the production of long-running series, commonly of an escapist adventure or crime nature, which often paid for themselves many times over through being sold on to the international market, particularly to America. This was an arena in which neither the BBC nor any of the other commercial contractors ever managed to come close to Lew's achievements. It had all begun with the sale of *The Adventures of Robin Hood* to CBS. The production company, Incorporated Television (ITC), was subsequently absorbed into the fabric of ATV as a wholly owned subsidiary, and by the early 1960s it was into its full stride.

Among the first off the production line was *The Saint*, starring Roger Moore as Simon Templar, a suave, tongue-in-cheek crimebuster, which would run for 143 episodes in Britain and the United States. Based on a character created by crime novelist Leslie Charteris, the series featured visual hooks such as Templar's white Volvo and the distinctive stick-man logo with a halo that adorned the character's business cards. *Danger Man* (retitled *Secret Agent* for the American market), starring Patrick McGoohan as British Intelligence officer John Drake, had a similar extended run.

These and the many subsequent productions churned out at ATV's Elstree studios facility may have lacked Pilkingtonian rigour, but they were enormously beneficial to Lew's image and ATV's public reputation. In a country long grown accustomed to importing most of its popular culture – in films, records and indeed much of television – from across the Atlantic, the spectacle of home product going the other way, and actually making money, was deemed to be highly bracing.

Milton Shulman, the grumpy *Evening Standard* critic, found it hard to say anything of a complimentary nature about ITV, but praised ATV for taking on 'the hazardous task of trying to make programmes which might be acceptable to the American market'.[28] And Lew did much better than just try. His frequent trips to the United States to set up his transatlantic deals were written up in the popular press with almost jingoistic fervour, while his dollar-earning talents usefully earned favourable mention in the House of Commons. Nor was Lew slow in pointing out that ITC's more routine sales efforts flew the flag for British television around the world. America was the main outlet but Lew would boast of *The Power Game* doing business in Zambia; reruns of Sir Kenneth Clark's arts programmes being much appreciated in Egypt, and one of his many crime series, *The Baron* (loosely based on a creation of the novelist John Creasey and featuring a secret agent working undercover as an antiques dealer), going down a treat in Poland and Nicaragua.

When Roger Moore, jaded by the length of the production process, expressed doubts about having to do yet another series of *The Saint*, Lew talked him round with the injunction: 'Don't think of yourself, my boy. Think of your country. Think of your Queen. We need the money.'[29]

In the parliamentary exchanges before the passage of the 1964 Television Act there was some mild acknowledgement that commercial television had made an effort to rebalance its output in a more responsible direction in response to Pilkington. But the big prize on offer, a third television channel, was, to nobody's surprise, allocated to the BBC. Lew had been at the forefront of the campaign for ITV to win it, but his disappointment was tempered by an agreeable consolation.

The new BBC channel was to be broadcast on 625 lines UHF, a standard which offered an improvement in picture quality and to which all channels would be obliged to change. Largely because of uncertainty about when the change should be adopted, all the existing ITV contractors had their expiring franchises renewed well beyond the original due date, until 1967. With a new government levy on advertising revenue beginning to bite, it was evident that the days of the commercial companies being able to rack up earnings of up to 100 per cent per annum on capital were effectively over. Even so, they all still had a licence to make a lucrative living for a bonus three years.

Meanwhile, the Grade Organisation, formerly the Lew and Leslie Grade theatrical agency, was surfacing in the City news pages as an exciting new public company with a market value of more than £2 million. In order to avoid an impression of divided loyalties, Lew had taken no part in its business since the spring of 1956. However, as the largest shareholder in his brother Leslie's agency interests, he was more than a disinterested observer of the rise and rise of the Grade Organisation.

Asked about the qualities of their more introverted younger brother, both Lew and Bernard would assert that Leslie was the really brainy one in the family. Originally, there seemed to be a touch of condescension in this accolade, but as the 1960s progressed there were objective indications that it might even be true. Leslie was the first of the brothers to make the breakthrough into the feature film business, and with an intriguingly diverse collection of movies, which he assembled in partnership with

Robin Fox, an agent friend and father of the film actors James and Edward.

It was Leslie who, in the face of initial resistance, put together the team that overcame the problem of how to achieve an effective cinematic presentation of the pop star, Cliff Richard. Songwriter Herbie Kretzmer, after ploughing through Richard's autobiography, *It's Great to be Young*, confessed to negative feelings about a film project on the grounds that 'the only thing that ever happened to this boy was that a microphone went down at the Elephant and Castle when he was eighteen'.[30] But the problem was circumvented after an intensive study of old MGM musicals for inspiration, and *The Young Ones*, an upbeat musical tale of young people getting the better of a rich property developer who threatened to demolish their youth club, was the outcome. Its success led directly to Leslie's and Cliff Richard's second film, *Summer Holiday*, shot mainly on location in Greece but with an off-route red double-decker London bus providing a familiar focus for British audiences. *Summer Holiday* did heart-warmingly good business in the icy winter of 1962.

With *Sparrows Can't Sing*, a jaunty Cockney drama directed by Joan Littlewood, Leslie was able to update impressions of the Grade brothers' once familiar East End. It did not find much critical favour, though some detected in its leading actress, Barbara Windsor, qualities that were built to last. *Sparrows* was soon oddly complemented by *The Servant*, one of the darkest films of the period, which portrayed the corruption of an effete upper-class young man of means (James Fox) by his sinisterly manipulating manservant (Dirk Bogarde) in a way that undermined conventional notions of established order in society. Its release, neatly coinciding with the crescendo of the 'Profumo Scandal' which was then rocking Harold Macmillan's Tory government, could scarcely have been more propitious. Scripted by Harold Pinter and directed by Joseph Losey, it impressed many critics, but somewhat depressed Leslie. As an apostle, like his brother Lew, of what he regarded as wholesome family entertainment, Leslie wondered if this film had overstepped the mark. He would later tell Hunter Davies, 'Actually, I thought it was revolting.'[31] But Leslie was able to accept very comfortably the industry plaudits accorded to him in his producer's role for bringing the picture in at £135,000, some £6,000 under a tight budget.

By the time the Grade Organisation went public in the summer of 1964, Leslie could claim to be among the few British film producers to have achieved an unbroken string of profitable movies. He had also branched out into the film distribution business, going on to acquire the Shipman-King chain of thirty-two cinemas around the country along with another twenty owned by Rive Films. Meanwhile, he continued to beef up the agency side of the business by purchasing the Harold Davidson agency. This gave him the right to present in Britain a range of evergreen American jazz and pop figures, among them Duke Ellington, Ella Fitzgerald and Frank Sinatra.

He also had a surprise acquisition up his sleeve. With Bernard at his customary full impresario tilt, presenting six shows in the West End ranging from Shirley Bassey in cabaret to Vanessa Redgrave in Brecht, Leslie politely wondered if his brother might like to disencumber himself of his theatrical agency business, in the interests of giving himself more freedom to pursue his many other projects.

The deal was done in the spring of 1965 when Bernard accepted £226,000 in cash and shares as recompense for handing over the Bernard Delfont Agency. This enabled Leslie to add to his books such names as Eric Morecambe, Ernie Wise, Norman Wisdom, Frankie Vaughan, Harry Worth, Leslie Crowther and Dickie Henderson, whose combined lustre had a bracing effect on the Grade Organisation's share price. However, the degree of freedom Bernard chose for himself proved to be somewhat limited, as he would almost immediately pop up again as deputy chairman of Leslie's expanded operation.

As his business star rose through the sixties, Leslie shed some of his earlier diffidence. He never appeared likely to emulate the personal flamboyance of his older brothers, but he did become more comfortable in his relations with the press, and more relaxed in his enjoyment of the expansive lifestyle that was now available to him. When Christie's sold a pear-shaped diamond of 15.1 carats for £19,000 at auction, Leslie was revealed as the successful bidder, shyly confessing it was 'a little something for my wife'.[32] And in December 1965 Leslie upstaged Lew and Bernard in terms of domestic style when he and Audrey took a shine to a large apartment in Kensington Palace Gardens, more popularly known as Millionaire's Row. With a then prodigious asking price of £120,000, it was described by the *Daily Sketch* as 'probably the most expensive flat in Britain',[33] though Leslie managed to secure it with a substantial discount.

Few of those who knew the Grade brothers intimately begrudged them their personal success. But the spectacle of Leslie's rise to front-line eminence in show business alongside Lew and Bernard did tend to concentrate the minds of the many who only knew of them by reputation, and with it came the thought – first articulated in the press but later taken up in the House of Commons – that they might just be doing too well for their own, or indeed anybody's, good.

THIRTEEN

Monopoly

FOR PUBLIC CONSUMPTION THE Grade brothers always claimed that family connections never influenced their commercial judgement, and that they competed fiercely with each other, just as they would with any other business rivals. In working practice, however, this posture was not always easy to maintain. Indeed, there were specific occasions when they were more than happy to give an impression of ruling Britain's show business roost.

As a young comedy scriptwriter, Eric Sykes heard Leslie Grade utter the dread words, 'Will you take a cut?' Having just worked around the clock for the best part of a week scripting a one-off comedy television show for Jane Russell, Sykes indicated that he felt that his agreed payment should not be in any way impaired. Leslie was insistent, however, on the grounds that importing Miss Russell from America, 'bringing a companion with her and everything', had proved more costly than anyone had expected. So the request was reformulated on more pleading lines.

'Do me a favour, Eric,' said Leslie

'I've already done you a favour, Leslie, by writing the show, rehearsing it and all in a few days,' replied Sykes.

'So you won't take a cut?' asked Leslie.

In receipt of Sykes's final 'No', Leslie promptly pronounced sentence. 'OK, but you'll never work again.'[1]

As Sykes indicated in his autobiography, such an edict could have been frightening to an actor or comedian, but it was not particularly intimidating for a writer, whose skill was much more easily transferable. However, he was intrigued when some years later, at the conclusion of another fractious pay dispute, this time with Leslie's brother, Bernard, he was given exactly the same minatory pledge: 'You'll never work again.'[2]

Sykes wrote, 'The only Grade who had yet to deliver this *coup de grace* was Lew. He was the eldest and realised that banging your head against a brick wall is not a healthy pastime.'[3] Yet Sykes may have been giving Lew a mite more credit than was his due.

Harry Secombe vividly recalled being offered a fast track into the Palladium by Lew, provided he accepted Lew's services as his regular agent on an agreed sliding-scale salary. When Secombe, after some hesitation, refused this offer, Lew was miffed and indicated that the comedian had injured his career prospects, telling him, 'All right lad. But one day you'll come crawling back to me.'[4] However, they were able to laugh about this exchange six years later when Secombe, with alternative agency assistance, did make it to the Palladium as the star of *Rocking the Town*.

It is perhaps true to say that all's fair in love, war and pay negotiations, but there's no doubt that, when it suited them, the Grades were not averse to implying that they had a writ that ran throughout show business.

Their general benevolence towards performers was well attested to, and not only by themselves. Given the enormous range of volatile talent on their books, the number of complaints publicly voiced against them was surprisingly few. Tommy Trinder, in sour mood after being bounced out of ATV's Palladium show, caused a bit of a stir at an awards ceremony by implying there had been some perfidy on Lew and Leslie's part related to his dismissal. Pat Kirkwood, the musical star, who was said to count Prince Philip among her admirers and whose legs were acclaimed by Kenneth Tynan as 'the eighth wonder of the world',[5] also had occasion to put the boot in. Her resentment was caused by her feeling that Lew had reneged on a promise to provide her with her own six-part TV series. Arthur Askey fell out with Leslie when he formed the view that he had been unfairly cut out of the role of dame in a Palladium pantomime, though their breach healed after a couple of years. But these were isolated instances, attributable most likely to a combination of disappointment and genuine misunderstanding.

In most show business reminiscence the Grades are portrayed in glowing terms, and not always for reasons related to mutual money-making. Max Bygraves, in his biography, said that they were not only efficient, but that 'the three of them were always generous with sound advice'.[6] Bruce Forsyth was most impressed by how 'all the brothers just lived for show business, though Lew was probably the most extrovert – he put his heart and soul into the work'.[7] Tommy Steele's only significant complaint against Lew was of once finding that his free cigar was of Jamaican origin – 'but after I pointed this out, he congratulated me for spotting it, and I got what he was smoking – the Cuban'.[8] The fastidious Roger Moore would complain about Lew always taking him for lunch to a fish restaurant in Soho – 'so pungent that you had to check your suit in the dry cleaners immediately afterwards to get rid of the smell'.[9] But in all other respects he found Lew wonderfully supportive. There can be no doubt that most of their starry clients, for most of the time, felt that the brothers were thoroughly on their side.

There had, all the same, long been ambiguities built into their role as creative showmen. These dated back to the 'packaged' Variety vehicles that Leslie had been the first to assemble in the early days of the war, and which provided a model for many of his older brothers' subsequent efforts. Previously, they, as agents, had been obliged to obtain the highest possible fee for their clients. Indeed, the interest of agent and artist could be said to be identical: the bigger the fee, the higher the commission.

This ceased to apply when they mounted shows featuring their own clients. In their capacity as 'packagers' of the entire show, they naturally had a keen interest in keeping down costs, including what was usually the biggest item – artists' fees – in order to maximise overall profit. Obtaining the highest possible fees for individual artists was no longer of the essence. This conflict of interest, however, excited little comment at a time when the Grades were seen as being among the saviours of Variety in dark and desperate times. They were also assisted within the business by being regarded, rightly, as men of their word – people who stuck to their verbal agreements, except of course in the occasional emergency when someone 'as a favour' might be asked to 'take a cut'. And even that wrinkle could be ironed out by their undoubted ability to deliver real favours.

With the advent of commercial television came a higher political sensitivity to business arrangements in the entertainment world. This much was evident in the ITV franchise applications. However, the ITA's expressed fears of monopoly that almost led to Lew's consortium missing out related not so much to the Grades specifically, but to the alliance of leading entertainment interests assembled for the bid. At that time, of course,

Bernard had no part in the enterprise and even the original stakes of Lew and Leslie could be deemed modest. But when the entertainment group emerged in the ascendant after ATV went on air, the role of the Grades excited rather more attention. Among the first to point out that the brothers had interests that, by accident or design, appeared to interlock in a mutually beneficial way was a bright young Liberal MP called Jeremy Thorpe.

Writing about what he described as 'an unchallenged family monopoly' in the *News of World* in July 1960, Thorpe asserted:

> Leslie and Bernard must control up to 80 per cent of the artists in this country (as agents). Today, whether you are an ITV or BBC producer you'll probably have to approach one of the Winogradsky boys for your stars . . . Lew has now left the agency but there remains a useful family link-up. Suppose, for example, actor John Smith is discovered. Leslie (agent) will put him on his books and could sell him to Lew (TV director). If the price is high Leslie (agent) gets his agency commission from the artist and benefits: if it's low, Lew (television) scores. If ATV then sell John Smith's programme to the network, Leslie (agent) will get a better rake-off and Lew (ATV) will get a bigger dividend.[10]

Thorpe rather overstated the reach of Bernard and Leslie as agents at that particular time, but his article did highlight an area of concern, if only hypothetically. Taking matters much further in real terms could well have been risky given the nature of the libel laws, and given the Grades' entirely proper desire to protect their reputations for honest dealing. Lew's personal vigilance on this score was firmly established in July 1963 when he won a libel action against the *Sunday Express*. Its combative columnist John Gordon had written an article suggesting that Lew had dumped a large quantity of his ATV shares through his prior knowledge of an adverse report by the Pilkington Committee, which was naturally expected to have a depressing effect on share values. In court Lew was able to establish that the last time he had sold any of his shares was some months before the committee had even been appointed. The newspaper was obliged to apologise and pay an agreed sum in damages, which Lew gave to charity.

There could be no defence, however, to the charge that the Grades were getting bigger and bigger, and at a breathtaking rate, by entirely legitimate business methods. 'You have to admit,' said a business rival quoted in the *Sunday Times*, 'that they work three times as hard as anyone else, and they're ten times as shrewd.'[11] In parallel with Leslie's and later Bernard's rapid enlargement of the Grade Organisation, Lew presided over a massive expansion at ATV that was a constant cause of fascination to the City pages. For the second time in his career, but now with more reason, Lew would hear the word 'monopoly' being bandied about in relation to his business interests.

Under Lew's guidance, the profits from the television franchise had been ploughed into a range of enterprises, creating what was said to be one of the world's biggest entertainment complexes. Along with the Stoll Moss group of twenty-two London and provincial theatres, and the ITC film-making operation, ATV's portfolio by the mid-1960s included a half share of Pye Records; a majority share in Bermans and Nathans, the theatrical costumiers; 100 per cent ownership of Muzak, the background music enterprise; a string of bowling alleys; a distribution company in Australia; and AP Films, which like ITC sold film to America, but specialised in animation projects of the *Thunderbirds* and *Captain Scarlet* variety.

'Where will it all end?' asked the *Financial Times* in April 1965, marvelling at the Grades' expansion in so many directions, though it indicated there was no intention to merge all the Grade interests into 'one big ball of wax'. Assured of this, the paper felt that working artists need have no fear of any combination that could damage their interests, quoting Leslie as saying, 'I get every penny I can out of Lew, he's only my brother.'[12]

The actors' union Equity was not so sure. Moreover, its concerns found expression in the House of Commons, to which Equity's former assistant general secretary, Hugh Jenkins, had recently been elected as the Labour MP for Putney. Jenkins, who later became Labour's minister for the arts, focused his attack on the divergence between show business practice in Britain and the United States. In 1960, the US anti-trust authorities had indicated their distaste for the mixing of agency and management, which of course was at the core of the Grade brothers' original rise and had been relevant ever since.

The target chosen by the American trust-busters was the giant Music Corporation of America (MCA), which had briefly, but crucially, been Lew's main ally in the United States in the late 1940s, and had since become the largest agency in the world. MCA was instructed that it could do agency work or production work, but not both. As a result, MCA chose to continue with production, selling off its agency business. On one level this process was helpful to the Grades. Among the experienced old MCA hands displaced by the anti-trust ruling was Robin Fox, who joined the Grade Organisation and partnered Leslie in his film-making adventures.

But the question naturally arose: should a version of America's anti-trust practice be imported to Britain? Hugh Jenkins and Equity were not for going the whole hog, but they were strongly in favour of limiting (or even eliminating) the agent's commission in circumstances where the agent also had a significant financial stake in the production. This could not be anything other than a dismal prospect for the Grades.

In the summer of 1965 Lew was confronted by another unpleasant prospect of a somewhat different type, relating to an ostensible misuse of Grade power and influence. Emile Littler, the brother of Prince, had a play called *The Right Honourable Gentlemen* running at Her Majesty's in the West End. Its run was suddenly disrupted when four of its stars – Anthony Quayle, Coral Browne, Anna Massey and Corin Redgrave – all gave notice to quit on the same day. As they were all represented by the Grade Organisation and as the theatre was owned by an ATV subsidiary, Emile Littler suspected that he was the victim of a stratagem designed to dislodge his show from the theatre, making it conveniently available for an ATV-supported production that wanted to move in. Littler wrote to the four stars accusing them of being part of a plot to close his show, and then released the letter to the press. The implication was that Lew had masterminded the alleged plot.

Lew promptly sued Emile Littler for libel, confident of success as his first knowledge of any 'plot' was when he read about it in a newspaper, but also with an awareness that the whole episode might be bad for business, regardless of any courtroom outcome. Even a victory could not mask the fact that paranoia about the hidden power of the Grades was by no means limited to disgruntled out-of-work actors, but something that reached into the upper levels of the entertainment world.

Lew's business horizon darkened still further in May 1966 when the *Sunday Times*'s investigative Insight unit produced a two-page spread under the headline, 'The Show Business Octopus'. A large diagram bearing a close resemblance to a map of the London Underground system was designed to illustrate the 'hydra-headed diversity' of the Grades' show business interests, which, the paper said, constituted 'probably the most powerful entertainment network in the world'.[13]

Lines radiated out in all directions indicating the blood and business tentacles connecting the brothers' many enterprises, with Lew's ATV assets marshalled on the right, Leslie's Grade Organisation and its satellites in the centre, and Bernard's more diverse operations listed to the left. It was an intricate and impressive display, though Bernard's listed holdings were, in fact, slighter than many had supposed them to be, given his wartime buying spree of theatre leases and his long friendship with the property developer, Charles Clore. Most of the wartime leases had long since expired or been sold on. Nevertheless, the diagram identified Bernard as having a solid interest in the Prince of Wales, Saville and Comedy theatres, along with the Talk of the Town. This combined with his six shows running in the West End – ranging from *The Killing of Sister George* to *Barefoot in the Park* – and regular summer shows in Blackpool, Great Yarmouth, Torquay and Weymouth.

Noting that the three brothers had 'complementary' empires, the accompanying article differentiated their characters:

> Lew is the early rising, cigar-chewing extrovert TV baron. Leslie, with a shy mask that conceals the shrewdest brain, runs the agency business. And Bernard Delfont, hopping out of his Rolls-Royce into his Prince of Wales Theatre headquarters with the mad dash of a hot Boy Scout, is the show-planning impresario . . .

As an example of 'the awe-inspiring comprehensiveness' of the Grades' operations, the article cited that year's pantomime at the ATV-owned London Palladium. Promoted by Leslie Grade and Bernard Delfont in conjunction with Leslie McDonnell, managing director of ATV's Moss Empires subsidiary, the show included Frank Ifield, Sid James, Kenneth Connor and Arthur Askey, all clients of the Grade Organisation or one or other of its subsidiaries – to which they each paid 10 per cent of agent's commission for booking them in – while the costumes, provided by Bermans and Nathans, also refreshed Lew's ATV interest.

The article did not assert financial impropriety, but it conveyed a strong message that the dovetailing of the Grades' interests was highly beneficial to their individual businesses, giving them a distinct edge over all rivals. While it did not challenge Lew's independence from decision-making in the Grade Organisation, it pointed out that, as its principal shareholder, he was ultimately bound to profit from the agency fees paid by the stars featuring in his ATV spectaculars, that is if they happened to be on the Grade Organisation's books, which most of them were. The article also saw the reform proposed by Hugh Jenkins, which was specifically designed to remove the fudging of agent and manager roles, as being likely to cause serious disruption to the Grade concept of business as usual.

Did all of this amount to monopoly? Bernard was quoted in the article giving a spirited defence of the brothers in business, insisting on their essential competitiveness in relation to each other. He had, he maintained, been obliged to cease doing business with ATV at one stage because his brother Lew was giving him such terrible deals. He had even complained to the ATV chairman, Lord Renwick, that 'Lew's bending over so far backwards to be fair, he's victimising me.' After Renwick had calmed him down, Bernard had resumed fraternal business, but on a strictly no favours basis. With regard to the monopoly argument, Bernard declared robustly: 'I like to think that the only monopoly we have is a monopoly of goodwill. Is it fair to have a go at us because of that? I mean I can divorce my wife, but how can I divorce my brothers?'

This was a valid point but, on close examination, it could also be construed as making a strong case for the opposition, as it suggested there was something indissoluble about a Grade connection, even across competitive business frontiers. Lew, more shrewdly, could not be lured into making any comment for publication. For a man of enormous loquacity, always ready to sound off publicly about aspects of his business – from the iniquity of the government's television advertising levy to the urgent need for another commercial channel – Lew was also remarkably adept at knowing when to keep his mouth shut. He had maintained a low profile through the controversy that surrounded the Pilkington Report, and a similar posture served him well in the monopoly debate.

The debate did go off the boil, though not directly through anything Bernard said or Lew did not say. Shortly before publication of the *Sunday*

Times article Leslie was admitted to Guy's Hospital. Initial reports suggested that it was a heart attack. At forty-nine Leslie was close to the same age as Bernard had been when he suffered heart problems. And Bernard had made a full recovery. However, it subsequently became clear that the man described in the *Sunday Times* article as having the 'shrewdest brain' of all the Grades had actually suffered a severe cerebral haemorrhage. With little prospect that Leslie would be able to return to work in anything remotely like a full capacity, Lew and Bernard were compelled to think of other ways of arranging the family's business interests. Leslie lived on for another thirteen years, but without being able to work again on more than an occasional part-time basis.

Lew's libel case against Emile Littler eventually surfaced in the Queen's Bench Division in February 1968, with ATV and the Grade Organisation joined in the action as his co-plaintiffs. The high point of the case was provided by the spectacle of Prince Littler testifying against his brother Emile in favour of Lew. In his own evidence, Lew's main contribution was to tell a story only obliquely related to the proceedings but which, he claimed, was an illustration of just how independently he and his brothers operated in relation to each other:

> 'For many years ATV had exclusive rights to the Royal Variety Performance, at which the Queen was present.
>
> 'After about seven years my brother Bernard Delfont became the president of the organisation which says who can have the Royal Variety Performance.
>
> 'He called me and said: "I have looked at the matter, you have had it for seven years. I think it is wrong for you to have it exclusively. You must alternate with the BBC."
>
> 'I kicked up an alarming row. But I just had to take it on the chin.'[14]

Emile Littler withdrew his 'plot' allegation in the course of the proceedings, which made it a formality that the judge would find in favour of the plaintiffs. Lew gave his share of the £2,250 damages award to charity.

FOURTEEN

Cashing In

WHEN THE SATIRICAL MAGAZINE *Private Eye* entertained its readers by portraying the boss of ATV as 'Mr Low Greed' no offence was taken. The wordplay was enjoyed inside ATV – not least by Lew himself – but few mistook the caricature for reality. Indeed, there was a perceptive school of thought in the organisation which held that Lew was not much interested in making money, nor, for that matter, really that much interested in television. What he loved about his calling was the business of having to sell and sell and sell again, and the rich opportunities for personal performance that went with that obligation.

It was certainly the aspect of his work about which he was prepared to make his proudest boasts. 'I've sold everything we produce except the weather forecast and the epilogue,'[1] he said, by way of explaining his first Queen's Award for Industry for Export Achievement in the summer of 1967. This was pardonable salesman's exaggeration, but with dollar sales of his TV films at twenty million a year, and fast rising, he had a lot to brag about.

On one trip to America with his youthful deputy managing director, Robin Gill, Lew asked for an update on how much they had sold. After consulting his list, Gill reported, 'We've not only sold every series we've got, you've sold two we haven't even made yet.'[2] Gill's next chore would be to cable London and set the unmade series in motion. This method occasionally led to complications. On another visit Lew over-enthusiastically pre-sold a series based on two words that popped into his head, 'The Skull',[3] but later had to confess his inability to think up a convincing story line to go with it. Never knowingly outflanked by other people's big ideas, he was once asked if the British could come up with a counter to the highly rated American situation comedy *The Flying Nun*, starring Sally Field. After a moment's reflection, he thought 'The Underwater Rabbi'[4] might do it.

By the late 1960s America sometimes found it more convenient to come to Lew. Martin Starger, who later became Lew's closest ally in his assault on Hollywood, has vivid recollection of his first encounter with the English showman.[5] As a rising young executive with the ABC network, Starger was sent to London in 1967 to reconnoitre the British television market. Lew's unique style of meeting and greeting made an indelible impression, as Starger later related in the columns of *Variety* magazine. Having landed at Heathrow Airport at 6 a.m. and been rushed to the front of the aircraft to disembark – much to the chagrin of the other passengers – Starger was whisked through the airport on a motorized cart, informed only that there was an 'important gentleman' to see him. He then recalled his first sighting of Lew Grade:

As we zoomed into the large Passport Control Hall, I saw a small, bald man in camel's hair overcoat pacing up and down by the immigration desks, puffing nervously on what seemed like a 14-inch cigar. The cart stopped in front of him, the official announcing, 'Here he is, Sir.'

The bald man in the camel's hair overcoat took his cigar out of his mouth, blew a thick cloud of smoke my way, smiled, and said, 'I'm Lew Grade. Welcome to London. Give me your passport.'

He showed my passport to a waiting immigration official who stamped it and said to Lew, 'The boys thank you for the tickets to the Palladium.' 'It's nothing, Harry. Glad to do it. I hope your wife feels better.' A porter grabbed my bags and before I knew it, I was entering a chauffeured Rolls-Royce approximately the size of a Greyhound bus . . .

I started to say 'Thank you' and words to the effect of, 'Mr Grade, you didn't have to come out personally at this hour to meet me.' Lew interrupted, 'Nonsense. Wouldn't have it any other way. Been up for an hour and a half anyway. I'll only be 45 minutes late to the office (it was now 6:30 in the morning!).

'Now, son, when you get to the hotel, take an hour or two sleep. My car will pick you up, take you to my studio. We'll show you some episodes of *Man in A Suitcase* [one of ATV's many detective dramas] . . . it will be a smash in America . . . I have six programme ideas I want to talk to you about . . . They are all fantastic! NBC and CBS are about to buy them, I'm sure . . . they're coming in to London next week . . . so you'll have to move quickly . . .

We arrived at the Dorchester. It seemed as if the entire staff was waiting for Lew. He hurried over to the reception desk . . . 'This is Mr Starger. He doesn't have to sign the register. Friend of mine.' The clerk nodded nervously and led us up to my room. Lew checked every corner of it.

'He pointed to the largest floral arrangement I have ever seen. 'These flowers are from Kathie and me. You must meet her. She's wonderful.'

'Now, son you get some rest and remember, my driver will be in the front of the hotel in two hours.'[6]

Most of the series that Lew lined up for export, like *Department S* and *Jason King*, both vehicles for the flamboyant Anglo-French actor Peter Wyngarde, and *The Champions*, a sci-fi adventure featuring a trio of agents with supernatural powers, were of the highly watchable but once seen easily forgotten variety. However, there were honourable exceptions, most notably *The Prisoner*, which exercised the talent of Patrick McGoohan after his long stint in *Danger Man*, and which became a cult series. In *The Prisoner* McGoohan plays Number Six, an intelligence officer held against his will in a mysterious village peopled with brainwashed characters from which he tries, forever vainly, to escape. During the course of the series he encounters several sinister incarnations of Number Two, played usually by notable character actors such as Leo McKern, Patrick Cargill and Eric Portman, but the identity of Number One remains a mystery until the last episode when he appears wearing a false face. His face is pulled off to expose the countenance of a monkey. This also proves detachable, finally revealing the familiar features of Number Six.

The significance of it all remains impenetrable to this day, as indeed it was in the beginning. Recalling the experience of selling the show's concept to Lew, McGoohan related:

He sort of said, 'Well, what's it about? Tell me.' So I talked for ten minutes and he stopped me and said, 'I don't understand one word you're talking about, but how much is it going to be?' So I had a budget with me, oddly enough, and told him how much and he says, 'When can you start?' I said Monday, on scripts. And he says, 'The money will be in your company's account on Monday morning.' Which it was.[7]

Lew prided himself on the lightning speed of his decision-making, though he was always disinclined to be rushed himself, if undecided. On those occasions his response was likely to be: 'If you want an answer straight away, it's No.'[8] Lew also praised himself for operating with an absence of visible paperwork, ratifying his deals, even the mega ones, with a flourish of his cigar and a prompt handshake. There was of course never any shortage of people at his command, ready to draw up any contracts that flowed from his decisions.

Lew's efforts as an exporter did not meet with universal approval. The BBC and most of the other ITV companies piously maintained that their programmes were made with the home market in mind, and offered abroad, if at all, only as an afterthought. Lew also had to accept regular ribbing from ABC's Howard Thomas, who suggested that his escapist adventure series were targeted on Birmingham, Alabama, rather than – perhaps more appropriately in view of his franchise – on Birmingham, England. However, almost everybody was impressed by the sheer scale of Lew's selling, and frequently pre-selling, of his company's products in the United States.

Among those most curious about how he did it was the *Daily Mail*'s Peter Black. The secret Lew told him was always to deal personally with the heads of the American TV networks. And always give them a good show. Black then asked Lew to reproduce the show that had managed to persuade the American bigwigs to buy *Randall and Hopkirk (Deceased)*, ATV's improbable series about a 'ghost' detective. Lew accepted the challenge, and Black reported:

I can assure you it was quite a performance. He leaves his chair, walks up and down behind the desk, takes dramatic backward steps, flings out his arms to emphasise a line, and all the while his pale blue eyes are blazing with a sincere desire to make you see it the way he sees it.

'I want you to visualise a small district, an ordinary middle class area. There's a block of offices. On the door it says "Randall and Hopkirk".

Then we see a line go through Hopkirk and it says 'Randall and Hopkirk (deceased).'

'There's two small private detectives who have always worked together. They are waiting for the big break. At last they get it. In the first five minutes of the case one of them gets killed. He's dead.

'The poor partner's hopeless. What's he going to do without his partner? Suddenly his partner reappears. Or he wakes up in a trance, or from sleep, and goes to the graveyard where his partner's sitting on the grave.

'He says, "What are you doing here, you're dead!" He says, "I know I am. But I don't want to leave you on your own." And that's how the story develops. But nobody else can see or hear him . . ."⁹

Not Hamlet perhaps, but wonderfully compelling stuff from a man in his sixties who was also always ready, on request, to liven things up by throwing in a quick Charleston, never losing the grip on his cigar. Few chief executives, even in show business, had the inclination or the ability to disport themselves in such a manner. To Lew it came naturally. Selling for Lew answered two basic needs, a stage for personal play-acting and a means of getting his own way. Money was the prize, but not the sole objective. The joy of television was that it required Lew's ability to sell in so many different directions – story concepts to his stars; product to the international market; programme scheduling ideas to the network committee; and ultimately of course ATV itself, as a worthy franchise holder, to the ITA.

This last necessity came into sharp focus in 1967 when the franchises came up for renewal in circumstances where the ITA's chairman, Lord Hill, had indicated a strong likelihood of significant changes. There was no lack of outside competition, with thirty-six serious bidders ready to contest the fifteen franchise areas, and no shortage of vociferous critics advocating the need for further improvements on Pilkingtonian lines. Confidence within ATV was high, but less than overweening.

The company felt it was moving with the times, even to the extent of being ready to drop its flagship Palladium show. It was, in truth, still remarkably popular, but the old Variety-style format was looking increasingly dog-eared as the 'Swinging Sixties' progressed. The unkindest cut was delivered by the playwright Dennis Potter, who wrote that the show had 'by now reached the particularly ripe kind of decay where one actually looks forward to the sudden drama of cheerful suds swirling through the high zone wash and slobbery dogs gobbling their tinned meat or liver'.[10]

It was known that Lord Hill was a personal admirer of ATV's boss. He had jovially presided over a celebration for the Queen's Award for Industry achievement at the House of Lords, where Lew had been presented with a piratical black eye patch for 'turning a blind eye'[11] to his critics. However, in his official capacity, Lord Hill happened to be one of those critics. To his way of thinking ATV's performance in the post-Pilkington era was patchy at best.

The franchise applications were controversially dealt with in secret by the ITA on the basis of written submissions and formal interviews, though Lord Hill later divulged the energising effect of Lew's ATV team on its deliberations. In his memoir *Behind the Screen*, he recalled:

> The interview was an exhilarating experience and many of the answers were given with a boisterous candour. More time was spent in this interview than in any other in lively exchanges on the successes and failures of the applicant's past programmes. It was an essay in superlatives. The successes were immense and the failures were dismal. Lew was the life and soul of the application. Behind the exaggerations and the indiscretions, here was a born showman whose enormous energies were being wholly devoted to his job. His judgement might from time to time be faulty but his honesty and dedication, to say nothing of his optimism, were unmistakable.[12]

ATV emerged from the process with a renewed franchise but with less than its heart's desire, which would ideally have been business as usual. In the interest of transfusing new blood into the enterprise, Lord Hill's ITA decided to reconfigure the whole operation. As part of the shake-up, it dropped the split weekend/weekday arrangement altogether, except in London, while the northern region was split into two, Lancashire and Yorkshire. This new franchise jigsaw had major consequences for all the original 'Big Four', and in one case seriously malign ones.

The worst sufferer was Rediffusion (A-R) which lost its lucrative London weekday franchise altogether. Its meagre consolation was to be accorded a half share in Thames Television, a new company formation in which the dominant partner was Howard Thomas's ABC. Thames, under Thomas's leadership, was allocated London weekdays. Sidney Bernstein's Granada maintained its strong position in the north, but was obliged to share the region with a new company, Yorkshire Television. Another new company, London Weekend Television (LWT), fronted by David Frost, which had exhibited an excellent grasp of public service rhetoric of the Pilkington style in its application, also featured in the line-up. LWT was awarded the choice London weekend berth, formerly the jewel in Lew's media crown.

This left the Midlands full week franchise, which was the one allocated to Lew's ATV. It was clearly less than a whole loaf, but it also represented much more than half. Lew still had every prospect of being a big player in ITV's network arrangements, though it would henceforth have to be in the arena of a 'Big Five' (Thames, ATV, Granada, Yorkshire and LWT). There were nonetheless predictions of troubled times ahead when the new outfits slotted into place later in 1968; these proved to be entirely correct.

Meanwhile, things were going quite agreeably for Lew elsewhere. In the spring of 1967 he became more than £1 million richer with a bare minimum of effort, beyond counting the money. The windfall was a consequence of the Grade Organisation's takeover, on a mutually agreed basis, by the giant Electric and Musical Industries corporation (EMI). At that time, EMI was flooded with incoming funds through sales of records by a pop group called the Beatles. The final purchase price was struck at £8 million, of which the major portion was shared by Lew, Leslie and Bernard.

The deal had originally been parleyed between EMI's chairman, Sir Joseph Lockwood, and the youngest of the Grade brothers shortly before Leslie was incapacitated by his stroke. In Leslie's agile mind it had had the charm of being a creative next stage in the development of the Grade family's fortunes, with the useful by-product of deflecting concerns about a Grade family show business monopoly. But it was Bernard, taking over as chairman of the Grade Organisation during Leslie's long convalescence, who brought the design to fruition. And Bernard became its prime beneficiary.

As part of the deal, Bernard was recruited by EMI on a salaried basis and given a mandate to extend the company's leisure activities. Although this meant forgoing his long-term freelance status, Bernard was encouraged to continue with his impresario activities in the West End, and given the finance to make judicious acquisitions in the entertainment sphere, countrywide. One of his first exuberant purchases was of the Blackpool Tower Company.

Lew did not begrudge Bernard his new eminence but he was perhaps more enchanted by the almost simultaneous progress, albeit at a much lower level, of his nephew, Michael, who showed signs of being made of the right stuff. Michael had been persuaded to join the family enterprise shortly after his father went into hospital. He was twenty-three years old, had no experience of agency work, and had exhibited no previous inclination to mount the show business ladder. He had been a modest scholar at Stowe public school, which he attended as a boarder and disliked intensely, but had displayed more promise after wangling a transfer to day boy status at St Dunstan's College, Catford, from which he emerged with a couple of A levels.

When Michael left school, his father had offered him a job but Michael decided to strike out in another direction, as a sports writer on the *Daily Mirror*. By the age of twenty-one he had a regular column, illustrated with his own mugshot, and was evidently going places in the newspaper business. After his departure, his boss, Hugh Cudlipp, accorded him high praise, saying, 'If Michael had stayed with the *Mirror* he could have ended up as sports editor.'[13]

Despite his lack of show business experience, Michael had a preparation for his life's work similar to that of his father and his two famous uncles, namely an upbringing by Olga. Indeed, his exposure to Olga was probably even more concentrated than theirs had been. It was certainly what he regarded as his most formative influence. Looking back in his autobiography, *It Seemed Like a Good Idea at the Time*, Michael wrote: 'She could be hilariously funny in the Jewish manner, firing off quaint sayings and curses in a mixture of fractured English and Yiddish. She could also be utterly impossible, stubborn to the point of mulishness, imperious, unforgiving and fiercely insistent on what she thought was proper behaviour.'[14]

Alongside Olga's implacable opinions, Michael noted her ability to bend the rules, if the cause was just. Feeling that Michael as a growing boy was too thin in comparison with the *goyim* in their Edgware Road neighbourhood, Olga deduced that their advantage was derived from the consumption of bacon. This called for action. Closing all the windows in the flat to prevent any Jewish neighbours from getting a whiff of her unorthodoxy, Olga plied Michael with bacon fry-ups to build up his strength. The offence was mitigated by her refraining from eating them herself and cooking in kosher margarine. Aside from such lessons in the art of concealment and compromise, Michael was indebted to his grandmother for her many pearls of everyday wisdom, of which one of the most useful was, 'From worry you don't die.'[15]

Michael was never in touch with his natural mother, Winifred, though it appears he may have had opportunity to establish some contact when he grew up. At one stage, when he became senior executive at London Weekend Television, he found himself working in proximity to Winifred's second husband, who, with his name professionally abbreviated to Kent Walton, and equipped with a mid-Atlantic accent, was ITV's *World of Sport* wrestling commentator, inviting Saturday afternoon viewers into the action with 'Greetings, grapple fans.' Michael explained in his autobiography that he could only have sought out his mother at the price of alienating his father and grandmother and, in any event, 'I didn't know her so I didn't miss her.'[16]

He regarded his relationship with his father as being close and loving, but it still had to bridge the gap created by their living, for the most part, in separate households. In mid-life, Michael consulted an expensive Hollywood psychiatrist who, after hearing the story of his early years, pronounced: 'You should either be gay or alcoholic – probably both.'[17]

Starting out at the Grade Organisation, Michael was taught the rudiments by Billy Marsh in a small, literally smoke-filled room; Marsh out-smoked even his Uncle Lew, though his preference was for cigarettes. The stock joke of clients reporting a recent meeting with him was 'I nearly saw Billy Marsh the other day.'[18] After a grounding in accounting procedures and a crash course in the art of assembling shows for seaside venues, Michael was let loose on the representation of some of the agency's bigger clients. One of them was Werner Schmidt, who had a German-originated concept called *The Golden Shot*, featuring contestants in crossbow shooting games, which he wanted to sell to British television. Michael was entrusted with the responsible job of presenting Schmidt and his idea to Lew Grade at Cumberland House. This first negotiating encounter between uncle and nephew was characterised by Lew telling the fresh young agent, 'Get your hair cut.'[19] Michael's client, however, had no complaints.

Schmidt emerged with an excellent deal and *The Golden Shot*, slickly hosted by Bob Monkhouse after Jackie Rae's attempts to front the show had fallen short, ran on television for eight years. The show was based around a series of shooting games in which, in order to win prizes, contestants would aim the crossbow at a target consisting of an exploding apple in front of a cartoon backdrop. The loading of the bolt into the crossbow was always a solemn proceeding, as the presenter instructed, 'Bernie – the bolt.' In the course of *The Golden Shot*'s long run there were three different 'Bernies' (none actually called Bernie or Bernard in real life), though the show's ultimate displacement by the even more popular quiz show, *Celebrity Squares*, precluded any need for a fourth.

Marsh later said of his apprentice, 'He started from scratch, but I could see very quickly that he had the Grade flair and the Grade capacity for hard work.'[20] Michael's ascent of the learning curve was unimpeded by the EMI takeover of the Grade Organisation, which was allowed to function very much as it had done before within the new corporate structure. However, the next major phase of EMI's expansion, initiated by his other uncle Bernard, was to signal major changes at Michael's level and many others besides.

Bernard's most ambitious project on behalf of his new employer became the takeover of the Associated British Picture Corporation (ABPC), which was then, after the Rank Organisation, Britain's largest film producer and distributor with 350 cinema outlets, along with the Pathé News library and a rich assortment of bowling alleys and squash courts. Additionally, the company owned ABC, which held the controlling half share in Thames Television. And it would be the television element that attracted the keenest interest of the Board of Trade and the ITA. Once again there loomed, in official minds, the spectre of what was called 'Gradopoly'.

Bernard claimed that there were no grounds for entertaining such suspicions, though Thames Television's boss, Howard Thomas, was among those who thought otherwise. As negotiations about the deal dragged on, Thomas remembered Lew giving him 'mysterious nods and winks' to the effect that one day soon, when the details were hammered out, 'We could all be together, in running a colossal conglomerate.'[21]

EMI did acquire ABPC at a cost of £63 million, but only after its acceptance of some stringent ITA-imposed safety features. These were designed to protect the original franchise arrangement from any predatory moves. The new conglomerate was required to sell off some of its Thames Television shares, reducing its holding to less than half, while those it retained had to be held in a hived-off company, chaired by Lord Shawcross. To further allay fears of a cartel of theatre, television and agency interests coming into existence, EMI was also firmly persuaded to divest itself of its theatrical agencies. This essentially meant getting rid of the Grade Organisation assets it had so recently acquired, aside from its cinemas which could be easily merged with the ABPC chain.

The method of disposal chosen was a series of management buyouts which enabled most of the old Grade agency operators to flourish under different company headings. Thus London Management Limited, financed principally by Leslie Grade, became the vehicle for the talents of his son and Billy Marsh. Nobody doubted that they would be anything other than a great success, particularly after Michael, stepping in while Marsh was away on holiday, picked up the reins on negotiations relating to Morecambe and Wise, long-time top stars for Lew's ATV.

Finding that their enthusiasm for ATV was on the wane, Michael alertly steered the comedy duo in the direction of Bill Cotton Jr, the son of the big band leader, who was then Head of Light Entertainment at the BBC. With the inducement of being able to stage their shows in colour on BBC2, at that time the only channel with the new system, Cotton persuaded Eric and Ernie to change allegiance and sign on with the Corporation.

Michael, in consequence, emerged from the whole negotiation with two extremely happy clients and one outraged uncle. Once he had recovered from the shock, however, Lew was able to see the episode as evidence of precocious initiative, in the traditional Grade family style.

FIFTEEN

Knighthood

L EW GRADE BECAME SIR LEW GRADE, though he still happily answered to plain Lew, in the New Year's Honours awards of January 1969. His elevation came as no great surprise, given his export achievements and the palpable hit made by his mother on being introduced to the Queen Mother at the Royal Variety Performance a couple of years earlier.

'I'm delighted to meet you at last,' said the Queen Mother. 'You must be so proud of your children, Mrs Winogradsky.' This gracious overture inspired Olga to clasp the royal hand in both of hers, and respond with great warmth, 'And you must be very proud of your children, too.'[1]

Lew's knighthood was accorded much good-natured approval in the press, even in its more highbrow reaches. The *Guardian* headlined its profile of him 'Lovable Lew', though a degree of ironic detachment was preserved by rendering the two capital letters as £ signs. Still, it enthused: 'Journalists love Lew Grade. Almost tenderly. He calls them by their first names, he hobnobs with them, and when he walks into a press conference he shakes hands with everybody. And most loveable of all, he talks about money . . .'[2]

And come Christmas, the *Guardian* could also have mentioned, Lew's company always laid on for the show business writers the most lavish luncheon of the year, at which champagne flowed like the Thames, while Lew himself wandered benignly and abstemiously around sipping his Coca-Cola.

Lew's lovability, however, did not go entirely unchallenged. As the new London Weekend Television enterprise, touted by the ITA as 'perhaps the greatest concentration of talent in one company ever seen in British television',[3] endeavoured to make its mark in what had been Lew's old franchise area, the predicted tensions arising from this new arrangement surfaced with alarming rapidity.

In its application for a franchise, the LWT group had made great play of its intention to lead public taste to the high ground. David Frost, the co-founder of the group along with the ex-MP and newscaster, Aidan Crawley, had argued that the British public was much more intelligent than it had been given credit for. Summing up his expectations for LWT, Frost promised less Variety with a capital 'V' and more variety with a small one. These uplifting sentiments were echoed by Michael Peacock, LWT's youthful managing director, who brought a cohort of well-regarded BBC production talent into the operation. Peacock, a former head of BBC2 and Controller of BBC1, was seen as a possible future director general before his defection to the commercial channel. He was quoted as saying, in relation to his plans for the future, 'You won't have to be a moron to get something out of London Weekend Television.'[4]

Observations of this type could hardly be considered music to Lew's ears. Essentially, he had created ITV's weekend viewing, and he had always gone to great lengths to preserve the lightness of its elements. One of his most celebrated networking triumphs had been the shifting of *Armchair Theatre*, ABC's drama showcase, from its prime Sunday-night spot on the grounds that viewers could not be expected to handle its level of seriousness while also having to think about going to work the next morning. His argument was: 'if they missed one important line of a play they wouldn't have a clue what's going on'.[5] As Lew saw it, at weekends, even more than at other times, ITV needed to maintain a high level of non-serious entertainment.

Despite the clear differences in programming attitudes between the young thrusters of LWT and what was called the old guard, led by Lew, the networking committee agreed that LWT should have its head for the first few months of scheduling, starting in August 1968. Alert to the change in direction at ITV, the BBC opportunistically seized the chance to entice viewers by packing more light entertainment into its own weekend schedule, thereby neatly reversing the traditional roles of the two main channels. Confronted with a choice between cultural and informational programmes on ITV and the lighter fare offered by the BBC, viewers switched over to the Corporation in droves.

From the first week it was evident that the conservatism of the viewers had been seriously underestimated. Many turned out not to have realised that any changes were under way. In consequence they were infuriated by the disappearance of old ITV favourites, and annoyed by the apparent eccentricity of the new schedules. Some of the difficulties were caused by an ACTT technicians' strike, expressing the union's displeasure at the disruption brought about by franchise changes. But it was also clear that, as Lew had predicted, LWT's basic strengths – in current affairs, the arts and children's programmes – were not best suited to a weekend franchise.

The new company's initial weakness on air was soon exacerbated by another problem. LWT's impressive line-up of mainly ex-BBC broad-casters and solid business interests, ranging from Pearl Assurance to the paper firm Bowaters, had a serious fault line which Andrew Crisell, in his book *British Broadcasting*, defined as being the fact that 'its business people had little understanding of television and its television people knew little of business'.[6] Memories of the original 'Big Four' companies losing large quantities of money before they managed to hit a winning formula had long since faded. The assumption by the late 1960s was that a television franchise should yield almost instant rewards. From the outset, therefore, LWT was saddled with a board impatiently expecting early profitability, which was not forthcoming.

After little more than two months on air, Peacock had the thankless task of having to warn his board that the company was already in a vulnerable position and that the advertisers were getting restive. In point of fact, the whole ITV network was beginning to feel vulnerable and restive. In failing to attract the size of audience needed, LWT's lacklustre start was seen as a crucial weakness at the heart of the whole enterprise. With the BBC suddenly taking up to 61 per cent of the ratings, ITV had to go back in their records to 1955 to locate more disastrous viewing figures. This gave rise to an apprehension that advertisers might decide to hold on to their money as they had done in the first year's transmission.

There was bound to be a network repercussion, and, almost as certainly, Lew Grade was bound to be the main instigator of change. According to a report in the *Sunday Times*, Lew signalled his dismay at

LWT's performance at a networking committee meeting late in 1968, where he was said to have blazed angrily at David Frost, 'I've succeeded in business by knowing exactly what I hate, and I know I hate David Frost.'[7] This episode was later cited, approvingly, in Jack Tinker's *The Television Barons*, as evidence of Lew's purposeful pugnacity at the time.

However, although Lew could be abrasive, he was rarely cruel. And he was not on this occasion, as David Frost was not even at the meeting when the remark was made. What Lew was expressing, in Frost's absence, was not antipathy to Frost himself, but his fundamental opposition to LWT's over-heavy reliance on programmes that featured its founding father. At the time ITV viewers were being asked to enjoy appearances by David Frost on Friday, Saturday and Sunday. There was some variation in what was offered: *Frost on Friday* aimed to be a hard-hitting current affairs programme; *Frost on Saturday* also strove for topicality, but was much lighter in tone; while *Frost on Sunday* was more overtly show-business oriented, with star guests such as Peter Sellers, Sammy Davis Jr and the renowned female impersonator Danny La Rue. But there was no escaping the fact that it all amounted to an overwhelming exposure to David Frost.

Lew used his muscle on the committee to create the first large-scale breach in what was now deemed to be LWT's unsatisfactory scheduling policy. Along with Yorkshire TV, ATV dropped Frost's Saturday slot altogether and replaced him with the Irish comedian, Dave Allen. The other two companies followed suit to a more limited degree by relegating the show to non-prime late evening slots. These moves were described by one newspaper as 'a Palladium counter-attack',[8] but they could, given the ratings situation, be more benignly seen as a defensive closing of ranks to mitigate the knock-on effects of the crisis in the London area.

As LWT floundered into the New Year, Lew also demonstrated that his less glamorous Midlands franchise was no impediment to high-powered show business projects as usual, scheduling fifteen Tom Jones spectaculars at a cost of £100,000 apiece. The swivel-hipped singing star may have represented a long backward step to the purists at LWT, but he cheered up adoring female fans and ITV's forlorn advertisers no end. By February 1969, Lew felt confident enough to say a few compassionate words about the newcomers to his world, laced with an element of 'I told you so'. He told the *Financial Times*:

We all make mistakes . . . you cannot feed people a continual diet of cultural or information programmes. You have got to have some, of course, and it is our responsibility to give them some, but if you give them too many they will switch off. . . . If you care about independent television you don't have to worry about where the programmes come from as long as they come from independent television. We all hoped that somehow or other the new companies [LWT and Yorkshire] would somehow produce a miracle . . . and miracles are not easily produced.[9]

In LWT's particular circumstance it was not so much a case of failure to perform miracles, but of basic promises not being kept. In March its much-trumpeted Public Affairs Unit, designed as the cutting edge of its breaking news coverage, was disbanded on the grounds that it was too costly. Further embarrassment was experienced in the summer when the radical Free Communications Group's magazine *Open Secret* published the confidential text that LWT had submitted to the ITA in pursuit of its franchise. It was now publicly all too clear that most of its original pledges had not been translated into reality.

Meantime, the established contractors were resisting any temptation to come to LWT's ratings rescue by old-fashioned means. Having initially been rebuffed by the newcomers, the other companies proved reluctant to expose their most popular programmes to heavy weekend competition when they could do so much better against the weaker BBC weekday schedules. The two bankers in the ITV system were the 'soaps' – Granada's *Coronation Street* and ATV's much derided but immensely popular *Crossroads*. Both were big money-spinners for all the companies, with the exception of LWT.

In September matters came to a head when the LWT's impatient board abruptly sacked Michael Peacock, precipitating a crisis which led six senior executives in the programme division to resign in protest. The attempt to kick-start a rise in the cultural standards of weekend television was effectively over. Some were tempted to view this outcome as a straight victory for Lew's old guard over new creative talent, but the more clear-eyed observers begged to differ. In its leader on LWT's troubles, *The Times* commented:

It would be too simple to regard Mr Michael Peacock's dismissal as Managing Director of London Weekend as a victory for the philistines of commercial television. For all the splendour of his reputation as a broadcaster, Mr Peacock was in fact running a company which was providing neither the commercial success which had been expected nor programmes of the quality that had been promised.[10]

Despite his scepticism about the LWT project, Lew never set out to bring the operation to its knees. He did not believe 'a miracle' was possible, though he was not averse to the performance of one. However, it could be argued that Lew's defence of ITV's traditional light entertainment values did enable LWT to self-destruct faster than might otherwise have been the case. And the conduct of this defence naturally enhanced Lew's role as the commercial companies' elder statesman, elevating the erstwhile networking supremo of the 'Big Four' to the status of prime mover of the 'Big Five'.

As the sorely wounded LWT limped into 1970, Lew allowed his sights to rise still higher, detecting that he might possibly be able to get back his lost London franchise by a more circuitous route. With LWT's principal shareholders signalling a willingness to sell, there were already money men circling the ITA with alternative notions of a way ahead. In this situation, Sir Robert Fraser was not surprised to receive an approach from a familiar direction. However, he deemed it significant enough to record it as a memorandum to file:

> I had better put it on record that the leaders of ATV asked me privately last Friday what I thought would be the likely attitude of the Authority if ATV entered into some form of association with LWT, which could include the outright purchase of LWT, followed by its operation as a fully owned ATV subsidiary.
>
> The question was put to me at a luncheon at which Lord Renwick, Mr Norman Collins, Sir Lew Grade and Mr Jack Gill were all present.
>
> Now the truth of the matter is that ATV had by 1967 been providing London with its weekend programmes for 12 years, and one of the reasons for the appointment of LWT was the strong feeling of the Authority that the ATV weekend performance had insufficient to commend it. The

Authority sought for the introduction of a greater distinction in the weekend programmes than, to judge from its record, ATV was ever likely to provide. I did not find it possible to say this in the presence of such a mixed company. It would have been too wounding to Sir Lew in the presence of his Chairman and Deputy Chairman and one of his subordinates . . .[11]

Given Fraser's delicacy about hurting his feelings, Lew was not to know that his populist past was the thing that negated his initiative in the present. Initially, he thought he had been thwarted by an aspect of the ITA's policy of separate development. At the time the ITA's public posture, maintained since its inception, was that it would not allow any one of the central companies to have a financial interest in another. This was deemed essential to the plurality of the enterprise, and was said to provide the network with a necessary degree of creative tension. In private, nonetheless, the LWT crisis was forcing a reappraisal of this once inflexible principle. In fact, a merger was secretly being contemplated by the ITA as a way out of its difficulties. However, it was one that envisaged LWT being conjoined with Howard Thomas's Thames Television, not with Lew's ATV.

Rumours to this effect induced in Lew what Fraser described as 'a chronic state of restlessness'.[12] A solution that created a unified London giant, capable of effortlessly dominating the entire network with Lew on the outside, was decidedly not what he wanted.

Lew's agitation on this score, however, soon faded into insignificance with the public furore that greeted the news that Sir Arnold Weinstock, the boss of the General Electric Company (GEC), had sold his 7.5 per cent holding of LWT's voting shares to Rupert Murdoch, the Australian newspaper proprietor. Murdoch had been a controversial figure ever since he had burst on the Fleet Street scene three years earlier with the acquisition of its sauciest Sunday paper, the *News of the World.* His subsequent purchase of a daily, the *Sun,* which he changed into a tabloid and took rapidly downmarket, swelled the ranks of his critics. The *Sun's* transformation proved advantageous to its circulation and balance sheet, but its sensation-seeking journalistic techniques were not deemed to be of the most responsible order. So when Murdoch, with what was seen as predatory intent, injected £500,000 into the ailing LWT operation to halt its slide towards bankruptcy, the ITA found itself embarrassingly on the spot.

Outrage at the possibility of the franchise falling into the hands of a foreign newspaper proprietor, known as 'the Dirty Digger', was almost universal, though Lew failed to join the chorus of disapproval. Relieved at the fast-receding prospect of his own operation being marginalized by a Thames-LWT alliance, Lew allowed himself the luxury of a dissenting view. 'For television to be a success,' he wrote in a letter to the *Sunday Times*, 'energy and enthusiasm are required – and I believe Mr Murdoch has both of these qualities.'[13]

Order was finally restored by the appointment of John Freeman, recently retired as the British ambassador to Washington, as LWT's new authority figure, with the all-encompassing title of Chairman and Chief Executive. A brilliant administrator and broadcaster, noted for his penetrating *Face to Face* television interviews of the early 1960s, Freeman took office with Murdoch pledging his support, but firmly renouncing any executive role. This proved to be an arrangement that the ITA could live with, and with which Lew could happily do business.

Not long after the establishment of amiable relations all round, LWT appointed a Deputy Controller of Programmes (Entertainment). The new man had no previous experience of television production, aside from glimpses of its operation from the sidelines, while working as a theatrical agent. Still, there were high hopes for him, on account of his name being Michael Grade.

Lew's parents: Odessa-born Isaac Winogradsky (left) brought his family to England in 1912. He was a sweet-natured man, but a poor breadwinner. Lew's mother, Olga (above), was the dominant force in the family. Her maiden name was Eisenstadt, meaning 'tower of iron'. *By kind permission of the Grade family*

At the Rochelle Street School in London's East End many of the pupils, like Lew, came from Jewish families in flight from Tsarist Russia and were initially equipped with little or no English. The picture (below) is of its Class 9 in 1916: Lew is back row, second left. *By kind permission of the Grade family*

Lew became a professional dancer after winning the amateur title 'Charleston Champion of the World.' The climax of his original stage act involved many frenzied gyrations performed on a tiny table. A critic described them as 'wondrous to behold'.
By kind permission of the Grade family

Lew came to prefer dancing with a partner as the solo act put too much strain on his knees. Here he is pictured in performance with his first male partner, Al Gold, also the son of Jewish immigrants. Lew is the Pierrot on the right.
By kind permission of the Grade family

By the early 1930s the Charleston was losing some of its popular appeal and Lew's agent suggested that his routine needed 'a new ingredient' – meaning a young woman. This is Lew in action with his first female partner, Anna Roth. © *TopFoto*

Kathleen Moody, a singer with a fine coloratura voice, was a regular performer on the BBC's *Variety Bandbox*, one of the nation's favourite radio shows during the Second World War. Lew successfully wooed her while also serving as an improbable soldier. *By kind permission of the Grade family*

Lew and Kathie cut the cake at their wedding on 23 June 1942, shortly after his discharge from the army on medical grounds. Kathie would taper off her singing engagements after the marriage, putting Lew's career first. *By kind permission of the Grade family*

Lew's younger brother Bernard on his wedding day, 22 January 1946. Left to right: Helen Delroy-Somers (the bride's mother), Leslie (the youngest of Olga Winogradsky's three sons), Bernard and his bride, Carole Lynne, Richard Tauber, opera singer and best man, Kathie and Lew. *By kind permission of the Grade family*

Leslie Grade pictured here with the children from his wartime marriage that ended in divorce; Lynda born 1940, and Michael, 1943. The two children were brought up by their formidable grandmother, Olga. *By kind permission of the Grade family*

Lew with other early ATV bigwigs, Val Parnell and Harry Alan Towers at a rehearsal for *Sunday Night at the London Palladium* in 1955. Towers would soon be eased out of the operation and Parnell eventually moved on, leaving Lew as sole ruler of the roost. *ITV/Rex Features*

Operating in characteristic style, Lew juggles a telephone, a cigar and a fistful of script. He himself produced very little paperwork, preferring the phone to any form of written communication. *Getty Images*

A rare photograph of the three brothers all together, resplendent in best bib and tucker. Lew and Leslie flank Bernard in the centre. This opportunity to dress up was afforded by the wedding of Leslie's son, Michael, in 1967. *Getty Images*

With Kathie and adopted son, Paul, on the day Lew became Sir Lew. They are pictured on the steps outside their Cavendish Square home immediately after Lew's investiture at Buckingham Palace in January 1969. *Mirrorpix*

In his element: Lew in 1973 making an immodest announcement of the return, after a six year interval, of his most cherished Variety show, *Sunday Night at the London Palladium. Mirrorpix*

Lew's mother, Olga, was a regular star of the Royal Variety Performance guest line-ups through the 1970s. Complimented by the Queen Mother on the accomplishments of her children, Olga warmly responded, 'And you must be very proud of your children, too.' *By kind permission of the Grade family*

On escort duty with Elizabeth II at the London Palladium in 1977. Lew counted the royals among his greatest fans, though his brother Bernard, who staged the Royal Variety Performances, was better acquainted with Her Majesty. *Doug McKenzie*

Clasping the Queen's Award for Industry trophy, awarded for his dazzling success in exporting British television shows, Lew is backed by some of the stars who made it all possible. From left to right: Roger Moore, Val Doonican, Connie Stevens and Des O'Connor. *Mirrorpix*

Among the more bizarre game shows that Lew's ATV brought to the nation's attention was *The Golden Shot*, testing contestants' skill with a crossbow. After an uncertain start, it flourished with the comedian Bob Monkhouse presenting. Here Monkhouse gleefully demonstrates the firing technique. *Rex Features*

Hollywood superstar Shirley MacLaine featured in an ATV series called *Shirley's World*, and hated it. This is her burying the hatchet at Mr Chow's restaurant in Knightsbridge in 1976, and declaring an undying affection for Lew, though not for all his shows. *Getty Images*

A friendly exchange with former Labour Prime Minister, Harold Wilson, at an awards ceremony in the Dorchester Hotel in 1977. A year earlier Wilson had braved some public disapproval by ennobling Lew, and his brother Bernard, in his Resignation Honours on leaving office. *Getty Images*

The blockbuster *Jesus of Nazareth* was the crowning achievement of Lew's TV career though its making was plagued with cost and casting difficulties. The relationship between Robert Powell (as Jesus) and director, Franco Zeffirelli, was not friction-free, but here they can be seen enjoying a convivial moment. *Rex Features*

Deeply impressed by *Jesus of Nazareth*, Pope John Paul II bestows the Order of St Sylvester (with star) on Lew at the Vatican, January 1979. Lew was also impressed by the Pope, telling reporters: 'He's got great charisma. I'd like to sign him up.' *Getty Images*

Lew and the Muppet Fozzie Bear indulge in some well-merited mutual admiration. Lew rescued the Muppets' brilliant creator, Jim Henson, from the despair of not finding support in America by providing an alternative home for his puppets in Elstree, and made a fortune. *Getty Images*

The easy part of filming *Raise the Titanic* was, as seen here, persuading the model of the vessel to sink efficiently. The hard part was bringing it up again, but Lew resolutely poured money into the achievement of this objective, and lost a fortune. *ITV/Rex Features*

Robert Holmes a'Court, seen here in deferential mode at the shareholders' meeting of Lew's ACC company in 1981, initially seemed like a friend in need before becoming Lew's business nemesis. Lew would later observe that the financier 'wasn't the warm-hearted Mr Nice Guy I'd thought he was'. *Mirrorpix*

Lord and Lady Grade at home in their comfortable penthouse in Knightsbridge. One of the apartment's many rooms had been stealthily converted, on Kathie's initiative, into a sauna (with telephone) as a nice surprise for Lew who, on first sight of the facility, announced, 'You'll never get me in there.' *Ian Bradshaw/Rex Features*

Baron Grade of Elstree, age 87, demonstrates a dance move in a London street for the delectation of his favourite nephew, Michael, who was then the chief executive of Channel Four Television. © *TopFoto/UPP*

SIXTEEN

The Beatles

THE PRIME ATTRACTION FOR THE posse of newsmen converging on the Amsterdam Hilton in March 1969 was the prospect of witnessing Beatle John Lennon doing something interesting in bed with his new wife, Yoko Ono. In the event, rumours that the couple might be prepared to exhibit some real-life lovemaking to underscore their message that love was all the world needed proved to be unfounded. The much-trumpeted 'Bed-in' demonstration for peace consisted of John and Yoko sitting demurely upright against plumped pillows in a suite ornamented with placards announcing 'Bed Peace' and 'Hair Peace'. Not a bad photo opportunity, but not really much of a story.

There was, however, one item of real news. Back in England the recently knighted Sir Lew Grade had launched a surprise bid for Northern Songs – the company that owned the copyright of the Beatles songs composed by Lennon and Paul McCartney – with a view to making it part of his ATV empire. The information was imparted to the voluntarily bedridden Lennon, who authorised 'a spokesman' to say on his behalf: 'He is definitely not selling his shares. And that is all he wishes to say.'[1] It soon emerged that Paul McCartney, who was away in the United States enjoying a more conventional honeymoon, was of the same defiant persuasion. Suddenly, and unusually, Lew was the bad guy.

The battle for Northern Songs, as a result of which the Beatles did lose ownership of their own songs, was the sternest test of Lew's popularity following the outpouring of sentiment that had greeted his knighthood. However, like most battles, it had a long and complicated prehistory, with evidence of imperfections and misjudgements on both sides.

The Grade brothers had for some time been fretting that they had no significant piece of the action relating to the most extraordinary entertainment phenomenon of the 1960s. Part of their frustration was born of what was seen as a lost opportunity. Before the Beatles arrived on the scene, the British popular music business was in poor shape, severely lacking in confidence.[2] Most of the big singing stars were American, as were most of the big songs. Any home-grown talent, like Cliff Richard and Tommy Steele, who hoped to prosper had to follow a traditional show business route, which almost automatically meant close acquaintance with either the Grade agency or Bernard Delfont's operation. And there was no reason, originally at least, why the Beatles should have taken a different tack. Bernard later recalled, on the subject of what he described as 'my greatest mistake':

> In February 1963 I was looking for a popular group to put in the Royal Variety Performance. My daughter Susan said: 'Daddy, why don't you put the Beatles in?' I said I had never heard of them. When I got back to the office I discovered they were doing a concert for us at the Princess Theatre in Torquay the following Sunday. So I rang to find out how the bookings were doing. Apparently people were sleeping in the streets waiting for ticket returns. That was good enough for me, so I booked them for the Royal Variety Performance in November.
>
> A short while later Brian Epstein [the Beatles' young manager] came round to the office to ask if we would like to manage the Beatles with him. One of my chaps said: 'Well, what do they want?' He mentioned something like £750 a week and we thought it was outrageous, so we turned them down.[3]

Bernard calculated that this rejection must have cost his business in the region of £10 million. He was able to mend fences with the group to a limited degree by having the Beatles star in the Royal Variety show, on the occasion when Lennon famously beguiled the audience by saying, 'Will people in the cheaper seats clap your hands? All the rest of you, if you'll just rattle your jewellery . . .' and the Queen Mother produced her famous one-liner in response to being told by the Beatles that their next appearance would be in Slough – 'Oh! That's near us.'[4]

As Beatlemania rose to its zenith, with a Beatles record being played on radio around the world every minute of every day, Bernard glimpsed another opportunity. He managed to establish excellent relations with Brian Epstein through their mutual interest in the theatre. Epstein purchased the Saville Theatre, in which Bernard had a major interest, and they put on shows there together. But Bernard's direct proposal that he should assist Epstein by buying-in as co-manager of the Beatles was turned down, apparently on the say-so of the Beatles themselves.

Ostensibly, Lew's connection with the Beatles was more tenuous than that enjoyed by his younger brother. But he did know Dick James, the group's music publisher, from way back. James, born Isaac Vapnik, the son of a Polish immigrant butcher who settled in the East End, had been a successful crooner with a number of big bands. After the war he became the first British vocalist to chart in America with 'You Can't Be True'. But his most celebrated hit in Britain was the theme song to Lew's seminal *Adventures of Robin Hood* television series. He was a client of the Lew and Leslie Grade Agency and when he gave up performing to start out as a song plugger and music publisher, he and Lew stayed in friendly touch.

Operating from premises on the corner of Denmark Street, then known as London's Tin Pan Alley, James struggled to make a living for several years. Shortly after Christmas in 1962, his way of life was transformed when Brian Epstein walked into his office. Epstein produced an acetate of the new Beatles single, 'Please Please Me', and said that if James could make it a hit, he could be in a position to secure the Lennon-McCartney music publishing contract. James was so excited by the song that he reached for the phone, in Epstein's presence, and rang an old friend, Philip Jones. At that time Jones was a producer on *Thank Your Lucky Stars*, ITV's answer to the BBC's *Juke Box Jury*. James had played only eight bars of the song down the phone before Jones came back with, 'OK, that'll do. They're on the show.'[5]

The first national television exposure of the Beatles duly followed in January 1963, and 'Please Please Me' rose rapidly to the top of the 'unofficial' *New Musical Express* chart, though it would stall at number two on the 'official' *Record Retailer* chart. Impressed by James' instant success in promoting the song, Epstein proved as good as his word and

Northern Songs was created a month later as a joint company representing the interests of Dick James Music and Lennon and McCartney, along with Epstein. Its sole purpose was to exploit the music rights of songs by Lennon and McCartney, most of which had yet to be composed. James, who shared Lew's gift for hyperbolic utterance, told the two Beatles that he would make them bigger than Rodgers and Hammerstein. They thought he was being ridiculous.

Of all the money streams attracted by the Beatles in their early days from recordings, television, live appearances and the like, the music rights represented one of the smaller tributaries. But as Lennon's and McCartney's prolific songwriting talent became apparent, so too did the value of the rights. The durability of music rights was something that was always beyond question, given their capacity to earn money well beyond the Beatles' lives as performers.

In Britain, there had long been an efficient mechanism for collecting royalties for songs through the Performing Right Society (PRS), which monitored their use, collected the revenue, and paid out on the basis of 50 per cent to the writer and 50 per cent to the music publisher. In addition to plugging songs on the radio and in other media, the music publisher took responsibility for registering the songs, producing sheet music, and chasing up overseas royalty monies.

By signing up with a publisher a songwriter essentially sold a proportion of his copyright in return for having his song marketed, splitting any income on an agreed basis. Although it was not customary to have the music rights vested in a separate company, as was the case with the Beatles, there was some advantage to them in that they could share in the profits from the publishing rights in addition to enjoying direct remuneration as songwriters.

There was, however, a distinct problem with Beatles remuneration at all levels. It was called tax. Though the full horror of its impact was tunefully lamented in the Beatles' song 'Taxman', written by George Harrison, the group's two more regular songwriters, Lennon and McCartney, had the larger problem with the Inland Revenue. By the mid-1960s, with Labour back in office, income and surtax levels could easily result in high earners having to pass on in excess of 90 per cent of their incoming wealth to the government. In an effort to avoid these punishing rates, the Beatles' advisors were constantly on the look-out for methods that might convert income into capital.

In February 1965, Epstein and James came up with what seemed like a bright idea for all concerned. It involved floating Northern Songs as a public company on the London Stock Exchange, offering one and a quarter million of the company's five million shares for sale. Fans could own a small piece of the Beatles by snapping up a share or two, while the return to the two Beatles as a direct consequence of the flotation was close to £100,000 each – tax free, as capital gains tax was not introduced until later in the year. James captured the euphoria of the moment by exulting, 'We have some of the greatest assets of any business in the world today – copyrights. You can keep your factories, plants and production lines – give me copyrights.'[6] Neither Beatle appears to have had any trouble with accepting the capital gain to ease their pressing tax problems, but there would be a question mark over how aware they were of just having put control of their music rights at risk.

By 'going public' the enterprise, like the many companies owning factories, plants and production lines, automatically became susceptible to being taken over. This consideration instantly crossed the mind of Lew Grade, who freshened up his old acquaintance with Dick James by calling him and congratulating him on his new venture, while mentioning in passing that if he ever felt at all inclined to sell his Northern Songs shares, he would know where to look.

Nothing so monstrous seemed likely to happen, at least as long as the unity and mutual esteem of the leading shareholders stayed intact. After the flotation, the alliance of James and Epstein and the two songwriting Beatles still controlled well over 60 per cent of the company's shares, with George Harrison and Ringo Starr having a meagre 1.6 per cent between them. At the time Northern Songs simply looked like a vehicle designed to make the songwriters more securely rich. A 1965 estimate of the Beatles' net worth had Ringo Starr and George Harrison hovering around $3 million, while Lennon and McCartney were said be in the $4 million bracket as a result of their stake in Northern Songs.

Problems with the arrangement began to arise when the Northern Songs shareholders lost their earlier band-of-brothers intimacy. There were signs that this was happening even before Brian Epstein's tragic death in August 1967. Brian Southall, in his book *Northern Songs*, wrote of the Beatles at that time 'both growing up and growing apart'[7] and suggested that Epstein 'was perhaps right to be worried about his future as manager . . .'

Dick James was also losing much of his original lustre as far as the group was concerned. From being the resourceful creative middleman who steered their early efforts up the charts, he began to appear to the Beatles more in the guise of another bean-counting 'suit' who was doing well out of them as the money rolled in, seemingly almost unbidden. At the same time, James was conscious of becoming more entrancing in Lew's eyes. He recalled Lew seriously 'romancing' him after Epstein's death, to the extent that it had become 'a standing joke between us. "Oh no," I'd say, "not that again, Lew!"'[8]

Lew was not the only person expressing an interest. Other parties, defined by James as 'the wolves', were also making approaches with an awareness that the rights to around 150 Beatles songs dating back to such early hits as 'From Me To You', 'She Loves You' and 'I Want To Hold Your Hand', could prove a lucrative addition to any portfolio of business interests. James kept Lew's designs on Northern Songs at arm's length, but he did form the view that Lew should have the first option if it seemed advisable to sell. Meantime, relationships between those involved in the company continued to deteriorate.

After the *Sgt. Pepper's Lonely Hearts Club Band* album was released it became increasingly clear that the Beatles were getting more restless, about their business concerns and with each other. Lennon developed a fascination with Yoko Ono that was perceived to be leading him in directions that the other Beatles were disinclined to follow. Their occasional get-togethers became more fractious, with Harrison and Starr walking out of one recording session, threatening not to return. Along with the slackening of the collective will to perform as a group came a more suspicious attitude towards their money and those who managed it. Early in 1969, Lennon, with the support of Harrison and Starr, recruited a rugged American showbiz operator called Allen Klein to review all their business arrangements, though even this initiative lacked unanimity. McCartney, less than enthralled by Klein, appointed John Eastman, the lawyer father of Linda, soon to become his new American wife, to handle his interests.

To Dick James it seemed as if the Beatles phenomenon was fast disintegrating, and in a way that might cause the share price of Northern Songs to plummet. Accordingly, he lifted the telephone and, without informing Lennon, then in bed with Yoko in Amsterdam, or McCartney away in America, rang his good friend Lew Grade with the request: 'Make me an offer.'[9]

Both men felt they were acting honourably. For Lew, James's call represented the reward for an exceptionally long business courtship, and an opportunity not to be missed. James was in the more equivocal position, but he thought, or had convinced himself, that a deal with Lew at that time was in the Beatles' interest as much as his own, protecting them from 'the wolves' and their own disunity, with a major capital gain into the bargain.

The deal was that Lew should launch a takeover bid of £9.5 million for Northern Songs. James and his partner, the accountant Charles Silver, would accordingly get a shade over £3 million in cash and ATV shares for their 32 per cent holding in the company. Combined with an earlier ATV holding of 3 per cent, this gave Lew a commanding, but less than decisive, 35 per cent in the company. His formal offer for the remainder of the Northern Songs shares was issued in April 1969 by Warburg and Co., the city firm which had bankrolled ATV at the birth of commercial television.

Lew emphasised the benevolence of his intentions as far as the Beatles were concerned and his reverence for songs that would 'live forever'. To no great emollient effect. Philip Norman, the Beatles' biographer, wrote that Lew epitomised for the group 'the hated breed of "men in suits"', and that his conciliatory noises 'might just as well have been the snarl of an alligator on the banks of the Zambezi'.[10]

With the assistance of another merchant bank, Ansbacher and Co., the Beatles signalled their intention to do battle. The statement they issued underlined their sense of betrayal:

> Despite the fact that The Beatles were collectively substantial shareholders in Northern Songs and that Northern Songs was, furthermore, largely dependent upon The Beatles for its prosperity, neither the Directors of Northern Songs nor the Directors of ATV discussed with, or informed, The Beatles of the proposed offer by ATV for the issued capital of Northern Songs.

Had they been so consulted, The Beatles would have informed the Directors of Northern Songs and of ATV that they would not be willing to accept the offer proposed by ATV in respect of their own shareholdings, nor would they be happy to continue, let alone renew, their existing contracts with Northern Songs under the aegis of ATV.[11]

With the Beatles resolutely hanging on to their 31 per cent holding in the company and Allen Klein shopping around for capital to acquire more shares on their behalf, there seemed to be no prospect of a clear winner. Lew's original offer closed on 14 May with his bid still well short of its goal of bagging at least half of Northern Songs' shares. By this time, the pivotal role in the company's destiny was seen to be occupied by a consortium of City brokerage firms, under the leadership of the theatre owners, Howard and Wyndham, which had quietly built up a 14 per cent stake. At an early stage the consortium had seemed ready to align itself with Lennon and McCartney, but exposure to Allen Klein's high-pressure methods tended to sap their enthusiasm. Some consortium members suspected that Klein was bent on securing Northern Songs for himself. This was a mistaken impression, but one that built in further delay and uncertainty.

The Beatles also did not help themselves overmuch, although they went into battle with some élan. 'It's like playing Monopoly,' said Lennon, 'but with real money.'[12] But they soon tired of the intricacies of the conflict, as Klein and Lew manoeuvred to try and obtain favourable responses vis-à-vis the uncommitted shareholders. There was also a sour moment of internal friction when a formal counting of the shares revealed that McCartney had over 100,000 more than his songwriting partner. Lennon, unaware that McCartney had quietly been increasing his stake in their joint enterprise, was said to be displeased by this disparity.

Despite these complications, Klein did edge close to a deal that could have effectively thwarted Lew's ambitions. The consortium agreed to pledge its support for the Beatles' cause, but with the stern proviso that Northern Songs should equip itself with an entirely new board of management with the Beatles having no direct voting power. Lennon, understandably, did not think much of this formula, but incautiously expressed his feeling of disgust publicly. He was famously quoted as saying, 'I am sick of being fucked about by men in suits sitting on their fat asses in the City.'[13]

Lew judged this to be a propitious moment to call Peter Donald, the head of Howard and Wyndham, and offer to buy the consortium's 14 per cent for £2 a share, a modest two shillings and sixpence up on his original offer price. The business was effectively concluded with the one telephone call, bringing Lew's total shareholding up to 54 per cent, enough to give him control of Northern Songs. Allen Klein rang him up soon afterwards to say, 'Well, I have to admit it. You beat me to the punch. We're now ready to sell the shares at the same price you paid to Peter Donald.'[14]

It was not quite the end of the story as ATV was not eager to stump up so much in cash. It would require an intervention by the City Takeover Panel to ensure fair play all round, as a result of which the two Beatles settled for a deal that gave them around £3.5 million in ATV loan stock. By December 1969, ATV had acquired 92 per cent of Northern Songs' issued shares and established an expanded music publishing division, headed by Dick James.

Lennon and McCartney never forgave James for his part in the process that led them to lose control of their songs. Lew, in contrast, managed to escape much in the way of direct censure, possibly because his role could be classed as business as usual, combined with a general awareness that there were much less sympathetic predators circling around the group at the time. And the Beatles did renew their contracts with Northern Songs, subject to amendments, in a way that suggested no more than a modicum of hard feelings. Lew, however, who hated to be on anything but the best of terms with the stars, may well have felt a lingering queasiness about his success in this venture.

Some years later the American Academy of Television Arts and Sciences honoured Lew with a special banquet at the New York Hilton, launched under the banner 'Salute to Sir Lew'. There were 2,000 guests including many of Hollywood's biggest stars, among them Bob Hope, John Wayne, Danny Kaye, Bing Crosby and Shirley MacLaine. And Lew was naturally delighted to see them all. But he was clearly most moved to see John Lennon, who had not performed publicly or even been seen around for some time, among those happy to render the salute.

SEVENTEEN

Family Matters

As Olga approached her estimated eightieth year, a decision had to be made about where might be the best place for her to live. She could still get about quite efficiently, attending Lew's functions as 'Mrs Grade' and Bernard's as 'Mrs Delfont', and, where there was some degree of uncertainty about who was in charge, as 'Mrs Delfont-Grade'. She still had her wits about her, becoming, after her initial warm encounter with the Queen Mother, a regular star in the guest line-up at the Royal Variety show. But when Michael left her home in Wimpole Street to get married, it became clear that she needed some additional help and support.

The solution devised by Lew in consultation with his brothers was to elevate her to the penthouse suite at the Grosvenor House Hotel in Park Lane, where all her needs could be, at least in theory, attended to by the hotel staff. This had the drawback of being on the expensive side even for what was now regarded as one of the wealthiest families in show business, but it had the merit of keeping Olga geographically close to all that was going on in the family. Lew, Bernard and Leslie often called by, though not so regularly as their wives, Kathie, Carole and Audrey, and Olga's daughter, Rita. Olga was never informed about the cost of this arrangement. If she had found out, Bernard maintained, 'she would have upped sticks and gone back to the East End'.[1]

There were some problems of adjustment, but of a minor sort. Although Olga had long since been extricated from the East End, it proved difficult to get East End concepts of frugality entirely out of Olga. Horrified by the price list for items on room service – 'How can they charge a pound for half a grapefruit?'[2] – she insisted on having her food supplies brought in. Thus Michael, as a rising television executive, had to apportion part of his working week to supermarket trawls, stocking up with items for his grandmother's Grosvenor House fridge.

Visitors were entertained in her flat, never in the hotel restaurant – 'See how much they charge for a cup of tea? Better we have one upstairs, where I can make it myself.'[3] In most respects, however, Olga handled her grand new external circumstances with aplomb, never letting them cramp her distinctive style. Sons and daughters-in-law would go up and down in her estimation with the same high degree of unpredictability, though Lew's wife, Kathie, rated by Michael as having 'an instinctive gift of tact',[4] was usually able to smooth over any family ructions.

It could be said that all the Grades had successfully adapted to living conditions to which their upbringing had not made them in any way accustomed. In addition to their fine London residences, both Leslie and Bernard had holiday homes in the South of France for rest and relaxation away from it all. Bernard and Carole also had a cottage in Sussex for interim family leisure at weekends. Even Lew and Kathie had branched out a bit by buying a house in Wimbledon, though their acquaintance with the property after leaving Cavendish Square was brief. Lew decided that, on balance, he was more comfortable back nearer the centre of things and the couple moved into a company-owned penthouse in Knightsbridge, close to the Royal Albert Hall, where he had once shone so brightly as 'the World Charleston Champion'. The Wimbledon house became the home for Kathie's elderly mother, though Lew sometimes referred to it ironically as his country place.

Lew also differed from his brothers in having no faith in the restorative powers of a holiday, though he could be penitent on the subject. 'I realise that this was selfish as far as Kathie and our son Paul was concerned,' he wrote in *Still Dancing*, 'I'm sure they would have loved to go on regular family holidays, like most people . . . On the other hand my idea of purgatory is sitting on a beach – in the South of France, or anywhere else for that matter – sunning myself with nothing to do and no phone calls to make. Pure Hell!'[5]

Lew's claim to abstinence on the holiday front is to a mild extent contradicted by the family photo album. There is an attractive study of

Lew at Davos in Switzerland, teetering on a pair of skis under the false impression that childhood proficiency as a roller-skater was preparation enough for the icy slopes. This exercise, like Lew's earlier golfing experiment, was never repeated. There is also a snapshot of a speedboat off the coast at Antibes, circa 1957, with Paul gleeful at the wheel, Kathie wreathed in the sunniest of smiles and Lew looking pensive. Kathie could remember another holiday in the South of France when Lew stayed inside all day making calls. On her suggestion they went home early – 'He was so pleased it was as though I had given him a present.'[6] Thereafter, the family made do with the occasional short three- or four-day break, usually to Paris where the telephones were wonderfully close to hand.

The Winogradsky family's social progress from poor refugee status, through East End hardship, to the front rank of show business aristocracy wrought major changes in their external circumstances but scarcely dented their attitudes. Losing the common touch was never a real option for the brothers, given the nature of their work. On the other hand, they were not at all averse to creature comforts. They certainly preferred to be driven about in Rolls-Royces, even for short distances they could comfortably have walked, but there was no contradiction in this as far as they were concerned. It was more, they claimed, a matter of business convenience than ostentation.

Of all the family, only Olga could be said to be highly partisan in political terms. Winston Churchill was her hero and admiration for him combined with a reverence, verging on adoration, for the royal family. Olga regularly kept her Conservative Party subscription up to date, though Michael thought that it was, in her mind, more a form of insurance than a badge of ideology. The Tory membership card was something that could be flourished as evidence of a patriotic disposition if, by some chance, the Grade family was invited to take to the road as refugees again.

Leslie was reckoned to be the most conservative of her sons in his general outlook, and was also the most observant of traditional Jewish customs. His wife, Audrey, was the only one of Olga's three daughters-in-law who adopted the Jewish faith. Lew and Bernard were proud of their Jewish heritage, but not religiously inclined in any formal sense. Lew did, however, confess to having an impression that 'somebody up there likes me'.[7] He also had no qualms about bringing God into any conversation, alluding to him, eyes raised heavenwards, as 'an advisor I don't pay'.[8] Bernard always maintained that luck was the prime determinant in human affairs. On the whole, he felt his was good.

Bernard rarely paraded a political opinion, though his wife, Carole, who was of Home Counties Tory lineage, thought that 'if pushed he might be a socialist'.[9] He could nonetheless display evidence of strong conviction, turning down the opportunity to produce Rolf Hochhuth's play, *The Soldiers*, because he thought its portrayal of Winston Churchill was grossly unfair. He also banned the Alec Guinness film, *The Last Ten Days of Hitler*, from being shown in any of EMI's cinemas, because its characterisation of the Führer was, in his opinion, too sympathetic. Both decisions were criticised in the liberal press, but Bernard never regretted either of them.

Lew's open political leanings tended to be shaped by the television advertising revenue levy: anyone who was for it, he was against. In the privacy of the polling booth, he reliably voted Conservative, though this affiliation was not the most reliable guide to his judgements. According to Marcia Stanton, his long-time personal assistant, one of Lew's most pronounced characteristics was 'being able to respond to any idea – if it was a good one. No matter where it came from.'[10] Outside the context of television, he never exhibited much appetite for political controversy. He could count leading politicians, in both the main parties, among his friends but the real stuff of politics, like current affairs in general, was not something that excited his interest. One of his great losing battles in the network committee was against the introduction of ITN's *News at Ten*, though he later publicly acknowledged the programme's success.

Aside from their shared ability to make money, the brothers showed an attractive readiness to part with it. Occasionally, in conspicuous fashion. At an emergency meeting of show business leaders at the Café Royal in Piccadilly convened to raise funds for Israeli welfare projects in the immediate aftermath of the Six-Day War of 1967, the Grades collectively pledged £40,000. Others who dug deep were Lew's friends, the Bernstein brothers of Granada Television (£35,000), and Albert Broccoli and Harry Saltzman, makers of the James Bond films with Sean Connery, who each gave £25,000. Soon afterwards, Leslie, by way of giving thanks to Guy's

Hospital, which had treated him for his stroke, presided over a £2 million public appeal to equip the hospital with a new wing, and started the ball rolling with a personal donation of £100,000.

Lew also excited public attention by organising charity events which raised £200,000 for the British appeal to send athletes to the Munich and Montreal Olympics, though he drew the line at raising money for the Moscow Games. Sister Rita also contributed by organising annual shows in aid of children's charities. These were mini-spectaculars, complete with cabaret of volunteer artistes furnished by her brothers, and staged at the Savoy, the Dorchester and other swanky hotels.

Yet the Grades were more noted for inconspicuous acts of generosity that were not designed for eye-catching mention in the press. For comedian and scriptwriter Denis Norden, Lew was simply 'the softest touch in show business'.[11] The drama critic Sheridan Morley, whose comedy actor father Robert Morley was one of Leslie's most valued clients, wrote of the Grades:

> Of course they were a mafia but one of the very best kind: when my father was trying to raise, very quickly, several thousand pounds and build a home for autistic children, it was Lew and Leslie and Bernie and, perhaps more surprising, John Lennon, who instantly sent the four-figure cheques. Other West End managements were out whenever he called them. There was a breathtaking generosity about . . . the brothers, coupled with a savage sense of what would work and what would fail when put up there in front of an orchestra.[12]

'I'd rather not talk about that,'[13] Lew told the reporter who discovered that he was financing much more than the education of his son Paul at Millfield, the independent co-educational boarding school in Somerset. By the time Paul left, Lew had discreetly assisted more than twenty of his fellow pupils whose parents had experienced difficulties in paying their children's school fees. Lew did however allow himself to be more open about the charitable endeavours of Kathie on behalf of the Red Cross, YWCA, Age Concern and the Royal National Lifeboat Institution. Kathie was also praised for organising Christmas and Easter parties for the children of ATV personnel based at Elstree Studios, where most of the company's lavish productions for the network and the international market were made.

This could be considered in the line of Lew's business, but Kathie's other Christmas party, for pensioners in Marylebone, did not remotely fall into that category. Conceived as a one-off, it became one of the borough's mega events and ran for well over twenty years, long after Kathie and Lew had left the neighbourhood. Eventually, with numbers approaching a thousand, it took over the Seymour Hall, where Lew danced attendance, paid the bills and ensured a better class of singalongs with such notables as Vera Lynn, Tom Jones and Shirley Bassey.

The charitable instinct seems to have been built into the Grades long before they had any serious funds to disburse, and possibly even before they had any acquaintance with the old Jewish proverb – 'Charity saves from death'.[14] In some ways, it seems to have been an almost necessary complement to their hard-headedness as businessmen. Leslie's first business partner, Albert Knight, said of him, 'Leslie would fight all day to take ten bob off you, to knock you down to the lowest price, but then he'd give you back £2 for the evening and not mention it again.'[15] Similar stories, albeit with much larger sums involved, attached themselves to Bernard and Lew during their business careers. A senior executive at ATV, quoted in the *Sunday Times*, said:

> There are two Lew Grades. One is the father of the family, who'll do anything for you if you're in trouble, or appeal to his sense of loyalty. The other is the businessman, who'll cut your throat to keep down your expenses, or make a neat deal. He'd always rather give money than spend it. Ask for £500 because of some personal crisis, and it's yours. Ask for £500 extra on the budget of some vital programme – not a chance.[16]

All the Grades learned very early on to be ruthless in their judgement of what would work on stage, and to be exacting in their assessment of costs, but this did not make them ruthless businessmen. While they clearly enjoyed getting the upper hand in any transaction, it was rarely in their own best interest to humiliate or impoverish those they dealt with. This was especially the case in the relatively small show business world, where they often had to do deals with the same people time and time again, and in which today's 'nobody' might unpredictably turn out to be tomorrow's star attraction. Whenever possible, they liked to leave a residue of good feeling, even after the toughest negotiations. Lew was once labelled 'a computer with heart',[17] which suited him well, though the heart was naturally well acquainted with the computer's calculations. Despite the mild schizophrenia suggested in the *Sunday Times*, there was essentially only the one Lew Grade, a man who succeeded in business without succeeding in losing his humanity.

The most openly charitable of the brothers was Bernard, who headed a raft of show business charitable causes and was a patron of the Attlee Foundation which ran a youth community project in Spitalfields, near the Winogradsky family's original Brick Lane home. Bernard's prime contribution was his presentation of the Royal Variety Performance, which passed on all its profits to the Variety Artists' Benevolent Fund. The money raised by this method maintained a home in Brinsworth House, Twickenham, for forty old performers who were down on their luck and provided discreet financial assistance for several hundred more in their own communities.

There were cynics who suggested that Bernard's fidelity to the Royal Variety show, which lasted for twenty-one years, was to some extent influenced by its being a lure for American stars who could subsequently be deployed around the British entertainment circuit. Bernard and Billy Marsh, who helped with the bookings, always denied any such low motivation, claiming that, in any event, American stars did not come cheap even at the prospect of seeing the Queen. Bernard, however, was never disposed to deny that the job had its perks, the main one being a stockpile of informal Queen stories to tell friends and relations, especially the ultra-royalist element represented by Olga and his sister, Rita.

The Royal Variety Performance was notoriously difficult to manage and there were frequent overruns which sometimes put pressure on Her Majesty's patience. After one particularly late show, the Queen told Bernard how very much she had enjoyed it, but in the likely event of her now not having time to change her dress before the state opening of Parliament on the next day, he would of course 'know the reason why'.[18] In booking the Kwa-Zulu dancing troupe from Natal in South Africa for the 1975 show, it had not occurred to Bernard, until the press asked questions, that the women would be dancing bare-breasted. He put in an apprehensive call to Buckingham Palace for guidance, but was reassuringly informed that the topless factor was unimportant as the Queen had witnessed many bare bosoms on her world tours. Another worrying time was when Maurice Chevalier could not be deterred from singing what Bernard regarded as an unsuitable song for the occasion. But, as it turned out, the Queen Mother was enchanted by Chevalier's rendition, delivered directly to her in the royal box, of 'You must 'ave been a beautiful bebe'.

Bernard's favourite story related not to the Royal Variety show, but to an occasion at the Talk of the Town, which had been commandeered for a fund-raiser for the World Wildlife Fund. This brought the royals out in force along with a large cast of distinguished guests, of whom the most spectacular by far was the romantic novelist Barbara Cartland. As Cartland swept past, the Queen beckoned Bernard's attention with what he construed as a twinkle in the royal eye. 'Who's that, Danny La Rue?' she asked.[19]

It would be Bernard's services to charity, as much as to the theatre, that led to his being knighted in 1974. Bernard hurried around to Grosvenor House to tell Olga about the honour before the news became public. He did not want his mother, now well advanced into her mid-eighties, to experience an excitement that was too much for her.

On his arrival, he found Olga already well excited. It was one of her days for kicking up a storm about the imperfections of her environment and she wanted Bernard to know all about it. She had allowed some of the hotel's smoked salmon into her life, and the experience had not improved her disposition. The maids were wonderful, but aside from that. For a start, couldn't they do something about the colour of the carpet? She was sick of dark green . . . As Olga's litany of complaint progressed, Bernard despaired of getting his good news in edgewise. Luckily, he spotted the mounted photograph of Lew and Kathie with their son, Paul, standing outside Buckingham Palace after Lew's investiture five years earlier. Manoeuvring it into Olga's line of vision, he managed to get out, 'You see this picture of Lew, Mummy? Well, you'll be getting one of me like that in a few weeks time.'[20] With that the penny dropped, and tearful happiness reigned.

It was sometimes assumed that Bernard operated on a more exalted intellectual plane than Lew and Leslie. As an impresario whose output, as both an independent operator and an EMI executive, featured many straight plays in the West End, this was partially true, but only up to a point. Bernard was famously quoted as saying that 'I'd rather see a good juggler than a bad Hamlet.'[21] But his friends suspected that he preferred a juggler to *any* Hamlet, good or bad. In the normal course of business, Bernard showed a proper reverence for his more serious productions, but his unfeigned enthusiasm was for musicals and theatrical extravaganzas that had their roots in Variety. Harry Secombe in *Pickwick* and Anthony Newley in *Stop the World – I Want to Get Off* ranked close to the top of his private hit parade.

Sheridan Morley felt that Bernard's skill as a showman was most expertly engaged by his 'standing at the back of the stalls, peering through his cigar smoke, and wondering if there should be a few more girls on the staircase'.[22] On one occasion Morley was asked to narrate the links in a television show called *Golden Hour of Drama* which featured highlights from a number of serious plays in the West End, including several put on by Bernard. After the transmission, Morley asked Bernard if he had enjoyed the show. 'Too much Shakespeare,' said Bernard. But, Morley protested mildly, there had only been one actual Shakespeare extract (from the Old Vic), the rest had been Terence Rattigan, Noël Coward, Anton Chekhov, Robert Bolt and even Harold Pinter. 'To me,' said Bernard, 'it's all Shakespeare.'[23]

This came straight out of the Lew Grade lexicon of self-mocking, though not entirely untrue, utterance on matters of high culture. Despite the divergence in their careers, their temperamental differences and their occasional business clashes, the brothers' basic tastes and attitudes remained remarkably similar. And Bernard, like Lew, was always keen to be appreciated for the impressive breadth of his endeavours, almost as much as for their quality. His long-held ambition was to produce more than the 128 West End shows credited to his impresario hero, Charles B. Cochran. This Bernard achieved by the early 1970s, after which even he lost count.

As the Grades ascended to national prominence, the popular press regularly ran, and re-ran, feature articles on the Winogradsky family's rags-to-riches story, usually padded out with a few of the latest Lew one-liners. Entertaining as these reads undoubtedly were, they had to be considered the journalistic equivalent of cheerleading, and not remotely analytical. However, when Lew achieved top dog status in television, a different type of coverage emerged. What was defined as the quality press took to assigning their best writers to finding out not merely what he was doing, but why he was doing it. In short, what made Lew Grade, the man shaping the nation's indoor viewing habits, tick.

Most discovered that, despite his volubility, Lew was an exceptionally hard tycoon to categorise. He could be jokily evasive, as *Campaign*, the advertising trade's magazine, discovered when it tried to get him to explain why he was the best-known person in television. 'That is,' Lew responded, 'because I'm the best looking.'[24] But even when he opened up frankly on the subject of his personal likes and dislikes, the thread of his logic was sometimes hard to grasp.

In expansive mood, shortly after the LWT threat had receded, Lew gave Hunter Davies of the *Sunday Times* what appeared to be a crucial insight into his well-known aversion to bad language on television. Since his public denunciation of the more colourful utterances in *Steptoe and Son*, Lew had adjusted his position to be more in tune with the permissive nature of the times, but not quite all the way. Lew acknowledged to Davies that he had come under pressure from his ATV colleagues to allow more explicit language in his dramas. But the way Lew saw it was:

> They go mad at me here, telling me I should let things be realistic. You shouldn't have bad language in realism. People at home, especially children, see these so-called realistic dramas and forget that it's really all fiction. So they think they can talk like that. Now in comedy shows, that's different. You know it's hokum, so it doesn't matter if there's a bit of bad language, as in *On the Buses*. It's all for laughs. It's not true.[25]

Pondering the quote, Davies realised that he had just been confronted with an intellectually arresting theory, which could be summarised as follows: realism on television was OK as long as it wasn't realistic, but fiction, being fiction, could therefore be realistic. Worth exploring further, he felt. However, any chance of elaborating on this interesting concept was defeated by the arrival of coffee and an urgent call from Shirley MacLaine in California coming in on Lew's private line.

In truth, Lew was not analytically inclined, either in relation to what he put on the screen or indeed to himself. He had no really coherent explanation for his unsurpassed mastery of fair to middling culture. Nor could he elaborate much on the reasons behind his individual decisions, which were almost invariably described as being based on 'hunch' or 'feel' or the prompting of his 'gut'. His gift was to have absolute trust in his instincts, allied to a firm belief that his taste was shared by the majority of viewers. Perhaps the most astonishing thing about Lew was not the gift in itself but that he should have preserved it, genuinely intact, for so long.

The *Observer*'s John Heilpern bravely tried to provoke Lew by suggesting that his favourite soap opera *Crossroads* was regarded by some as 'a programme of mind-blowing idiocy', while ATV's quiz show *Celebrity Squares* constituted 'an insult to anyone's intelligence'. The latter show was based on the game noughts and crosses; each of the nine squares on the screen contained a figure from the world of entertainment, such as Leslie Crowther, Terry Wogan or William Rushton, who would answer a series of general knowledge questions on behalf of contestants whose role was to guess whether or not the responses were correct. Lew remained cheerfully upbeat about the criticism, pointing out that he thought such shows were great, as did an awful lot of viewers. 'And another thing,' said Lew. 'With *Celebrity Squares* you can go out of the room for five minutes and come back without the worry and anxiety of missing anything. It's relaxing. You understand what I mean?' It's clear that Heilpern did not consider this a weighty intellectual point for presentation to the *Observer*'s highbrow readership, but he did conclude his article on mildly admiring lines: 'Those who say that Grade's innocence is his strength are right, for there's no cynicism in him . . . Everything's great.'[26]

Lew of course was not as innocent as all that. And it does appear very much as if on these occasions he enjoyed playing the part of Lew Grade, the forever wise-cracking, unwavering optimist, if only to fend off any probing that went too deep. On the other hand, Lew's well-cultivated persona was not too far distant from his real personality, which certainly helped the credibility of the act.

He did have a useful preservative that helped him to maintain the outlook and enthusiasms of his youth. Unlike most up-from-the-bottom tycoons, he never experienced a dysfunctional divorce from the tastes and attitudes of his original family. Nor, as a consequence of achieving wealth and fame, did he feel any need to assume the colouration of an ostensibly more socially refined peer group. To an extraordinarily large degree Lew took the family with him. This provided him with a firm grounding even in the highest places, and even under interrogation by the most saucily inquisitive wordsmiths. Asked by Paul Dacre, now the editor of the *Daily Mail* but then a *Daily Express* feature writer, how he had managed to adapt and change with the times so efficiently, Lew rewarded him with the reply, 'By simply not changing. I'm just the same as I always was.'[27]

Of all the fine journalists who tried to get the measure of Lew, the most perceptive was probably Nicholas Tomalin, who was not a regular show business scribe but a war correspondent who was later killed covering the Yom Kippur war for the *Sunday Times* in 1973. Clearly enthralled after interviewing ATV's remarkable boss, Tomalin wrote of him:

> Lew Grade is the most powerful man in Britain's most sophisticated and neurotic medium because he is neither sophisticated nor neurotic. For other more complex tycoons, it is disastrous sentimentality to talk of 'good family entertainment' or 'great-hearted drama' or 'lovely spectacles'. For Lew it is merely honest sentiment.[28]

If the Grade brothers had ever got together to write a primer on how to succeed in business, its subtitle would almost certainly have been 'By extending the concept of the family'. For Lew his colleagues in the television world were always part of 'one big family',[29] even when the numbers employed at Cumberland House and the Elstree and Birmingham studios swelled close to two thousand. Leslie's agency staff also had the sense of being admitted into a family with a mission to cheer up other families nationwide. There were limits to how far this informal ideology could be applied. One of Leslie's braver ventures in his later years was an effort to establish a cinema chain that only showed films that all ages of the family could see together. It never made much headway. Even so, the Grade brothers' idea of themselves as family men, operating family businesses for the benefit of other like-minded families, held good, though the 'family' businesses were ultimately called ATV and EMI.

In Lew's case, however, possibly because he was the eldest, it seems to have been difficult for him to envisage any family circumstance of which he was not the unchallenged paterfamilias. He really did have to be the man in charge. He was the one most driven not simply by ambition to succeed, but by the need to be seen as Number One. There were only occasional glimpses of the steel behind Lew's parade of jokiness, but it was always there, defending the proposition of who really had to be the boss.

Enormous fun and enjoyment could be derived from working for Lew. Equally, the experience of having Lew working on your behalf if you were a performer could also be wonderfully bracing. But actually working with Lew as a coequal, or something approximating to that status, was freighted with hazard. Leslie could do it but, even with the advantage of consanguinity, it was never easy. Both Joe Collins, Lew's original patron as an agent, and Val Parnell, his first ostensible boss at ATV, would in the end find themselves marginalized by Lew's energy and relentless thrust for pole position. Kathie of course soon came to realise that her best prospect for a happy marriage was one that accorded her husband centre stage.

This consideration applied very much to Lew's corporate existence. Within ATV the general level of job security and satisfaction was high, though most lived with an uneasy awareness of one of Lew's more ominous one-liners – 'when people get too big for their boots, it's time for them to walk on other people's carpets'.[30] It was certainly an organisation where it was possible to fly too high, too soon.

For some years Robin Gill and Lew had seemed inseparable. The Oxford-educated Gill, who had been recruited as a promising high-flying executive from Border Television, accompanied Lew on many of his trips to America. He rose swiftly to become ATV's joint managing director and held the unofficial title of Lew's favourite son. This led to press speculation about his being Lew's natural successor, and Gill showed signs of believing this might indeed be the case. Soon afterwards, Lew made a late discovery that they were 'not compatible'[31] and Gill was sent on a long holiday that would extend into a full parting of the ways. Reflecting on Gill's career, Lew told Stephen Aris of the *Sunday Times*, 'For a long time I thought he was brilliant. I am so illiterate and he spoke the English language so beautifully. He wrote wonderful memos. The trouble was he thought that when I was knighted I would retire and he would take over. He was wrong.'[32]

Gill's role in the company was almost instantly filled by the Australian, Bruce Gyngell. His obvious popularity and familiarity with the boss also led him to be hotly tipped as the most likely candidate for the top job. Although Gyngell was twenty-five years younger than Lew, it was well noted that the two men seemed to share common values on the score of bad language and much else in television. He seemed admirably well suited to carrying the torch for family-oriented entertainment should Lew ever decide to pass it on. But after three years' enjoyment of most favoured status, Gyngell found himself bypassed for an anticipated promotion in a way that, he felt, left him with no option.

Gyngell also left ATV's employ abruptly, though he later resurfaced in brave style as the man who rescued TV-am, the breakfast television company. His finest hour was the introduction into the morning schedule of a puppet character called Roland Rat, who became known as the rat who saved a sinking ship.

In retrospect, Lew always spoke most fondly of Bruce Gyngell, and indeed of Robin Gill. Inside the ATV 'big family', however, their sudden departures underlined the message that of all the potential routes up through the organisation the riskiest, by far, was the one signposted 'heir apparent'.

EIGHTEEN

Changing Times

SHAKESPEARE, AS LEW PERCEIVED HIM, needed the boost of star quality, and the Bard certainly got it in ATV's production of *Twelfth Night*, which was screened in 1971. Alec Guinness played Malvolio to Joan Plowright's Viola; Ralph Richardson provided an eccentric Sir Toby Belch; while the pop star, Tommy Steele, equipped with guitar, contributed a lively Feste. There was nonetheless some concern among the cast about the mixture of acting styles involved. One of its members mentioned, regretfully, to ATV's boss that perhaps one actress was more suited to performing Noël Coward than Shakespeare. 'Thank God,' said Lew, breathing a mock sigh of relief, 'They'll understand that better in Wisconsin.'[1]

Shakespeare may not have needed Lew Grade, but having British television's leading exporter on his case did refresh memories of the great playwright's achievement in some out of the way places. By 1970 it was clear that ATV's lavish productions were being appreciated in parts of the world that no other broadcasting outfit could reach. The company's dollar earning around the planet in that year amounted to more than thirty-six million, with some twenty-four million coming from the United States. By comparison, the BBC, with the output of two channels to draw on, earned a modest six million dollars from overseas sales.

In the wake of *Twelfth Night*, ATV launched star-studded productions of *Hamlet* (with Richard Chamberlain and John Gielgud), the National Theatre's *Merchant of Venice* (with Laurence Olivier) and the Royal Shakespeare Company's *Antony and Cleopatra* (Janet Suzman and Richard Johnson). Lew also concluded a deal with the National Theatre to record its major productions on video cassette for distribution worldwide. In the course of these endeavours, Lew often met up with what could be described as the intelligentsia of the theatre world, but without any detectable change of style. After lunching with Lew at Cumberland House with a view to discussing further collaboration between ATV and the National Theatre company, of which he was the new artistic director, Peter Hall confided to his diary:

> He gave his well-known Yiddish comedian performance for two hours and I laughed a lot. He speaks the same language as his brother, Bernie Delfont, but is even more self-deprecating. 'I'm not very good at scripts, I can't read a script, well you know I skim through a few pages, I get a feeling, a flavour. What's important is the package. What it's about. Who's doing it. Who's in it.' I should think he told thirty stories during the lunch.[2]

The essential Lew may not have changed, but he certainly knew how to adapt to changing times. There had been an important regime change at the top of the ITA. Lew got on well with Lord Aylestone, who succeeded Lord Hill as ITA chairman. Better known as 'Bert' Bowden, Aylestone was the son of a Cardiff baker who had risen through the ranks of the Parliamentary Labour Party as chief whip and Commonwealth Secretary before his ennoblement. But Lew enjoyed a much closer friendship with Sir Robert Fraser, the defender of 'people's television' and properly regarded as the main architect of ITV. When Fraser announced his retirement, effective in October 1970, the prospects of Lew enjoying a similar level of intimacy with his successor looked extremely dim.

Brian Young, the newly appointed director general of the ITA, soon to be rechristened as the Independent Broadcasting Authority (IBA), was a rank outsider in television terms. He had been a schoolmaster at Eton and headmaster at Charterhouse before ascending to the directorship of the Nuffield Foundation. This was not a career trajectory that gave Young much acquaintance with light entertainment. Early on in his reign Lew complained of being bullied over aspects of his schedule and privately moaned that the new director general 'did not understand the entertainment business'.[3] However, Young did understand Shakespeare.

As Lew saw it, his efforts on the cultural front should have the consequence of enlarging indulgence for what he was trying to do in other areas. Like *Crossroads*, for example. Although his cherished soap had been cut down from five to four days a week in the interests of improving production quality, it still encountered heavy flak. In 1972 the IBA's own General Advisory Council gave the show what seemed like a life-threatening bad report. Lew responded by inviting the GAC to a banquet – on the *Crossroads* set. He also personally drew up and distributed an impressive catalogue of social issues that had, he claimed, been sensitively covered in its story lines:

> drugs, alcoholism, unmarried mothers, gypsies, prisoners and their after-care, colour problem, foster children, orphans, widowhood, juvenile delinquents, mental health, kleptomania, gambling addiction, malnutrition (old age), drunken driving, motor accidents, paralysis, suicide, flood victims, atheism and agnosticism, illegal immigration, crime and criminals, frigidity, miscarriage, problems of birth and death, abduction, child molesting, doctors and nursing, police.[4]

After digging their way out of this avalanche of justification, the IBA admitted defeat, though they would subsequently regroup and come back again before the end of the decade insisting on a further reduction in *Crossroads* programmes, to no more than three days a week. Lew also expected the IBA to tolerate, if not exactly enthuse over, some of his excursions down memory lane in programme terms. *Emergency Ward 10*, one of Lew's original hospital drama winners, came back into the ATV schedule, thinly disguised as *General Hospital*. And even *Sunday Night at the London Palladium* returned for a while before Lew finally and regretfully accepted that it had truly had its day.

If there was something elegiac about these enterprises, it was perhaps only to be expected. The IBA had a rule that dictated that the chief executive of any franchise operation had to retire at the age of seventy. Lord Aylestone delicately explained to Lew that it was accepted practice for top executives to retire between sixty and sixty-five and that this occurred 'even in the case of people like yourself, who seem to be immune from the normal aging process'.[5] So the rule would apply in his case. This gave Lew until December 1976 to realise all his heart's desires in television, though he was able to maximise uncertainty about his actual birth date in a way that allowed him to continue until September 1977. Meantime, even Brian Young came to appreciate Lew's usefulness as man who could beat the drum for commercial television and raise morale in times of trouble.

In 1972 a Parliamentary Select Committee gave ITV a thorough mauling. In a series of hearings at the House of Commons it vented strong criticism of the commercial channel, and published a report that was reminiscent of Pilkington in its tone. Both Young and Aylestone felt their enterprise had been unfairly treated but were disinclined, for political reasons, to kick up too much public fuss. Lew's response was more florid. He hired a BOAC Jumbo jet which flew seventy American journalists to Britain to see 'the finest television in the world'.[6] Many were impressed with the wonders of ITV and were widely quoted on the subject.

This grand gesture begat another. Twelve months later forty British journalists strapped themselves in for an encounter with Lew's America. Peter Fiddick of the *Guardian* reported:

> A twelve-hour jet flight direct to LA followed by oysters and a side of beef before you could decently get to your bedroom and the scotch, gin and grapes on the side-table. Two days' slog around the film-city of Universal and the video empire of CBS, with Hitchcock, Rock Hudson, Mary Tyler Moore, Raymond Burr wheeled out for distraction, and a free ticket to the Playboy Club in the Press Kit just to get you in training for the next day. Disneyland, the theatre, a late night dinner from ABC attended by so many of the company's stars without their husbands they were beginning to wonder why the local gossip columnist was invited. And then, Las Vegas . . .[7]

And relentlessly on. Given the prodigious nature of his public relations budget, it was perhaps unsurprising that Lew was inclined to get the benefit of any doubt in the press. Lew may not have killed off all criticism with his kindly largesse, but it certainly impaired a journalist's will to speak ill of him. However, even the more independent observers would come to the conclusion that some of Lew's best programmes were made during his last television stand in the 1970s, and not all them in predictable areas.

Unexpectedly, ATV began to acquire a positive reputation for its current affairs programmes, a product, at least to some degree, of Lew's expressing a late-developing, but apparently genuine, liking for a good documentary. The original breakthrough on this front was attributed to Neil Armstrong's 'giant leap for mankind' in 1969. The ITN news team, rather nervously, had approached Lew with a view to disrupting his precious schedule by extending its coverage of Apollo 11's touchdown on the moon, and found him to be wonderfully, and unexpectedly, acquiescent. Thumping the table with his fist, Lew pronounced: 'This is the biggest story since the birth of Jesus Christ.'[8]

Thereafter ATV's previously less well regarded current affairs division assumed a much higher profile. In general terms though, all the ITV companies, under pressure to improve the seriousness of their output, were undergoing significant change. At middle and even higher levels, the old show business figures, so dominant in the early days, were giving place to a new breed of television professionals. Fast-rising management stars, like Charles Denton at ATV, Jeremy Isaacs at Thames and Barry Cox at LWT, were people who had come up through the ranks of television journalism and documentary production. So ATV was essentially going with the flow, though with active encouragement by Lew.

Some of its documentary programmes undeniably had a cutting edge. The Burmese Embassy tried, and failed, to prevent the screening of ATV's *The Opium War Lords*, a product of Adrian Cowell's long sojourn in the Burmese jungle. It won a BAFTA award. Even more impressively, ATV provided generous air time for reporting by the combative Australian journalist, John Pilger. This could hardly be regarded as playing it safe, as Pilger's hard-hitting programmes, about Vietnam and Cambodia and the imperfections in Britain's political system, regularly ruffled feathers at the IBA. In the end, the Authority insisted that his output should be preceded by a screen caption which read: 'In the programme that follows the reporter is expressing a personal view.'[9] Despite his problems with the IBA, Pilger had no complaints about the support he received from the top tier at ATV. Lew sent him personal notes of congratulation after even the most controversial programmes.

There was, however, one documentary that Lew felt unable to defend. *Hang Out Your Brightest Colours*, written and narrated by the Welsh actor, Kenneth Griffith, was the story of Michael Collins, the rebel-patriot leader killed in the Irish Civil War in 1922. The programme was commissioned by ATV and the British government did not come out of it in an attractive light. Though historical in content, it was seen by some in the IBA as being potentially inflammatory in contemporary terms; British troops were trying at the time to contain a fresh upsurge of IRA violence in Northern Ireland, brought on to a large extent by the government's policy of internment without trial. In view of what he termed 'the present delicate political and military situation',[10] Lew decided against offering the programme for transmission.

In the ensuing furore over the censorship of the programme, Griffith maintained, after a long talk with Lew: 'It is my conviction that the Independent Broadcasting Authority pushed responsibility for a decision on to Sir Lew Grade.'[11] It was certainly felt by many in ATV that Lew had received an official warning to the effect that the franchise could be at risk if he put the programme on air. The IBA always publicly denied putting pressure on Lew, though the official history of ITV did subsequently concede that Lew's action 'relieved the Authority of an awkward responsibility'.[12]

Lew took a less full part in the networking process than had previously been the case, but he was still regarded as the master of its nuances. Howard Thomas, the boss of Thames Television, was impressed by how Lew conducted himself in a networking struggle that involved Lord Louis Mountbatten, Prince Philip's uncle, who had been Britain's last Viceroy to India and who was later assassinated by the Provisional IRA. Both Thomas and Mountbatten were keen to have the Thames documentary, *The Life and Times of Lord Mountbatten*, transmitted as a fully networked programme in the 9 p.m. slot.

This created a problem for Lew, who counted Mountbatten as one of his closest chums in the royal establishment. On the occasion of the 'Salute to Sir Lew' by America's show business stars, Mountbatten had flown over specially to New York and given a warm speech in praise of Lew, saying he would not have missed the event for the world. Lew's delicate difficulty now was that he could not see a programme about Mountbatten's life as being prime-time network material. On the other hand, he did not want to do or say anything that might be hurtful to his distinguished friend.

With the scheduling issue still in flux, Thomas and Mountbatten cornered Lew at a social event, where Lew adroitly decided that attack was the best policy. 'Howard must be mad,' he said, addressing Mountbatten, 'putting on your programme against the BBC at nine! That's when they put on all those sexy plays with bad language. You'll get slaughtered. Now when I put on the programme, after the news at 10.30, there'll be no opposition.' With Mountbatten unconvinced by this logic, Lew clinched his argument by asserting, 'I'm so sure, I'll bet on it. If Thames gets higher ratings than ATV, I'll pay you £500.'

Mountbatten could see no flaw in this, though as Lew, unlike Bernard, was not regarded as a betting man, it was an uncharacteristic offer. In the event, Thames did achieve higher ratings for the programme at 9 p.m. than ATV did at 10.30 p.m. Not long afterwards, Thomas asked Lew if he had paid up. 'I've already sent the cheque to Mountbatten,' said Lew, adding mischievously, 'Cheap at the price, wasn't it?'[13] Lew had achieved exactly the outcome he wanted while concurrently enhancing his friendship with Mountbatten, by making him feel like the winner of a wager who had outsmarted the great Lew Grade. And it had all been done – in television prime-time terms – at trivial expense.

Lew was less often seen at the regular Monday programme controllers' meetings where the 'Big Five' horse-traded over the programme mix in the network schedule, preferring to send along Bill Ward. As Ward's relationship with Lew went back to the earliest Palladium show days, he was reckoned to know the boss's mind better than most. But not completely, as it turned out. Jeremy Isaacs, who attended the meetings in his capacity as Director of Programmes at Thames Television, recalled: 'As a colleague at controllers' meetings, Bill had one drawback: to any controversial proposal he could make no meaningful response; promising an answer next week, he would depart to Great Cumberland Place to consult Lew. No one ever remarked on this. We just waited.'[14]

Lew's relative downgrading of this once obsessive area of concern was not dictated by any detectable slowing down or through any contraction of his long working day. But his priorities had changed. With the more limited Midlands franchise, Lew's path to glory seemed to be even more dependent on his big blockbuster series, which could not only get almost guaranteed network exposure, but also sell throughout the world. And there was another important impetus propelling him in the same direction.

Brother Bernard was making a modest name for himself as the boss of EMI's film division. It was undeniably the case that the movies had lost some of their mass appeal, mainly for the reason most succinctly expounded by Sam Goldwyn: 'Who wants to go out to see a bad movie when they can stay at home and see a bad one free on television?'[15] In Britain audiences for the cinema had been in sharp decline for many years, almost entirely due to the impact of television. At the peak of cinema's popularity in 1946, the average Briton went to the pictures more than thirty times a year, compared to just three by the early 1970s. But the movie business still commanded a huge amount of newspaper attention and coverage, particularly in relation to its stars. There was no open declaration of fraternal war, but it rapidly became apparent that any stars Bernard could get for his films were likely to be eclipsed by the ones Lew attracted into television, and that this was no accident.

This was not a guaranteed recipe for success. Indeed, Lew's first coup in this arena, which involved obtaining the services of the bankable Hollywood star, Shirley MacLaine, came close to being a disaster, though it had all started in optimistic fashion. In her book, *You Can Get There from Here*, MacLaine testified to Lew's compelling quality as a man 'who has the ability to revive flagging enthusiasm simply by walking into a room. And if you walk into *his* room, he is likely to change your life. Give him a captive audience, and he can sell anything. He sold me television.' After her formal recruitment at Cumberland House, MacLaine recalled, 'Sir Lew walked me to the elevator, saying hello to everybody in the office, calling them by their first name . . . his employees treated him as if he were some wonderful, respected, powerful and rich uncle.'[16]

The series that Lew had fashioned for her, entitled *Shirley's World*, had MacLaine careering around the planet as Shirley Logan, an alluring but none-too-bright photojournalist. MacLaine, on being acquainted with the actual scripts, described her character as 'a nosy, irritating, empty-headed little banana head',[17] which did not bode well. Twenty-four episodes were planned, many of them to be acted out in exotic parts of the Far East, but seventeen was deemed to be quite enough. Looking back on *Shirley's World*, MacLaine wrote of 'an experience something akin to what Vietnam must have been for Kennedy, Johnson and Nixon. You begin by sticking a big toe into the water and before you know it, you are up to your neck in a cesspool.'[18] It says much for the forgiving natures of both Lew and MacLaine that they would kiss and make up, and declare undying affection for one another, after these words were published. But Lew, never inclined to dwell on past upsets, had already moved on to the wooing and winning of another stellar Hollywood character, Tony Curtis, and was brimming with renewed confidence.

Curtis, as a fun-loving Brooklyn millionaire, was teamed with Roger Moore – formerly of *The Saint* and subsequently a James Bond – who played Lord Brett Sinclair, a languid English toff, in a series entitled *The Persuaders!*. Introduced by a memorable theme tune from John Barry, the plot involved unorthodox crime-busting in some of the world's more glamorous locations, and this time all twenty-four episodes did get completed on schedule. *The Persuaders!* was not a success with the critics, of whom the most cutting, Morton Moss of the *Los Angeles Herald Examiner*, felt that Curtis's performance 'really reached new heights of mediocrity'.[19] Nonetheless, the series did excellent business in 1972 and might have done much more, but Lew was never able to persuade Curtis and Moore to reunite for a second series. He deduced that their rivalry as male sex symbols could have been at the heart of the problem.

In 1973 Lew reached for and got another superstar, Burt Lancaster, and things moved on to a more uplifting plane. Lancaster was commissioned to play the lead in *Moses – The Lawgiver* in a co-production that Lew had fashioned with the Italian state broadcasting service, Radiotelevisione Italiana (RAI). Fidelity to the biblical story was held to be essential to the enterprise, though Lew did make one of his rare incursions into the production process. As originally scripted the film was to begin with Moses meditating alone in the wilderness, but Lew suggested it might be better to open up with Pharaoh's massacre of the innocents. And this did come to pass.

The most significant event of the year, at least in retrospect, was the death in August of Lord Renwick, who had flanked Lew as ATV's chairman for more than twelve years, for the most part unobtrusively without attempting to steal his chief executive's limelight. Showmanship was not Renwick's strongest suit, but he did have a quality said to be unique in the organisation: he was the one man capable of choking off Lew's more extravagant enthusiasms for enterprises that carried too much risk.

With Renwick's demise Lew almost automatically became chairman of the ATV Corporation, while continuing in his normal executive capacity. Some time later the ATV Corporation changed in form to become the Associated Communications Corporation (ACC), which was deemed a more efficient holding vehicle for the group's widely diversified, and still rapidly expanding, non-television business interests. In this new structure, the television element, ATV Network, became one of ACC's many subdivisions as a wholly owned subsidiary company. Lew also became chairman of the ACC overall holding company, thus ensuring a powerful corporate role for himself that was capable of extension long beyond his IBA-enforced retirement from hands-on television work.

None of these arrangements was deemed controversial. It was generally felt that Lew, as the founder and energiser of the whole enterprise, merited every promotion he could get. As he climbed ever higher, with his reputation further embellished by the production of Bible-based blockbusters, Lew could be forgiven for having an inkling that even God was on his side. Nevertheless, later events would suggest that Lord Renwick might have been a better choice.

NINETEEN

Moses, Jesus and the Muppets

The inspiration for *Jesus of Nazareth*, the six-hour television film version of the story of Christ that represented Lew's greatest blockbuster effort, can be jointly ascribed to Kathie and to Giovanni Battista Montini, better known as Pope Paul VI. This project, subsequently described by Lew as 'the best thing I ever will do',[1] had never achieved any prominence on his list of entertainment priorities. But one thing had led to another.

The filming of his *Moses – the Lawgiver* series had generated great interest in Italy, to the point where its government decided that it would be a good idea for Lew to meet the Pope. Lew remembered being quite flattered by the suggestion, but no more than that. This level of insouciance failed to survive that night's pillow talk with Kathie, as recollected in *Still Dancing*:

> 'Did anything special happen today?', she casually asked me. 'Nothing of any great importance,' I said, 'I had lunch with the Italian Ambassador and he suggested I have a private audience with Pope Paul.'
>
> BANG! On came the bedside light. Kathie sat up. 'What did you say?' she said.
>
> To Kathie, a Catholic, this was a momentous occasion. 'I said I'd let him have some dates.' She looked horrified.
>
> 'Kathie, don't worry,' I said reassuringly. I'll call him tomorrow and fix the date.'

Next day I called the Italian Ambassador, and told him we would be very happy to go to Rome the following week.[2]

Lew and Kathie were alone in a large reception room at the Vatican when the Vicar of Christ walked in accompanied by two Monsignors. Some rearrangement of his robes took place before the Pope turned to them with a smile, holding both his arms outstretched, and Lew recalled, 'after that I was gone'.[3] Suddenly finding himself unnaturally deficient in both powers of speech and hearing, Lew experienced the occasion in an almost trance-like state. Glimpses of the Pope as a rather austere figure on television had not prepared him for the pontiff's warmth in person. Throughout most of the 25-minute audience, the Pope held Lew's hand, while telling him how pleased he was with the Moses project. They found a firm bedrock of agreement in the benefits of an enterprise that powerfully reacquainted people with such things as the Ten Commandments. The Pope told Lew and Kathie that he was happy to bless the Moses production and that they had his permission to use this endorsement for the purpose of publicity if they so wished. He also hoped, in conclusion, that sometime in the future Lew might consider another production, possibly called 'In the Footsteps of Jesus'.[4]

By this stage Lew was so paralysed with awe that he was unable to take a word in. On leaving the Vatican he had no memory of what was said in the final stages of the audience. Fortunately, Kathie was able to remind him of Pope Paul's proposal, and of the fact that her husband had nodded his assent to it. At a high level – indeed, as Kathie perceived it, at the very highest – an implicit deal had been done.

Lew held off from making any public announcement until the way had been prepared. First, with his Italian co-producers, RAI, and second with General Motors. It took a high degree of lateral thinking to link the capitalist behemoth with the Gospel story, but Lew was right in divining that GM's chief executive, Richard Gerstenberg, might be interested in a sponsorship arrangement. A fast pilgrimage to Detroit established that this was indeed the case. And Lew returned from a swing around America with glad tidings for his ATV board: NBC was keen to network the programme, and was especially delighted to have General Motors occupying the sponsorship berth. 'Jesus' had effectively been pre-sold.

The ceremonial unveiling of the proposed production took place at a press conference in Rome in July 1974, with Lew in tiptop form. 'I'm Jewish,' he declared, 'Jesus was Jewish, and we both share the same birthday. But that's not why I'm making the series, I'm making it for all mankind.'[5] No expense was to be spared and, although roles had not yet been assigned, he wanted everybody to know, 'If we need George C. Scott to play Barabbas, I'll ask George. If we need Olivier to play Pontius Pilate, I'll call up Larry. I'm sure nobody will turn down the chance of being associated with this project. It is something the world needs. A programme to remind people of sacrifice.' When someone enquired if by chance the programme would go out in a religious slot, Lew emitted a shriek of outrage. 'Peak times,' was his stern promise, 'or I'll shoot everyone in independent television.'[6]

The chosen director, Franco Zeffirelli, was someone whose work was for Lew a byword for quality. The same could be said of the writer, Anthony Burgess, who had co-scripted *Moses – The Lawgiver*. Burgess was also England's most prolific novelist with, as Lew was somewhat indelicately reminded by one journalist, the less than sacred *A Clockwork Orange* as part of his oeuvre. Undeterred, Lew ploughed on to heap praise on the concept of co-production as a way of building Common Market sentiment through cooperation across national frontiers. People should know that the market was 'not just to exchange goods, refrigerators, motor cars and ties with each other, but to provide the best of everything for everyone'.

The only serious interruption to his flow was achieved by an American journalist who asked, 'Do you think this is a non-profit venture?' There was a shocked silence before Lew could come up with 'Non-profit, I wouldn't ever use that word.'[7] Nevertheless, there must have been times over the next two years and more, with the film's cost climbing from an estimated £3 million to close to £12 million, when Lew must have felt that Jesus wanted him to incorporate it into his vocabulary.

There were problems from the outset. Zeffirelli's preferred Jesus was Tom Courtenay, who was already an established actor, or possibly a big American star. Lew, however, prompted by Kathie, was drawn to Robert Powell, a relatively unknown English actor, said to be equipped with naturally mesmerising eyes. Zeffirelli gave way, but only after Lew had offered himself as the compromise candidate. Thereafter the Italian director won most of the production battles. Israel was logically the most authentic location, but the Moses project had run into difficulties there, not the least of them being interruption by the Yom Kippur war. Zeffirelli therefore decided that, on balance, it would be more practical to recreate the Holy Land in Tunisia, with some scenes being shot in Morocco.

The stars recruited by Lew flew in and out of these North African locations as and when required: Rod Steiger (Pontius Pilate) from Malibu, Anne Bancroft (Mary Magdalene) from New York, James Mason (Joseph of Arimathea) from Switzerland, Anthony Quinn (Caiaphas) from Italy, and Ralph Richardson (Simeon) and Laurence Olivier (Nicodemus) from London. As it became apparent that Zeffirelli was trying to impart an Old Master-like quality to each frame, it also became manifest that all the actors would spend an enormous amount of time waiting around in full make-up in outdoor locations with the blistering heat sapping their energies. Olivier felt compelled to mention the problem, only to have Zeffirelli point out the benefits – just how wonderful each frame looked. Olivier ironically conceded that the actors' distress was 'nothing compared to the suffering of Our Lord',[8] but thought it should definitely be borne in mind.

Of all the actors Robert Powell, in the title role, probably suffered the most. Zeffirelli, who had begun his career in opera, was painstaking in terms of visual composition, but not over-concerned with the minutiae of the actor's craft. While he would accord some deference to the Hollywood stars flown in by Lew, Powell, as a young actor questing for knowledge, was not so readily tolerated. Peter Ustinov (Herod the Great) recalled a time when Powell sought guidance from his director on the subject of how he should register different degrees of pain and transcendence while in the process of being crucified. 'Darling,' was Zeffirelli's response, 'you are boring me, get back on the cross.'[9] On another occasion, Powell's request for advice was met with, 'Darling, just go and watch Larry [Olivier] and ask him to give you some acting lessons.'[10]

On occasions Lew would fly in, partly with a view to bolstering his protégé's confidence, but mainly concerned to try and cut down what seemed like the open-ended expense of Zeffirelli's operation. Lew had to accept that some expenses were vital to the enterprise, among them the four hundred sets of armour imported from Rome and the thousands of crowd scene costumes for the Arab extras passing as biblical Jews, which all had to be scrupulously dyed from local berries as they had been two thousand years before.

Still, he felt some economies were possible, without violating the integrity of the project. In his memoir *Acting My Life*, Ian Holm (Zerah, of the Sanhedrin) recalled one of Lew's tours of inspection as being characterised by his 'snapping at Zeffirelli's heels while the rest of us stood around getting hot'.[11] Having failed to persuade Zeffirelli to contemplate limiting the number of apostles in the Garden of Gethsemane, Lew cast around for possibilities of cost saving elsewhere. Holm remembered Lew moving on to the problem of over-running, suggesting cuts in the words spoken by each actor. With Olivier acting as an unofficial shop steward some modest cuts were achieved, though umbrage was taken by Anthony Quinn who deliberately drawled Caiaphas's residual lines to take up virtually the same amount of time. As far as the overall costs of the production were concerned, Lew came to the realisation that he had no real option but to grin and bear it.

There were compensations. The long drawn out process of making *Jesus of Nazareth* provided Lew with a wonderful platform. The very notion of a Jew being in league with the Pope to spread God's word upped Lew's personal publicity value several more notches. It is true that there were some aspects of the publicity he felt he could have done without, like the *Sun* newspaper's revelation that his 'Jesus' was living out of wedlock with Pan's People dancer Babs Lord. 'What are you trying to do . . . Crucify me?' was said to have been Lew's initial response to the reporter pursuing the story.[12] However, Robert Powell, encouraged by Lew, soon neutralised the embarrassment by resorting to marriage.

More unwelcome was a report by Nigel Dempster, the *Daily Mail*'s resourceful gossip columnist, intimating that Burgess and Zeffirelli did not see eye-to-eye over the presentation and characterisation of Jesus Christ. Burgess was quoted as saying, 'I am fed up with seeing Jesus made into a fairy figure.'[13] But this problem was also well contained, in part by including Zeffirelli in the screenwriting credits.

These little local difficulties aside, the reflected glory of the Gospel project seemed to cast a warm glow over Lew's other enterprises in times that were outstandingly glum for most of his compatriots. The power cuts and spiralling oil prices of 1974 provided the prelude to rampant levels of socially disruptive inflation under a new Labour government. At the same time, fresh manifestations of terror engendered by the conflicts in Northern Ireland and the Middle East came close to home in the cities of mainland Britain. In the case of Lew's brother Bernard, frighteningly close.

In the summer of 1975 the Metropolitan Police raided a Bayswater Road flat linked to a terrorist, code-named 'Carlos', and discovered not only a large cache of weapons but also what appeared to be a hit list of prominent Jewish public figures, among them violinist Yehudi Menuhin, former Tory minister Sir Keith Joseph and Sir Bernard Delfont. Subsequently, Lew, without any supporting evidence, claimed that he too was on the list, though it was Bernard's sardonic view that his brother just could not abide the thought of being left out of a celebrity line-up, even one of potential assassination targets.

This was also a restless period in terms of industrial relations, but Lew rode it out better than most, at least partly thanks to his relatively benign record as an employer. Peter Plouviez, the long-term general secretary of the actors' union, Equity, could not remember Lew ever ratting on a union agreement, though negotiation with him could be tough. Of all the employers in television Plouviez reckoned that Lew was probably the best; he was certainly the funniest.[14]

Lew had no great expectations for the money-making potential of *Edward VII*, one of ATV's historical drama series made with an eye to prestige rather than profit. It was judged that the life and loves of Queen Victoria's son were not likely to be of much interest to anyone outside Britain. However, with some scenes being filmed in Osborne House and Sandringham and at other authentic royal locations, all with the Queen's permission, the series turned out to be more sumptuous than anyone had expected. Encouraged by this outcome, Lew decided to test its saleability on one of his American trips and found himself happily embroiled in what amounted to a bidding war between the CBS network and the Mobil Oil Corporation, which sponsored transmissions on independent broadcasting stations. Mobil Oil eventually secured the rights as a preliminary to ordering further series from Lew's Elstree production line. *Edward VII* was retitled *Edward the King* for transatlantic audiences, to prevent any confusion with the story of another English royal Edward whose abdication had been forced by an association with the American Mrs Wallis Simpson. With this modest adjustment, it went on to become one of Lew's bigger dollar earners through 1975.

A year later, while the re-creation of the Gospel story was still unfolding in the Tunisian desert, something even more wonderful befell. Lew discovered that Jim Henson had a problem. Henson, already well known as the creator of the marionette and puppet characters for the popular American children's educational series *Sesame Street*, wanted to put together a show of his own, but was still looking for a suitable studio as a base for operations. The American networks all seemed uninterested. Lew alertly offered him Elstree, which Henson gratefully accepted, and the Muppets duly became part of ATV's extended family.

From the earliest transmissions it was clear that the Muppet characters – Fozzie Bear, Miss Piggy and Kermit, the fast-talking frog – had an appeal that was destined to last, and not only within ATV, where some detected in Kermit several of Lew's more distinctive character traits. Within a few months *The Muppet Show* was commanding an audience of thirteen million, and Muppetmania had truly arrived. Although it was originally intended mainly for children, its combination of slapstick humour and verbal dexterity, set within the loose framework of a Variety show, gave it a devoted following among all age groups. The guest spot for a subservient human element in the production had any number of celebrities fighting for inclusion. Among those who made it were Peter Sellers, Elton John, Rudolf Nureyev, Peter Ustinov and Raquel Welch. *The Muppet Show* was a programme that genuinely made people feel happy, both to produce and to watch. Lew also ensured, through his ITC sales operation, that no part of the globe that could afford to pay for it missed out on its good cheer.

Lew's impression that somebody up there must like him was further confirmed by another development in the same year. Of the two brothers, Bernard had better contacts with politicians at the highest level. As a member of a government working party set up in an attempt to arrest the decline in the British film industry, Bernard had met Harold Wilson, the Labour Prime Minister, on a number of occasions, and they got on well. Lew could claim a friendly connection with Marcia Williams, Wilson's imperious political secretary, who had been elevated to the peerage as Lady Falkender. He had once beguiled her with an impromptu Charleston at a party given by Wilson's publisher, George Weidenfeld. However, his acquaintance with her boss was only slight, though having received his knighthood during Wilson's earlier administration, he had no reason to think himself out of favour.

In the spring of 1976, Bernard was summoned to Wilson's presence with the expectation of another informal chat about the movie business over a glass of sherry. As it turned out, Wilson wanted Bernard to accept a peerage in what was to be the Prime Minister's list of resignation honours, on his impending departure from office. An astonished Bernard managed to splutter his grateful acceptance, only to be treated to what he described as 'a second bombshell' on his way out. 'Oh, by the way,' said Wilson, 'You're not the only member of the family who's been here today.' On arriving back at his office, Bernard rang Lew.

'Were you in Downing Street earlier today?'

'Yes.'

'Did he offer you what he offered me?'

'Yes.'[15]

The ennoblement of Bernard and Lew as respectively Lord Delfont of Stepney and Lord Grade of Elstree, though instantly popular in the world of show business, did not meet with universal acclaim. The proposal to include them among those to be honoured had originally featured in the famous 'Lavender List', so called because the names it contained had been penned by Marcia Falkender on her lavender scented and shaded notepaper. And the allegation was that it was essentially Marcia's honours list, to which the Prime Minister had cravenly and misguidedly given his assent. As it was indeed the case that Marcia had long been among those urging Wilson to inject more glamour into the honours system, there were some grounds for taking the charge seriously.

Most offence to purists was caused by the peerages allocated to Lew and Bernard, along with those granted to publisher George Weidenfeld and to Joseph Kagan, whose chief claim to fame was as the manufacturer of the Gannex weatherproof coats to which Wilson was partial on rainy days. Joe Haines, Wilson's press secretary and no fan of Lady Falkender, emerged as the most bitter critic. He objected to the 'song and dance'

personalities as being too lightweight, and let it be known that he had
personally refused an honour on the grounds that 'I can't sing and I can't
dance, and I can't do impersonations.' No less than 100 backbench MPs
signed a motion of protest against the list. Some Labour members felt it
constituted 'the less acceptable face of capitalism', and there were Tories
who chimed in with strong support. To Robert Adley, Conservative MP
for Christchurch, Wilson's farewell honours list seemed like 'a spiv's
charter'.[16]

Lady Falkender conducted a spirited defence on her own behalf,
disclaiming any undue influence on her boss, and lambasting critics of the
honours for being 'sanctimonious', prone to 'unadulterated snobbery' and
more seriously, in some cases, exhibiting 'covert anti-Semitism'.[17] There
was never a clear-cut conclusion to the row. But since those lively times
both Philip Ziegler, Wilson's authorised biographer, and Ben Pimlott, the
Labour historian, would, after scrutiny of all the evidence, arrive at the
opinion that, regardless of whose hand originally penned the list, Wilson's
resignation honours had gone to the people that Wilson himself wanted
to see have them.

It was said of Lew that he fell off his cigar on learning of his
ennoblement, but he never seems to have been unbalanced by the ensuing
'Lavender List' controversy. He was well sustained by the voices of people
who most mattered to him: by Olga, reported as saying excitedly, 'I'm so
proud to have lived to see two of my sons become lords';[18] by Prince
Philip, who wrote to Lew, in a letter made public, 'I hope you will forgive
me for taking this chance on behalf of all the people you have helped in
the past to acknowledge our great debt and give you our thanks';[19] and by
the senior ATV executives in Great Cumberland Place, who presented
Lew with a framed photograph of themselves over the caption: 'Lord
Grade is my shepherd, I shall not want.'[20]

Lew could also claim to be engaged on matters on a much more exalted
plane, well above frivolous concerns about the reasons for his and
Bernard's ennoblement. Always adept at sidestepping criticism by moving
briskly on to his next enthralling project, Lew was soon in a position to
declaim to the world that *Jesus of Nazareth* really was, after all the delays
in the desert, truly in the can and definitely coming. As Lew saw it, in his
role as the project's John the Baptist, spreading the glad news:

It's the greatest thing we've ever done. It's a masterpiece. There has been nothing like it in the world before. It will last forever. I can't wait for you to see it. And we'll get our money back. But we don't think of the money. The point is, it's the greatest thing we've ever done. It's got delicacy. It's got taste. It's fantastic. I cry every time I see it, me, a grown man . . .'[21]

There were nonetheless some causes for concern before the actual launch. Lew's earlier biblical epic, *Moses – the Lawgiver*, had done well enough in Italy and adequately in the United States, but less than wonderfully around the world. It had not been the prodigious success that was hoped for, so Lew was on edge about its successor. And there was a distressing late hitch in America, where a section of fundamentalist Baptist opinion held (without having seen the product) that *Jesus of Nazareth* was sure to be 'blasphemous'. This caused General Motors to get cold feet about its sponsorship arrangement, and Lew was informed they wanted out on grounds that the subject matter was 'too sensitive for commercial purposes'.[22] But NBC held firm to its transmission pledge, and Lew was able to effect the high-speed recruitment of another multinational giant, Proctor and Gamble, to take the place that GM had so nervously vacated. Finally, over the Easter of 1977, *Jesus of Nazareth* was delivered to the viewers' judgement, ably sent off by Lew's new-found friend, the Pope.

From the vantage point of the Vatican balcony, Pope Paul VI told the crowd assembled in the square below, 'Tonight I'm going to look at the film *Jesus of Nazareth*. I want you to look at it not only with your eyes but also with your heart.'[23]

Early ratings figures for the film, broadcast in two three-hour segments, indicated that thirty-two million people had watched in Italy, more than twenty million in Britain and around ninety million in the United States. Even with the rest of the world yet to be conquered, Lew knew he had pulled off his greatest popular success in television and that he would indeed get his money back, and much more besides.

While the film might not have quite measured up to Lew's lauding of it as one that would 'last forever', most critics had to concede that it was exceptionally good and, in some parts, quite beautiful. Zeffirelli's exasperating attention to detail and visual composition had paid off, while

Robert Powell made a convincingly moving and eloquent Christ. And the galaxy of stars involved managed, in most instances, to eschew the ponderous style of utterance that had become so boringly familiar in the many Bible-based epics churned out by Hollywood. Lew had good reason to be proud, though he was inclined to overestimate the film's persuasive power. Peter Ustinov was flummoxed by Lew telling him that if the film had been available in biblical times there would have been 'no need for the Crucifixion to have taken place at all'.[24]

In the eight months up to September 1977, the date of Lew's enforced retirement from television's front line, his enterprise broke all previous export records, reaching 107 countries and selling four times as much as the BBC and the fourteen other independent television companies all combined. Sales to the United States alone topped $100 million, with *Jesus of Nazareth* and *The Muppet Show* heading the list of highest earners. *Forbes* magazine eulogised Lew's efforts, saying that 'Grade has probably done more to raise the standards of US TV than most of our domestic moguls.'[25] In Britain, the Royal Television Society's awards for the most outstanding programmes of the year went to Lew's ATV – for *Jesus of Nazareth* and *The Muppet Show*. It could be said that the fusion of popularity and quality, long sought by Lew but not so often objectively achieved, had been triumphantly realised.

Had Lew actually retired at this point, aged seventy plus, it would have been possible to write sentimentally of his career having a magnificent and fitting climax. However, Lew had absolutely no intention of giving up such a thoroughly enjoyable way of life. Though grudgingly reconciled to his loss of executive authority at ATV, he did not anticipate being entirely without influence as chairman of its holding company. As he said, 'just as Jesus is always there so my presence will always be with the TV company'.[26] He also had the consolation of knowing that there would still be a Grade family member very much active in one of the 'Big Five' at independent television's networking level. This was the natural consequence of his nephew Michael's emergence, in May 1977, at the tender age of thirty-three, as Controller of Programmes at LWT after a rapid rise up its light entertainment ladder. This promotion led to his being dubbed 'Nephew of the Year'[27] by a whimsical friend, but nobody saw it as unmerited. According to Jeremy Potter in ITV's official history,

Michael already 'shared his uncle's flamboyance, flair for publicity, devotion to hard work and delight in doing deals'.[28]

To this delight Lew himself could now add yet another – playfully teasing reporters assigned the task of pinning down his intended ultimate retirement date. Yes, he would say, he had a firm plan to retire in the year 2000, well maybe make that 2001. Though, perhaps on reflection, better revise that and say that when 2001 came around he might then 'consider retirement'. Be sure to check with him then.

In the meantime, what he planned to do was no big secret. Even before the Muppets arrived, Lew was hard at work on a career move that would circumvent the IBA's irritating age restriction and provide all the loyalists in Great Cumberland Place with a thrilling, if unnerving, new series of adventures.

TWENTY

Movie Mogul

A T AN AGE WHEN MOST PEOPLE are well into retirement, Lew Grade, one-time professional dancer, theatrical agent and television supremo, embarked on a fourth career that eclipsed all those that had gone before, at least in terms of glamour. His simple objective was to become, as he put it, 'the biggest film producer in the world',[1] and he came mighty close, producing some eighty films, many featuring Hollywood's biggest stars, in little more than six years. Few of his films would achieve high ratings for artistic merit, but most were anything but cheap and two of them – *On Golden Pond* (staring two Fondas, Henry and Jane, with Katharine Hepburn) and *Sophie's Choice* (Meryl Streep) – featured prominently among the Oscar awards.

This was big-time movie-making of a type that post-war Britain had not seen before, and history would show that it all ended in tears with Lew's elaborately constructed business empire in a shambles and Lew himself being ushered towards the door marked 'Exit'. In *The Once and Future Film*, his book about British cinema in the 1970s and 1980s, John Walker wrote of Lew's efforts: 'the classic trajectory of tragic hero was to be his, beginning with overweening pride and challenge to the gods and ending in humiliation and total disaster'.[2] During the cruel decline of his career as a movie mogul, it was suggested by some commentators that Lew's films had almost invariably been 'stinkers',[3] which was not true, and that the whole exercise had been evidence of the recklessness of an old man in a hurry, which was only partly true.

In reality, Lew had originally approached the movie business with some caution. While appreciative of his younger brother Leslie's success as a film producer in the early 1960s, with *Summer Holiday* and *The Servant*, Lew had not been tempted to proceed in the same high-risk direction until much later, and then only on a limited basis. His initial efforts could be classed as being more in the category of helping out old chums, rather than any pursuit of world domination, though he did vouchsafe to *Time* magazine at an early stage, 'I'm going to make a fortune in the film business, and I mean a fortune,' adding, as an afterthought, 'Whenever I say I, of course, I mean the company.'[4]

The first film he backed was *Crossplot* (released in 1969), a modestly priced spy drama based in London with the lead played by Roger Moore. This could fairly be construed as support for an actor whose long, loyal service in *The Saint* had placed him uniquely high in Lew's estimation. Warm, if rather more ambivalent acquaintance characterised his next significant film venture, with Shirley MacLaine. As part of the equation for luring MacLaine into television and the tribulations of *Shirley's World*, Lew had pledged his backing for two films she wanted to make. Despite the problems with the television series, Lew was as good as his word. *Desperate Characters*, which excited some favourable comparison with *Midnight Cowboy*, went on to win a Berlin Film Festival award in 1971. MacLaine's other Lew-financed movie, *The Possession of Joel Delaney*, explored demonic concerns and the occult in a way that anticipated *The Exorcist*. Both movies were set in New York and both were low-budget operations, and neither was a stinker.

Soon afterwards, Lew entered into a similar arrangement with another friend. He had first got to know Julie Andrews and her family when she auditioned for a singing role, aged six, and Lew had detected in her talent which 'had a future'.[5] This had been realised to the extent that she later became a movie queen in California, though her career had faltered slightly since her mid-1960s triumphs in *Mary Poppins* and *The Sound of Music*. Still, she was a huge catch for television and Lew, presuming on old acquaintance, managed to secure her services for a series of twenty-four spectaculars on ATV, which were also screened on the ABC network. As a subsidiary aspect of the television deal, Andrews asked Lew to commit himself to making two films with her American husband, Blake Edwards, as director. Lew, growing in confidence as a movie financier, readily promised to do so.

The first, *The Tamarind Seed* (released in 1974), starring Julie herself and Omar Sharif in a story that blended romance and espionage, did unremarkable business. But the second, *The Return of the Pink Panther*, was another matter. Made possible by Lew persuading Peter Sellers, an old client of the Lew and Leslie Grade agency, to give it another go as the supremely incompetent Inspector Clouseau, *The Return of the Pink Panther* yielded a profit for Lew's ITC operation of well over $10 million, and extra revenue was derived from a smaller percentage in its prompt follow-up, *The Pink Panther Strikes Again*. More importantly, it was the experience of putting the *Panther* enterprise together that convinced Lew that feature films need no longer be a by-product of his television activity. Instead, they could become his prime business focus. There was also another logic propelling him in this direction.

By 1974, with Lord Renwick recently deceased, Lew found himself in the peculiar position of having supreme authority in the company but with only short-term career prospects. The IBA made it clear in 1974 that Lew could not, under any circumstances, expect to exercise his authority in television beyond their imposed retirement date. According to Bernard, as reported in *Last of a Kind*, Quentin Falk and Dominic Prince's entertaining account of Lew's movie-making exploits, the IBA's intransigence had a profound impact on his brother:

> It was suddenly as if age had become a barrier to him. He thought, 'Well, I'll go into films instead.' He had to do something. So you could say he went into films totally for the wrong reasons. There's no doubt about it. It was just for the work . . . had he still been sixty, he would never have gone into films, because he was perfectly happy with what he was doing in television . . .'[6]

Bernard himself almost certainly contributed another strand to Lew's movie-making motivation. As head of the film division at EMI, Bernard had originally enjoyed only modest success. His first initiative had been to appoint Bryan Forbes, one of the industry's most respected directors, as head of production with a mandate to produce quality family films, geared to the domestic market. An ambitious programme was announced and a quantity of such films were made, but apart from *The Railway*

Children and *The Raging Moon*, both released in 1970, few were successful. Forbes resigned with a year of his three-year contract still to run, in circumstances of some bitterness. He complained that some of the films he produced had actually been turned down by EMI's own distribution and exhibition division, which also operated, albeit with a large measure of independence, under Bernard's ultimate authority. Forbes applauded Bernard for his 'act of courage' in appointing him in the first place, but left with a wounding parting shot: 'Perhaps in retrospect I wished Bernard Delfont had had the courage of my convictions more often.'[7]

Forbes' miserable departure, however, would afford much more prominence for the previously undervalued efforts of Nat Cohen, who also produced films for EMI as head of its subsidiary Anglo-EMI. Cohen had a more populist edge, having served a long and robust apprenticeship that included backing some of the more rumbustious *Carry On* films. His first contact with Bernard dated back to the 1930s when, as manager of the Mile End Empire, he had engaged 'Delfont and Toko, Syncopated-Steps Appeal' as the lead dance act. Their movie-making association, however, began much later with *Up Pompeii* (released in 1971), a madcap, innuendo-ridden romp highlighting the comic talent of Frankie Howerd. Then in 1973 Cohen came up with *Murder on the Orient Express*, based on the Agatha Christie novel, and exhibiting a stellar line-up. Cohen managed to persuade Ingrid Bergman, Lauren Bacall, Anthony Perkins, and many more besides, to agree to work for a low flat fee in what amounted to an assemblage of cameo roles for all those taking part, aside from Albert Finney as Poirot. To both Cohen's and Bernard's surprise it became absolutely huge.

In Britain it was said to be one of the key movies, along with *The Sting* and *The Exorcist*, that arrested the decline in cinema attendances in 1974 for the first time in twenty years. But it was also a massive success overseas, grossing around £200 million worldwide. Its international success was a comforting indication that market resistance to non-American English-language movies could, with the right product, be overcome. This happened to be precisely the area Lew wanted to penetrate. Lew was also most probably powerfully inclined to cap Bernard's success. Sibling rivalry may not have represented their prime motivation, but it seems to have been unfailingly the case that whenever one brother had a successful surge, the other instinctively pressed his foot down on the accelerator.

Lew's acceleration into movie mogul status, from close to a standing start, was phenomenal. Between late 1974 and 1977 he announced, usually with a large fanfare at the Cannes Film Festival, plans to produce almost fifty films, nominating the stars, and boasting of the width of the budgets at the directors' disposal. Overall budgets for each batch of films started around £20 million, escalating upwards to £50 million and later to £100 million and more, which always made for grabbing headlines.

Alert commentators did notice that the orbit of the stars sometimes changed in their course from one projected movie to another, and occasionally went into total eclipse. Some suggested, furthermore, that Lew's star selection was a bit on the conservative side, favouring old-timers said to be embarked on the way down, rather than the rising variety. It was also correctly detected that several amazing 'new' ventures were, in fact, old ones in freshly ironed attire.

It was certainly the case that nobody in the business took Lew's figures entirely at their face value. Howard Thomas, his old sparring partner at Thames Television, wrote of him: 'I used to say that at his television press conferences Lew usually doubled the figure he first thought of; but when he got into films the multiples got even higher.'[8] Even so, many of the pictures were actually completed with something close to their predicted complement of expensive stars, and often at high speed.

The key advantage Lew had over other British movie-makers lay in the contacts and credibility established by ATV worldwide, and particularly in the United States. It was the success of ATV that provided the secure knowledge that the movies that Lew promised could actually be delivered. In this way, he used his TV-based corporation in much the same fashion as a Hollywood outfit deploying its production record. Lew's word was famously his bond, but its guarantee was the business.

Lew claimed that he was normally able to recover 60 per cent or more of his film-making costs from advance sales of television and distribution rights on the basis of ATV's prestige and the reputation of the director and stars assigned to each movie. Half of this money could be paid before a film was finished, with the rest being received in the form of firm guarantees. In this way the financial risk borne by ATV could be reduced to less than two-fifths of the cost. Initially at least, this appearance of a safety net was sufficient to calm the nerves of Lew's fellow ATV directors in a way that enabled their leader to take flight. The risk was also, it was thought, further minimised by ATV's eggs going into so many different movie baskets. On this analysis it was not just a matter of the more films the merrier, but seemingly the more films the safer.

Much of this, however, had to be taken on trust as few of Lew's colleagues were able to master all the intricacies of the boss's pre-selling arrangements. Alexander Walker, the doyen of film critics at that time, wrote in *National Heroes*, his book about the British cinema industry: 'Lew found himself quickly locked into a bewildering variety of deals which would have taxed the brain of a master cracksman to keep track of the combinations.'[9] Some of his productions were pre-sold straight to an American distributor; others were financed territory by territory around the globe by Lew's ITC Distributions operation; yet others were contracted to be shown first (and only) on American television and then sold outside America by Lew's own companies. And there were subtle variations on all these methods, of which the details were sometimes little known outside the circumference of Lew's head.

The possibility that Lew might be taking on too much never seems to have crossed his mind, though it did cause apprehension to some close acquaintances. The film director, Michael Winner, a family friend of the Grades since his childhood, remembers begging Lew not to get too deeply involved in movie-making. 'He shouldn't have gone into films,' said Winner, 'different entirely from television. He was too nice a guy. His word was his bond, but that was not always the case with the people he shook hands with. But Lew thought everybody was as honest as he was. I said to him "dream on, Lew", but he took no notice.'[10]

Like any Hollywood tycoon, Lew reasoned that it only required one big hit a year to cover the losses of a run of less successful movies. Lew's rule of thumb was that he could stand the strain of breaking even, or even losing a little, on nine films provided he could get a blockbuster hit in the $100 million box office category with his tenth. Of his ability to deliver on that basis he had absolutely no doubt. 'I believe in the law of averages,' he told a *Financial Times* journalist, extolling his range of upcoming movie projects. 'One of these has to be a blockbuster.'[11] What was needed was momentum of the kind that would lead to the desired, but not entirely predictable, big hit.

The flavour of Lew's style of operation at this time was most efficiently captured by the British film director, John Boorman, in his memoir, *Money into Light*, in which he recalled:

> When Lew started making movies he approached me with a script about Livingstone in Africa. It was intriguing but needed a lot of work and research before you could get to the point of knowing if it was makeable.
>
> Lew would have none of my doubts and reservations. We were lunching in his office suite together with the writer and a couple of Lew's executives. 'How much do you want to make it?' he said. 'A quarter of a million?'
>
> 'Lew, please,' I protested.
>
> 'All right, make it $350,000.'
>
> 'I don't know if it can be done, even if I did want to do it.'
>
> Lew bellowed out for his cheque book. He made out a cheque for half a million dollars and signed it. He handed it to me. I refused to take it. He got up from his chair and tried to stuff it in my jacket pocket. I fended him off and we sparred for a moment, when with a deft movement he stuffed it between my backside and the chair. I tried to ignore it, but I felt at a distinct disadvantage from then on with half a million dollars of Lew's money sticking up my arse.
>
> He refused to talk about the project itself, the story, the script, the casting – these were details for writers and directors to take care of.
>
> 'Let me tell you how I work, John. I don't want to read the script – haven't got time. I don't see rushes. Don't show me a rough-cut.' He waved away such a trifle. 'You make it. You have the final cut.'
>
> I felt if I let him go on any longer, my silence would be construed as agreement. I made a feeble attempt to interrupt. I reached out a protesting hand. He thrust into it a cigar that looked capable of sinking the *Belgrano*.
>
> 'I know what you're going to say, John. Other studios have given you the final cut, right?'
>
> 'But nobody has gone as far as I'll go. I don't even want to see the picture when it's finished!'[12]

Boorman confessed to being completely won over by Lew's unusual brand of sales charm, though he did manage to extricate himself without concluding a deal on this occasion. Still, there were many other directors ready to profit by Lew's largesse even before he could slip a large cheque under their backsides.

Although Lew kept all the threads of the movie-making business in his own hands in London, he operated with close allies in other territories. His closest on the continent of Europe was Carlo Ponti, the film producer husband of Sophia Loren, Italy's most luminous star. Loren had previously rendered her services for Lew's TV remake of *Brief Encounter*, in which she, somewhat bizarrely, played the love-torn housewife opposite Richard Burton. It was not thought to be an advance on the original. Lew and Ponti put together eight films in all, with Loren taking the leading role in four of them.

In California, Lew's man-on-the-spot came to be Martin Starger, who as a young executive had been so entranced by the ATV boss's welcome-to-London technique back in 1967. Since those days, Starger had risen high in America's ABC network, becoming head of its Entertainments Division. The string of spectacular programme concepts to his credit included *Rich Man, Poor Man* and, most famously, *Roots*. Soon after Starger left ABC in 1975 to develop his own business, Lew took him on. He became the best-paid man on Lew's payroll at $100,000 a year, with a healthy percentage cut on each realised film idea to supplement his immodest salary. It was early recognition of the fact that Hollywood was crucial to the enterprise.

Lew always maintained that his movie-making initiatives were just great for the British film industry. But the degree to which he assisted the home-grown film business was open to question. As his objective, from the beginning, was to crack the international market, this inevitably dictated a preponderance of American directors and of highly recognisable American stars, even though the films had their financial origin in London. He employed a few British directors, Michael Winner being one of them, but they were in a distinct minority. Lew also did genuinely try to steer some of the action in the films towards British studios, but again this was not always feasible. As he disarmingly explained in relation to his Western, *The Legend of the Lone Ranger*, 'Unfortunately, I can't make it here because I can't find enough cowboys.'[13]

The decision to expand film output on the basis of international pre-selling naturally upped the workload of his ITC operation, although this was a chore that the boss was very happy to share in. Ian Jessel, ITC Distribution's managing director, travelled all over Europe and later to Hong Kong, Australia and Japan with Lew as his companion and sales assistant. Jessel said of this experience:

> Almost everyone knew him by sight or by name, even if they didn't know him personally. He always spoke to them as if they did, and even in countries he had never visited before he was welcomed as a kind of jovial ambassador. It wouldn't take him long to tell tales of his Charleston dancing, and it wouldn't take him much longer to actually perform.
>
> He had the ability to make people want to be in business with him, to be associated with him. They would often suspend belief as far as the films were concerned just because they somehow felt he was an important force in the industry and he made them feel like family. If the films were not perhaps as irresistible as they should have been, or I wasn't as irresistible as I could have been, he always was.[14]

Good personal vibes around the planet, however, were no adequate substitute for good audiences for Lew's films. History has judged them harshly as being, for all their expense, essentially unoriginal. Many of them were based on the best-selling pulp thrillers of the day. Others were often remakes of popular old classics. Lew's aversion to having his films X rated also helped to ensure a lack of intellectual adventure. Even so, he did accept that films should be accorded more permissive latitude than he deemed desirable on television. Nudity was not out of bounds, if discreetly employed. He was also conscious of the need to appeal to a much more youthful audience. And while most of his film output now ranks as old-fashioned, it was not conspicuously more old-fashioned than most of the Hollywood movies being produced at the time. Nor, it must be said, was it conspicuously much better.

By the spring of 1978, with Lew officially out of the television loop and giving almost undivided attention to the movie side of the business, he must have felt some apprehension, or at least have experienced a twinge of uncertainty, about whether his vaunted ability to please most of the people, most of the time, could be transferred from television to film. Not that anyone else would have noticed from his demeanour. Publicly, he was still feeding a fascinated, and almost entirely uncritical, press with a concentrated diet of wonderful, new, exciting upcoming movie projects – all destined, he would assert, to be big winners. At this point Lew could claim to have more films in the promised production pipeline than Metro-Goldwyn-Mayer, Twentieth Century-Fox or any of the traditional Hollywood names. However, it cannot have escaped Lew's keen arithmetical attention that he had already gone past the ten completed movies mark, while the big hit that would justify a series of low earners had yet to put in an appearance.

There was an element of bad luck in this. One of Lew's certain winners, as he thought, should have been *Road to the Fountain of Youth*, the provisional title for the movie that would reunite Bob Hope and Bing Crosby in another classic 'Road' movie. It had been fifteen years since their fifth and highly profitable last – *Road to Hong Kong* in 1962 – and Lew was delighted to be the man to bring them together again. A date to begin filming in England was agreed. Then Crosby fell into a twenty-foot-deep orchestra pit in Pasadena while taping a CBS special commemorating his fiftieth anniversary in show business. No bones were broken, but the crooner emerged in a groggy state, though valiant with it. It was reported that he sang for the paramedics on the way to Pasadena's Huntingdon Memorial Hospital, a hopeful sign for Lew. But when Bing came out of the hospital three weeks later, diagnosed with a ruptured disc at the base of his spine, his enthusiasm for movie-making had expired.

This could be counted as a misfortune, but the Hope–Crosby film venture was only one of a number of Lew's most favoured projects that had not worked out, at least in box office terms. *Voyage of the Damned* had a strong contingent of stars (Faye Dunaway, Max von Sydow, Oskar Werner and Orson Welles), and an ostensibly powerful true story line about a ship that left Hamburg in 1939 laden with Jewish refugees and headed for Cuba, which refused to take them in. Yet it did only modest business. The same was true of *The Cassandra Crossing* (Burt Lancaster, Ava Gardner, Sophia Loren and O.J. Simpson), featuring terrorism and other forms of mayhem on a speeding transcontinental train that had to be isolated because there was a deadly virus on board. Some thought the action element a mite over-egged. *The Domino Principle* (Gene Hackman, Candice Bergen, Mickey Rooney and Eli Wallach), a political thriller; *March or Die* (Gene Hackman and Max von Sydow again, plus Catherine Deneuve), a steamy melodrama set in a dusty French Foreign Legion outpost; and *Russian Roulette* (George Segal and Denholm Elliott), an espionage caper, all did poorly, and deservedly so.

On the other hand, *Farewell, My Lovely*, with Robert Mitchum playing Raymond Chandler's gumshoe, Philip Marlowe, was an excellent film, even though it was a remake. But it did sound rather than spectacular business. The follow-up, *The Big Sleep*, another remake, again with Mitchum but set incongruously in London, was neither good nor lucrative. Joan Collins, who played opposite Mitchum, was impressed with how dextrously the American actor had knocked her about for the purposes of one violent scene, without hurting her one little bit. Afterwards, she asked Mitchum what was the secret of this gentle skill. 'Honey,' was the laconic reply, 'I've been doin' this stuff for a hundred years so I'm not about to hurt an actress in a scene, 'specially not in *this* piece of crap.'[15]

Capricorn One (Elliott Gould, James Brolin and O.J. Simpson) rose well above this level, exhibiting some originality of conception. The story of how a manned space flight to Mars was stunted up as a hoax in a television studio was naturally pleasing to the many conspiracy theorists who had always entertained doubts about the moon shot. And the film was among the few to show a profit.

Of the first tranche of Lew's big films to be released, one of the most successful was the quirky *The Eagle Has Landed*, based on a best-selling novel by Jack Higgins which featured intrepid German soldiers invading an English village with a view to assassinating Winston Churchill. With Michael Caine as an almost sympathetic German officer and Donald Sutherland as a wonderfully crazed IRA man, it was an altogether unlikely story though one with an engaging twist at the end. But even *The Eagle Has Landed* was no way near being in the blockbuster business class of the *Panther* film that kicked off the whole enterprise. What Lew needed by now, with the law of averages proving less helpful than originally expected, was something more of the order of a *Star Wars* or a *Saturday Night Fever* or a *Grease*.

There was no hint in contemporary press reports of there being any major structural flaw in Lew's grand design, but he must have been acutely aware of it. Indeed, there can be no other explanation for the extraordinary move he made to bolster his credibility as a big-time film-maker in the summer of 1978, still with no big hit on the near horizon.

In August 1978 it was revealed that Lew had almost quadrupled his salary, upping it from £59,000 a year to £210,428. This made him by some distance the most highly paid company chairman in Britain. At that time the chairmen of ICI and BP were both paid less than £100,000 a year. Even more relevantly, pay restraint was one of the prime items on the domestic agenda of the economically distressed Labour government to which Lew of course owed his peerage. It was claimed that a large proportion of Lew's rise would come out of the coffers of ATV's subsidiary in America, but this failed to render it more acceptable in the eyes of many left-wingers. 'Obscene'[16] was the verdict of William Molloy, a Labour backbench MP, who started off a chorus of public protest that had echoes of the 'Lavender List' controversy. But this time the damage to Lew's long-cultivated image of being just an ordinary man-in-the-street, though writ exceptionally large, seemed to be wholly self-inflicted.

Lew considered it a risk he had to take. People across the Atlantic, he explained, just could not believe he was on only £59,000 a year, when their top executives in the movie business were hauling down a million dollars a year and more. It just made them laugh. And that wasn't good for business because, and this was said with much feeling, 'it made them think British productions were not so good'.[17] In essence, it was the symbol of the salary, not the reality, that was so important to Lew. How the big-league Hollywood people saw him had become, in many respects, a more vital concern than how he was viewed in Britain.

Lew was also quoted as saying, some thought rather insensitively, 'The money doesn't mean anything to me. I live for my work and have no expensive tastes or hobbies.'[18] This was a hard concept to convey to most of his fellow countrymen to whom, in wage-strapped times, money did mean something. However, aside from a cigar bill that would tax the full width of any working man's weekly pay packet, Lew was only telling the unvarnished truth. He really didn't need or particularly want the money, and there was no indication of his lifestyle suddenly evolving in a more extravagant direction. Between business trips to New York on Concorde, which he was said to use the way most people hop on a bus, Lew invited reporters to scrutinise the unvarying nature of his working day in Great Cumberland Place: at his office desk as usual around 6 a.m., open all the post before any of the help arrived, business meetings and phone calls through the morning, light lunch, the time-honoured Winston Churchill-style nap – 'the secret of my success'[19] – from 1.15 p.m. till 2.30 p.m., more business in the afternoon until the Rolls came around to take him home to Kathie around 6.30 p.m.

Occasionally, more privileged writers were invited to the two-storey penthouse in Knightsbridge that was his and Kathie's home. This also exhibited signs of being a working environment, though one with many pleasantly decorative aspects. With no immediate access to a garden, Kathie had rendered the terrace superbly colourful by planting shrubs in a richly assorted collection of antique chimney pots. Indoors there was much evidence of comfort, deep sofas and armchairs piled high with tapestry cushions, and more than a few delicate hints of romance. Many of the bowls of crushed flowers on display were the residue of the roses that Lew presented to Kathie every Valentine's Day.

An incredibly youthful-looking Kathie was often around on these occasions to bear witness that her husband spent most of his evenings leafing through scripts, watching TV or cassettes (other people's output, not his own), and punishing the telephone – first with calls to New York and then later on in the evening to California. Every room had three telephones, but there was one in Lew's high-tech study – his top persons' priority line – that even Kathie didn't know the number of, and didn't want to know, in case she accidentally let it slip. It was not possible to spend long in their joint company without detecting that Lew was one of those fortunate men who was still, after many years of marriage, a hero to his own wife.

Not that Kathie was at all deferential. She was ready to chat freely, even irreverently, about matters relating to her husband's domestic habits. Although Lew ruled a technologically advanced empire and spent a lot of time dickering with his TVs and VCRs, he was not much of a technician himself. If any of the appliances failed to respond to his touch, which happened quite frequently, it would be her duty to come to his rescue.

Still, he was not difficult to cater for. Never a big eater, Lew liked chicken, liver and bacon, veal and smoked salmon especially. Fruit too, though he was not big on vegetables aside from raw carrots and radishes, and cucumber, raw or pickled. But he did have a sweet tooth and, as he had to watch his weight, this meant that Kathie was sometimes compelled to hide the ice cream. Chocolate was not allowed in past the front door.

It was also interesting to learn from his wife that Lew, perceived by many to be one of the nation's leading extroverts, was in fact really a shy man. And that he could have a problem unwinding after a tough day. Kathie had given some thought to how to help him relax a bit more, particularly during his nights, which were sometimes restless. The sauna in one of the small upstairs rooms was designed to help him in this regard. She had arranged to have it installed, complete with telephone, as a nice surprise. But Lew had taken one look at it and said, 'You'll never get *me* in there.'[20] Fortunately, the housekeeper liked to use it from time to time.

The abiding impression of Lew and Kathie at home was of a couple who were thoroughly comfortable with their living arrangements, and even more comfortable with each other. Still, it was hard not to wonder what exactly it was that was keeping Britain's best-paid business executive awake at nights.

TWENTY-ONE

Two Titanics

Two months after his spectacular hike in salary, Lew was back in California armed with a bold new plan with an interesting, and entirely novel, family twist: he and Bernard were going into business together. It was to be on a limited basis, but on a project of prime importance to both brothers. Speaking at a specially convened press conference at the Beverly Hills Hotel in October 1978, Lew announced to the world in general, and to Hollywood in particular: 'I have a tremendous relationship with my brother, but we fight like mad. We are in competition in many areas of the entertainment industry. But after all these years we have decided to form our own distribution company for North America. We will still go our various ways in the rest of the world.'[1]

Those assembled for the conference were impressed by the bullish confidence that characterised Lew's delivery, though some of their reports exhibited scepticism about the feasibility of his plan. By announcing that he, in alliance with Bernard, was prepared to mount a direct British challenge to one of the most impregnable aspects of the American movie business – its distribution system – Lew was raising his movie mogul profile to a much higher level than ever before. From being one of Hollywood's most welcome outsiders, he was riskily edging close to the position of becoming an external threat.

It seemed like a good idea at the time. By the late 1970s the film-making enterprises of Lew and Bernard had become similar in many respects. In 1976 Bernard's EMI had acquired the British Lion film company and with it the executive abilities of Barry Spikings and Michael Deeley, who were already well versed in the ways of Hollywood movie-making. And the films they set up for Bernard, usually from a Hollywood base, were designed to have international appeal. They had their greatest success with *The Deer Hunter*, released in 1978 and the winner of five Oscars, including Best Picture, in the following year. Like Lew's man, Martin Starger, Spikings and Deeley did most of their angling for directors and star talent in California. Bernard also scored a big financial success for his company by putting up some of the seed money for Columbia's runaway hit, *Close Encounters of the Third Kind*. In terms of outlook and production, the film-making side of both Bernard's EMI and Lew's ITC could now fairly be described as highly Americanised.

America was the driving force in the industry with a home market that represented 50 per cent of the world gross for films, compared with a fragile British figure of around 5 per cent. It was inescapably where the big action took place. But in America, Lew and Bernard were normally obliged to distribute their films through the routes established by Universal, Columbia, Fox, Warners and the other Hollywood majors. Lew had derived some short-term advantage from a co-production link-up with the General Cinema Corporation of Boston, but its reach in terms of controlled cinema houses was limited. To achieve anything approaching coast-to-coast distribution a deal had to be done with one of the majors, who customarily took 30 per cent of box office revenue for the service. It was Lew's impression that this represented a raw deal, and he reckoned that he and Bernard could do better for themselves.

Instead of paying the American outfits, Lew invited Bernard to consider the idea of their going in together and handling their own film distribution in the United States and Canada. Bernard could see its logic and the Associated Film Distribution Corporation (AFDC) was formed with Lew as chairman, Bernard as deputy chairman and Martin Starger as president. It was capitalized at $38.5 million, with much of the initial investment to be spent on opening and staffing branch sales offices throughout North America to help blaze the trail for British product. It would not take very long before the brothers realised that they had bitten off more than they could chew. Looking back in *East End, West End*, Bernard wrote:

> Maybe we made too much of it. In any event the fanfare of announcement
> of our alliance . . . was interpreted by our American rivals as a declaration

of war. Suddenly there were problems at every town. If our film output had been stronger we might have withstood the pressure, but while we were big on our own ground, our combined output could not outclass the Hollywood studios. We needed *The Deer Hunter* ten times over to do that. Consequently, we were not taken seriously by the other distributors. With them having first choice of screenings we were left with whatever they did not want. It was no way to run a business.[2]

The operation limped on for two costly years before it was phased out, and Lew and Bernard thankfully went back to having their films distributed through Universal, their most favoured, or more precisely least resented, American major.

It was sometimes suggested that Lew thought that *mea culpa* was the name of an Italian movie starlet, but in the context of AFDC he was prepared to accept full responsibility for the debacle. In his obituary notice for the enterprise Lew blamed himself for underestimating the massive overhead costs required for branch offices, film prints and advertising that were essential for distribution in the United States. He called it 'a fatal mistake'.[3]

It would take more than one large error, even one said to be of a lethal variety, to undermine Lew's authority. But he made another only a few weeks after launching AFDC, though nobody gave it much heed at the time.

Raise the Titanic was, for all the wrong reasons, Lew's most famous movie project. Based on a contemporary best-selling novel by Clive Cussler, it concerned a race between the Americans and the Soviets to recover a mysterious element, byzanium, of crucial importance to an intercontinental weaponry system. To complicate matters the byzanium was located in the vaults of a devastated liner six thousand feet under the Atlantic. 'I went to America,' Lew excitedly recalled, 'and locked the author and his agent in my hotel room, and wouldn't let them out until they'd signed a deal with me.'[4]

The book's imaginative, fresh slant on the old, but still awe-inspiring, disaster story about the 'unsinkable' SS *Titanic*, which went down in 1912 after hitting an iceberg with the loss of 1,513 lives, was that it was primarily about bringing it up again; and in a condition to complete its maiden voyage to New York. This element, combined with a plot involving Cold War derring-do under the sea, convinced Lew that he had acquired a property with blockbusting potential. By his standards it was not an especially star-studded vehicle – the leading roles were eventually allocated to Jason Robards, Richard Jordan and Alec Guinness – but technically it was the most challenging. And the business of making the movie was rendered even more difficult by the technological equivalent of inadvertently placing the cart before the horse.

The original intention was to shoot most of the action at the CBS Studio Centre in Los Angeles. By the summer of 1978 a magnificent collection of beautifully crafted models had been assembled to recreate the flotilla required for the enterprise. There were eight models in total: four United States warships, two tugs, a New York Harbour fire ship and the *Titanic* itself, fifty-five feet long and twelve feet high and weighing in at ten tons. With the cost of the project already approaching $6 million, enough to cover the entire budget of many of Lew's other films, it was realised that there was nowhere on the studio site, or anywhere else that sprang to mind, that could accommodate a tank large enough to house a 55ft model in the simulation of a depth of more than six thousand feet in a manner that could be efficiently filmed.

At this point there was the possibility of junking the models and building smaller ones, or even of pulling the plug on the whole enterprise. Both options would have been expensive, but immensely cheaper than the one that Lew actually took, which was to transport the existing models to the island of Malta, which appeared to present the best prospects for a site where a tank could be custom built to the desired specifications. This proved to be a protracted operation and one that was made even more expensive by an edict of the island's Prime Minister, Dom Mintoff. On Mintoff's insistence the tank had to be fully landscaped in order not to deface the panoramic view of the island afforded to tourists as their planes came in to land at Luqa Airport. As Lew later lamented, the time frame on the movie got more and more out of hand – 'So we found a plot of land in Malta, and they built a bigger tank. I asked when it would be ready and they said January. But they didn't say *which* January.'[5]

Back in December 1978 Lew simply announced that he had sanctioned moving the *Titanic* project, in which he had unbounded confidence, to a Mediterranean location, and that the budget for the film had been increased from $10 million to $20 million. By now Lew's relationship with *Raise the Titanic* was being compared by nervous colleagues in Cumberland House to the one he had previously established with *Jesus of Nazareth*. That had gone way over budget several times, and Lew had still thrown money at it, but in that instance of course it had all come out right in the end. *Titanic* was seen as the boss's new act of supreme faith, though some already thought the miracle incapable of being wrought twice. It's even possible that Lew's faith in the project might have been shaken had he known that his steeply upgraded estimate of the film's eventual cost would prove to be another $20 million shy of the mark. And cost was by no means the only problem.

Shortly after making his fateful Malta decision, Lew learned that Bernard's EMI operation was also making a film about the *Titanic*, though one of a more conventional variety. In Bernard's case the ship was only required to go down. Although the brothers were now conjoined in their American distribution project, they had somehow overlooked the possibility of duplication in their separate production processes. Lew rang Bernard to insist that his brother should cancel his *Titanic* film, and delivered one of his characteristic 'What are you trying to do to me?' tirades. 'We had the idea first,' he shouted down the line. 'How would you have liked it if I had made "Assassination on the Orient Express" when you were finishing *Murder on the Orient Express?*'[6]

Surprised but unrepentant, Bernard said that he had not been aware of Lew's project and that, in any event, his own *SOS Titanic* had been in the making for some time. There was no way of stopping it. In the end the brothers had to console themselves with idea that the world film market might be big enough to accommodate both movies. Lew put a brave public face on things by saying there was really no comparison to be made; the models alone in his film cost more than Bernard's budget for his entire production. But he seethed in private, 'just what I could have done without at that time – another Titanic'.[7] In fact, the coincidence of their coming up with similar film ideas was not that extraordinary. The doomed voyage of the *Titanic* had featured in at least a dozen earlier films, and would later inspire more. All the same, it was rather strange that Bernard should not have been aware of Lew's project, which first figured publicly in one of his brother's many long catalogues of upcoming big treats more than two years earlier.

The explanation probably lies in their different methods as movie moguls. Lew was personally involved in initiating most of his films, and while he may not have spent an excessive amount of time actually poring over the scripts, he mastered the outline of all his movies to the extent of being able to sing their praises on a credible basis; he was always the best publicist of his own films. Bernard, in contrast, was more laid back, an arbiter of film ideas rather than an initiator, tending to respond to those thrown up from below, usually by Nat Cohen or Barry Spikings. He was also inclined to leave publicity for individual films to the publicity department. Bernard could be very hands-on in the theatre, but he tended to hover in the background where film-making was concerned. He was always ready to concede that there were products emanating from his own EMI film factory which he did not know much about. So he could well have accidentally missed what was coming through his brother's pipeline.

It could be argued that Bernard's approach made for a less hectic style of film-making, though it did have its pitfalls. In 1978 the Monty Python comedy team were under the firm impression that they had a deal with EMI to finance *The Life of Brian*, their satirical take on events related to the Gospel story. Spikings and Michael Deeley had appraised the project on Bernard's behalf and were both enthusiastic, verging on ecstatic. Emissaries were accordingly sent off to scout for locations in Tunisia, where there was a deep reservoir of local biblical talent and expertise left unemployed since Lew's *Jesus of Nazareth* television caravan had moved on. Then word came through that Bernard, rather late in the day, had got around to reading the script and decided it was all far too risky.

'I'm not,' Bernard told his film men, 'going to be accused of making fun of Jesus Christ.'[8] Deeming it possible that EMI could wind up in court on a charge of blasphemy, he pulled out of the deal in a way that made him the butt for much satirical comment, though Bernard's position as the brother of a Jew who had publicly won the commendation of the papacy had to be considered rather more delicate than that of most other film producers.

No great harm was done according to the recollection of Terry Jones, the Python who went on to direct the film.[9] Beatle George Harrison assumed the role of producer by creating a company called Handmade Films, and came through with the initial £2 million required to make the movie. It went on to make a great deal of money and now ranks in many people's estimation as one of the funniest films of all time. Shortly after the movie's release, Bernard encountered George Harrison on a transatlantic flight and experienced the warmest of handshakes, accompanied by the words, 'Thank you so much for turning down *The Life of Brian*.'[10]

Lew, meanwhile, was able to commence another year in an invigorating way by basking in a new endorsement by a new Pope. In January 1979, Lew and Kathie were invited to Rome for an audience with Pope John Paul II. The Pope had been among those most impressed by *Jesus of Nazareth* and wanted to show his appreciation for Lew's 'contribution to the arts and working to keep the nations together'.[11] Less awestruck than on his previous papal encounter, Lew had a clear recollection of the Pope saying what a wonderful thing the film was 'for all Christianity', and of his own response, 'No sir, for all people.' This was rewarded with a pat on the hand as the Pope readily conceded, 'You're quite right.'[12] Lew came away from the audience as a new Knight Commander of the Order of St Sylvester (with star), and with a ringing endorsement of his own for the new man in the Vatican. 'He's got great charisma,' Lew told reporters, 'I'd like to sign him up.'[13]

Lew was now easily the most decorated man in British show business, but honours for his output of films proved elusive. With almost twenty films completed and released, Lew made no secret of the fact that, in the continued absence of a blockbuster, an Oscar or two would not come amiss. For a while he was able to entertain fleeting hopes for *The Boys from Brazil* with Laurence Olivier playing a character based on the real-life Nazi hunter, Simon Wiesenthal, and Gregory Peck as the fugitive Nazi, Dr Mengele of Auschwitz infamy. Ira Levin, who wrote the novel on which the film was based, set the action in Paraguay but the movie was shot in Portugal, albeit with passable credibility under the guidance of Lew's chosen director, Franklin Schaffner. Lew was thrilled when it received a nomination for an Oscar, but that would turn out to be the full extent of its acclaim.

A similar fate befell *Autumn Sonata*, one of ITC's few more cultural ventures in film, for which Lew enterprisingly engineered a cinematic marriage between the two famous Bergmans, with Ingmar as its director and Ingrid as its star. True to the director's gloomy but searching vision, *Autumn Sonata* was a film of some quality and it also was nominated for an Oscar, but received nothing when the awards ceremony came around in April. *The Medusa Touch* (with Richard Burton and Lee Remick), which was also viewed by Lew as a candidate for honours, soon slipped into oblivion without troubling the judges. At this stage in his career, Lew's closest brush with the Oscars was provided by Shirley MacLaine's brother, Warren Beatty, who told Lew that he had just the right part for him in his remake of *Heaven Can Wait*. But Lew felt unable to accept the challenge of yet another career in front of the cameras. Beatty's film, *sans* Lew, subsequently went on to collect an Oscar for its art direction.

Lew was far too busy to be cast down. In February 1979 his holding company, now calling itself the Associated Communication Corporation (ACC), had done a £12 million shares and cash deal to take over the chain of eighty-one Classic cinemas. With the integration of this purchase into the operation, the number employed on the payroll of Lew's conglomerate swelled to more than five thousand. To its traditional holdings in television, overseas sales operations, theatres, records and music publishing there had also been substantial additions in insurance, property and travel, and a useful earner called Ansaphone. The only mild diminution of Lew's generally expanding empire had been occasioned by the selling off of Muzak. This was thought to be not entirely unconnected with Lew finding himself trapped in the Cumberland House directors' lift for three hours, back in 1977, with nothing but Muzak for company.

With the acquisition of the Classic cinema chain, Lew seemed likely to achieve some of the benefits of vertical integration of his film business – controlling the means of production, and to some degree, the means of distribution and exhibition of his product, at least in Britain. This did not put ACC in the same class as EMI, which controlled the largest chain of 315 cinemas; many of which had, on Bernard's direction, been converted into three- or four-screen auditoria. Even so, Lew's acquisition had to be deemed strategically useful, especially in conjunction with the establishment of Black Lion Films as yet another new division in the ACC empire. The original purpose of Black Lion was to churn out comparatively low-budget British films, mainly with a view to cashing in on the popularity of well-known television series. Its first film, which enjoyed some success, featured Ronnie Barker, television's most renowned prison inmate, in a comedy called *Porridge*.

These advances, however, were offset in the quiet recesses of the counting house at ACC by reports of developments in Malta. The good news was that a feasible tank for the *Titanic* model 300ft long, 250ft wide and 35ft deep had been built, and landscaped to Dom Mintoff's satisfaction. The bad news, as subsequently related by Bernard Kingham, Lew's production chief, was:

> Unfortunately, it leaked. No sooner had we filled it with water, than it ran out. We had to keep a large stand-by staff on full pay while we were plugging the holes . . . We started production in the Malta tank six months late. And no sooner had we put the models in the water than we had to take them out and reconstruct them – their relation to each other was on the wrong scale. Then we sank them, and they kept bursting – the water pressure was too much for them. It was endless. It was expensive![14]

With money being guzzled away in the Mediterranean and no actual movie in sight, Lew still desperately needed a blockbuster of some description. And in the summer of 1979, he got one. Seriously late by Lew's calculation of the law of averages, but for that very reason all the more welcome.

The cavalry arrived in the form of *The Muppet Movie*, which did outrageously well, as the Muppet television series had previously done, and for that matter still was doing, all around the world. Shot mainly in Hollywood, the plot was fairly rudimentary with the Muppets travelling eccentrically across America before lighting upon the movie capital of the world, where they are offered a film contract by an impresario called Lew Lord. Many of the stars Lew had deployed on his other movies put in guest appearances among the puppet characters, along with a few more including Mel Brooks and Telly Savalas. The extent of the Muppets' contribution to Lew's cause could be judged by the American figures; from eight movies released in 1979–80 by Lew and Bernard's new AFDC distribution system, no less than $38 million of the total $42 million grossed came in via *The Muppet Movie*.

As Lew publicly rejoiced in what he described as the 'unbelievable business'[15] being done by the Muppets, Bernard's executive career entered one of its trickiest phases. EMI was strapped for cash. Bernard's own barony, called the Leisure division and which included the film, cinema and theatre interests, was performing adequately. But the two other, more traditional areas of the corporation's business – records and medical electronics – were both in difficulties. High hopes for the company's future had been invested in EMI's costly exploitation of the invention of a new 'miracle' body scanner which had already been marketed in the United States. But the American electronics industry, not unlike its film industry, had no intention of lightly surrendering a large chunk of its immense home market to outsiders. EMI found its progress in the States impeded, while the American firms refined their own alternative invention. EMI's profits went into free fall – down to £11 million compared to £65 million only two years earlier – along with the value of its stock. In May 1979 there was a boardroom reshuffle and Bernard took over from Sir John Read as chief executive, assigned with the grim task of piloting the corporation out of its perilous situation.

Bernard's first effort to achieve a life-saving cash injection by doing a deal with Paramount Pictures, then owned by the giant American conglomerate Gulf and Western, failed publicly and rather humiliatingly. But by the autumn of 1979 he had steered the business into safer territory, with EMI accepting the embrace of Thorn Electrical, the leading makers of television sets, hi-fi and record players and white goods. Thorn stumped up £174 million in a takeover that created Britain's biggest show business conglomerate. These financial adventures curtailed Bernard's film-making activity to some degree, but never completely. When the freshly constituted Thorn-EMI board was formed, Bernard accepted an invitation to join it, and was granted oversight of film and theatre interests in the new arrangement as head of Entertainment and Leisure.

On 15 October, Leslie died. The long struggle with illness of the youngest of the Grade brothers ended at a hospital in Fréjus near his holiday home in Sainte Maxime in the South of France. He had been admitted after suffering another stroke. Both Lew and Bernard had flown in to see him in the last weeks; his son, Michael, visited him on the last days, and

Leslie's wife, Audrey, and his two children by her were with him when he died. Michael arranged the transfer of his father's body back to England, where a cremation ceremony took place at Golders Green, north London, in the brisk Jewish manner with family and a few close friends in attendance. Sheridan Morley, who was among the mourners, remembered there being some confusion, as people filed out from Leslie's service, with other people coming in for the next. Lew, he recalled, hesitated for a moment and was jostled along by his brother. 'Come on Lew,' Morley heard Bernard say, 'I'm not staying for the second house even if you are.'[16]

The occasion when all the stops were pulled out was Leslie's memorial service, held at the Liberal Jewish Synagogue in St John's Wood in December. It had been thirteen years since Leslie's heyday as Britain's leading theatrical agent, but many of his old clients turned out to celebrate his life and work. Robert Morley and the BBC's light entertainment chief, Bill Cotton Jr, led a succession of show business stars and other dignitaries in paying tribute to him as a family man, a resourceful agent, a quietly effective showman, a charitable benefactor, a loyal supporter of Leyton Orient Football Club, and as the first of the Grade film producers. Mireille Mathieu provided a vocal interlude in French, Edward Fox gave a reading from the Bible, Frankie Vaughan intoned Psalm 121 – 'I will lift up mine eyes unto the hills' – and Cliff Richard sang 'God be in my head . . .'[17]

It was a lively and moving celebration, but not one that shed much light on the central riddle created by Leslie's death. According to his will, Leslie, who had been regularly referred to in the press as an extremely wealthy man, left an estate valued at £40,562 gross, which was reduced to a total of £445 after the subtraction of death duties. This sum was to go to his widow, Audrey.

On these figures, it appeared as if Leslie had lived close to penury while Lew and Bernard were coining it. Only a few weeks prior to his brother's death, Lew had ironically complained of a drop in his income to £195,000 a year due to the fall of the dollar against the pound, which affected the American content of his monthly paycheck. 'I think it's a liberty cutting my salary like that,'[18] said Lew, making buoyant moan. Yet there was no objective evidence that Leslie, or indeed any of his nearest and dearest, were ever close to the poverty line at the end, or through any of his years of chronic illness. Nor was there any sign of impoverishment in his family after Leslie's death.

The solution to the puzzle was indicated in a column by Robert Head, City Editor of the *Sunday Mirror*. Head pointed out that Leslie was accorded an unusually long period of time in which to take advantage of all the legal ways of disposing of wealth before death, through the transfer of assets to family, friends and/or charities. Once regarded as the shrewdest of the Grade brothers at amassing money, Leslie had the opportunity to make it all melt efficiently away, so that a net 'petty cash' figure could be arrived at by time of death.[19]

It was always known that Leslie's powerful charitable impulses did not extend as far as the Inland Revenue. In *Still Dancing* Lew recalled the disconcerting experience of going through the agency's books after Leslie had been posted overseas: 'My little brother, I was soon to discover, did not believe in paying income tax, and for the next couple of years I had to work particularly hard to pay off the debts he'd incurred.'[20]

This aversion to tax never quite expired. Many years later, after the brothers had achieved the comfort zone of multi-millionaire status through the sale of the Grade Organisation, Leslie had another difference with the tax authorities. This was resolved after the Commissioners of Inland Revenue had issued a writ against him for payment of £28,000 in outstanding tax. For all his reluctance to pay, Leslie never appears to have got the better of the revenue commissioners through skirmishes with them during his lifetime. In death, however, his triumph over the taxman seems to have been virtually complete.

The impact of Leslie's death was felt most grievously by Rita, who had always been closest to the youngest of her three brothers and who was already in mourning for her doctor husband, Ian, who had died only a few months earlier. Rita's desolation became the main concern of the family, but she eventually extricated herself from depression by writing a lively memoir, *My Fabulous Brothers*, and finding a new career as a radio presenter.

TWENTY-TWO

Chutzpah

By EARLY 1980 LEW'S MOVIE-MAKING operation was delicately balanced. The Muppets had been able to save the day as crisis loomed in the previous year, but it was beyond even their powers to save *every* day. In the wake of the screen success of the puppet characters, Lew needed the big follow-up with real people taking the leading roles. And his hopes were high, though he felt it would be invidious to mention which was his personal favourite among his upcoming productions – 'They're all my favourites,'[1] he said.

Still, he was known to entertain great expectations for offerings along the lines of *Escape to Athena* (starring David Niven and Roger Moore), *Love and Bullets* (Charles Bronson, Jill Ireland and Rod Steiger) and *Blood Feud* (Sophia Loren and Marcello Mastroianni). And even higher ambitions for *Saturn 3* (Kirk Douglas and Farrah Fawcett), ITC's response to the new enthusiasm for sci-fi movies. But, like most of their pre-Muppet predecessors, none of them hit the spot at the box office.

Ironically, the best clue to where Lew was going wrong was provided by one of his own enterprises. Lew rarely paid much heed to the output of the Black Lion film division, which was mainly geared to providing movies for the domestic market, but in late 1979 one of its productions, *The Long Good Friday*, attracted approving attention at the London Film Festival. Put together by producer Barry Hanson and director John Mackenzie with a relatively modest budget of £1.2 million, the film was a tense and exciting thriller with Bob Hoskins playing an East End gangland boss at odds with more serious heavies in the IRA. It was undeniably violent and expletive-ridden but well paced and with an excellent sense of style and place. Lew's initial response was to have it cut in length and pruned of its bad language with a view to showing it on television, which would be less expensive than releasing it through the cinema circuit.

The movie was saved from this cruel fate by a mini campaign launched by some of the leading film critics, with the *Guardian*'s Derek Malcolm and BBC Television's Barry Norman among the most prominent. They had seen the film at the London Film Festival, and thought any mutilation of its content a thoroughly bad idea. As a direct result George Harrison's Handmade Films, which had previously rescued *The Life of Brian*, was drawn into the debate. Harrison's outfit eventually bought the cinema rights from Lew and organized the film's distribution. On general release *The Long Good Friday* did well in Britain and abroad, and was generally approved of by the critics. In his book, *The Once and Future Film*, John Walker described it as 'probably the best film that Grade made', though Lew personally had little to do with it. Rather more harshly, but not too far off the mark, Walker added that the movie 'showed up Grade's other films for what they were, rootless productions of no relevance to any nation, lacking purpose or passion'.[2]

Lew may have absorbed something of a lesson from this episode. There was some slight change in his rhetoric. Originally he had highlighted the quality of the stars in his productions. But his emphasis later was more often on the sensitivity and calibre of his directors, trying to underline that his films were well made rather than just showcases for familiar Hollywood names. However, with almost thirty films completed, and at least another thirty already announced or in some stage of production, there was no possibility of any significant change in direction. It had to be a matter of keeping on keeping on until the law of averages kicked in again.

Meantime, Lew was still sustained by what is generally known as a good press, but one of the type that can often have unhappy consequences through the buoying of false hopes. The inherent weakness in Lew's fast-track movie-making strategy was perceptible after his first ten completed films had failed to yield a hit way back in 1978. Yet the flattering coverage of his endeavours continued unabated. His method of taking the battle to the Hollywood majors was deemed to be one of the nation's great success stories, at a time when, admittedly, such stories were in short supply. As late as June 1980 the *Sunday Times* could write of Lew's already suspect

American distribution system as being a potential 'masterstroke'.[3] With hindsight, not only the newspaper's readers but Lew himself might have been better served by more sceptical assessment.

There was a high degree of jingoistic wish-fulfilment in all this. But there was also an element of compassion. Newspapermen really did like Lew very much, and even those shrewd enough to entertain doubts about his grand design could do no other than wish him well. Barry Norman might take Lew to task for his attempted mutilation of *The Long Good Friday* but he would still feature as 'the great and wonderful Lew'[4] in Norman's memoirs. Alexander Walker of the *Evening Standard*, probably the most clear-eyed observer of the scene, could write sardonically of Lew's (and Bernard's) operation as boiling down to a business that required them 'to mail off cheques to talented folk in Hollywood and wait for *them* to deliver the goods'.[5] Yet he was unfailingly nice about Lew, whom he described as having 'chutzpah of the most genial kind'.[6]

Inside ACC, however, it was beginning to seem like chutzpah of the more alarming kind, particularly after the board was joined by Sir Leo Pliatzky in February 1980. Pliatzky, a former permanent secretary at the Department of Trade, was accustomed to a relatively orderly flow of business. In ACC he found much that was orderly, with the various divisions presenting detailed figures about their operations on a regular basis. But there was virtually no paperwork relating to the high-spending film division, coupled with very little awareness of what the chairman had in mind. Efforts to obtain elucidation from Lew could prove unrewarding, as Pliatzky recalled: 'He'd say, "Leo, let me tell you a story," and end up miles from the point I was trying to make. He did things by gut feeling, and didn't care for figures. We never knew whether he was talking in pounds or dollars and, sometimes, nor did he.'[7] Pliatzky soon learned that the board not only had no control over the film-making side of ACC but that it was expected to have no control. Although ready to acknowledge that he was new to the weird and wonderful ways of the world of entertainment, Pliatzky did find this worrying.

In business terms, the best that could be said of Lew's relentless big-budget output was that it provided a flow of movies that was essential to his American distribution operation, that is if its high overhead set-up costs were ever to be justified, let alone recouped. On the other hand, the lengthening parade of films that were evidently not winners, and were often clear losers, made it more difficult to pull off the failsafe pre-selling deals that provided the underpinning for the whole enterprise, and reassurance for Lew's co-directors. Distributors around the world were less inclined to offer guarantees of upfront money when their audience expectations had to be markedly lowered. Lew needed to start raising those expectations again, and the *Titanic* project looked like his best prospect for doing so. In terms of credibility, he had a lot riding on events in Malta.

By the spring of 1980, there was some encouragement to be had in that the tank-related difficulties had been overcome and there was an end in prospect, getting on for four years after Lew had first been seized by the idea. *Raise the Titanic* ultimately came in at a cost of around $40 million, and would be bracketed by *Variety* among the front rank of the most expensive films ever made, along with *Cleopatra* and *Heaven's Gate*. It opened for business in the United States in the summer and quickly closed, and this pattern would be repeated around most of the world. The most charitable estimate of the eventual return to ACC was around $20 million, providing the substance for Lew's most enduring one-liner – 'it would have been cheaper to lower the Atlantic'.[8]

In truth, it was a remarkably boring movie. It was as if the ingenuity that had gone into raising the model *Titanic* had drained invention from all other aspects of the film, like plot, dialogue, character development and even basic visual appeal. Even the film's prime special effect had only a limited impact. Given the level of pre-publicity, it was hard to suspend disbelief sufficiently to feel that it was the *Titanic* that was truly being raised, rather than a model in a tank being craftily winched up. Looking back, it was possible to argue that things might have turned out better if the movie's first designated director, the distinguished Stanley Kramer, had not jumped ship even before the tank complications set in, or if Steve McQueen or Paul Newman, Lew's original first preferences, had been available for its leading role, which, perhaps presciently, they were not. But there was little comfort in such speculations.

Despite his brave witticism, Lew was hurt, and more than financially.

He always insisted on seeing more merit in the film than was apparent to most viewers, and was disposed to ascribe its lack of success to market saturation as a consequence of Bernard's *SOS Titanic* being released earlier in many parts of the world. But as Bernard's film had also done poorly, it did rather suggest that it was just generally a bad year for *Titanic* movies. Lew did have a modest point, however.

The Japanese distribution firm, Toho-Towa, which had put up $1 million in advance money for the *Raise the Titanic*, actually did well out of the film in a market which had not been diluted by having Bernard's production shown previously. In Japan, almost alone in the world, it was a genuinely popular movie. And reciprocally, Japan was very popular with Lew, though not entirely for cinematic reasons. As he put it, after returning from clinching the deal with Toho-Towa: 'In England I stand only 5ft 6ins but in Tokio I am so tall I feel like Clint Eastwood or Gregory Peck. It is a great feeling.'[9]

It would take some months before the full financial impact of the *Titanic* film disaster could be absorbed and delineated in the ACC holding company accounts. By the end of 1980, however, it was already clear that Lew was heading for trouble, and at risk of being cut down to Norman Wisdom or even Mickey Rooney size, which cannot have been a great feeling. There had, after all, never been any provision in Lew's original grand design for the almighty flop that annihilated all known pre-selling safeguards. While it was just possible to joke about the movie, there could be no joking about the corporate bottom line.

TWENTY-THREE

Power Game

SHORTLY BEFORE CHRISTMAS 1980 Olga fell down and fractured her wrist and had to be admitted into hospital. The family was alarmed, but her recovery seemed to be miraculously swift. She was soon back in her Grosvenor House apartment and, with the benefit of extra nursing care, seemed to be making further good progress. The men in the family felt that global business could be resumed as usual.

Her grandson, Michael, went to the United States with the aim of selling a new LWT documentary series there, while Lew felt that it was safe to go off and fulfil a prior engagement in the Philippines where, as the guest of President Marcos, he was scheduled to open the Manila Film Festival. Soon after Lew's departure, however, Bernard visited Olga and came away with the impression that their extraordinary mother had made another of her strong-minded decisions, and almost certainly the last. 'It's so hard to die,' she had told him, 'it takes so long.'[1]

Lew was in his hotel room in Manila on the night of 16 January 1981 when he received a call from Kathie at 2.30 a.m. reporting on the circumstances of his mother's death in Grosvenor House. Her daughter, Rita, had been with her at the time, as had Kathie and Kathie's sister, Norah. Towards the end, Olga had talked contentedly with them about her pleasure in having two of her wonderful three sons become lords, about the pride she felt in having her daughter marry a doctor, and about how lucky she had been in her long life. Her last words were, 'Oh! My lovely *kinder*...'[2]

'In a strange way,' Lew wrote in *Still Dancing*, 'although I had lost my precious mother, it eased my sorrow to know that her last moments were spent with such happy reminiscences . . .'[3] Nobody knew exactly how old she was when she died, but *The Times* in its obituary of Olga Winogradsky settled for 'approximately ninety-four'.[4]

No death can be regarded as timely, but had Olga lived to approximately ninety-five, it is hard to imagine that she could have died with the same degree of equanimity. The period following Olga's death would rank as the most traumatic in her eldest son's career, with the power and prestige he had built up over so many decades slipping inexorably away. It would have been intriguing to know how Olga would have coped with the experience of seeing Lew in the process of being toppled from his public pedestal. But it was probably a mercy that she was spared.

As a television tycoon, Lew's rare errors of judgement about public taste and the buying proclivities of the American networks had not proved expensive. The ratio of successes easily outweighed any loss-makers. But any lingering hope that this pattern was to be repeated in the film division was now on its last legs.

'ACC shock results hit shares', was the *Guardian* City page headline of 19 December 1980, giving the first official intimation of Lew's trouble in store. His holding company had been forced to halve its interim dividend due to reduced profitability, and the slump in City confidence could be judged by the movement of the share price, sliding to 48p from a year high of 117p. The December figures also revealed a seemingly irreducible company debt of £77 million, related in some measure to the underperformance of the film division.

It was the first, but by no means the last, evidence of the impact of the *Titanic* debacle. Among those anticipating worse to come was Sir Leo Pliatzky. He told fellow directors that in his glum opinion, '*Raise the Titanic* is just the tip of the iceberg.'[5]

The immediate internal consequence of the alarming figures was the discreet establishment within ACC of an 'inner cabinet' consisting of three senior directors under the chairmanship of Lew's deputy, Jack Gill. They were allocated the task of vetting all the company's spending activities. When news of this arrangement inevitably leaked to the press, it was reported that this triumvirate would be taking over most of Lew's functions and that he would soon be elevated to an honorary position as company president. 'That's rubbish,' Lew was reported as saying in rebuttal, with Gill chiming in loyally, 'Nobody is trying to push Lew out. It is ludicrous – he set up the committee. Our sole purpose is to rationalise our financial strategy.'[6]

That Jack Gill (no relation to Robin Gill, the earlier joint managing director of the ATV Corporation who had departed so abruptly) hoped to take over the company eventually on Lew's retirement can scarcely be doubted, but neither could the fact that he was a long-time Lew admirer and super-loyalist. After joining ATV in 1956 as an accountant, Gill had been entrusted with a series of responsible jobs including that of chairman of ATV Network television when Lew had been forced into retirement by the IBA.

Through the late 1970s, as deputy chairman of ACC, Gill had supervised the reporting methods of all the separate divisions to the board, with the exception of Lew's feature film domain. Lew's praise of Gill in the company's annual report was never less than generous. In the June 1980 report, Lew wrote, 'In Mr Jack Gill, who is both Deputy Chairman, and Deputy Chief Executive, I have someone who is closely beside me in all major decisions affecting the Corporation, and once more I am happy to acknowledge my debt to him.'[7] This accolade had been followed soon afterwards by Gill's assumption of yet another title, that of group managing director. In short, Gill, almost uniquely in Lew's long company history, was an heir apparent who apparently did not make him feel threatened. And Gill, who was then sixty-one compared to Lew's seventy-four, felt that time was comfortably on his side.

There was one aspect of Gill's rise that had caused Lew irritation. In recent years Gill had shown a desire to see his own name up in lights over some of ACC's more minor productions. Lew felt that showmanship was not one of his old friend's areas of competence, and made no secret of the fact. ATV's programme chief, Charles Denton, remembered being in Lew's office one day and finding him in a state of exasperation. Lew had just seen a billing for one of Black Lion's new releases, *Hawk the Slayer*, which happened to be preceded by the words 'Jack Gill presents'. 'I tell you this, Charles,' said Lew, 'Jack Gill Presents is a joke.'[8] It's also possible that Lew had been irked by the praise accorded to *The Long Good Friday*, which had originally been produced under Gill's aegis at Black Lion. But these aggravations seem to have been slight in the general context of a relationship which functioned smoothly in all other areas.

However, as Gill and his two 'inner cabinet' co-directors, Bill Michael, head of the property division, and Ellis Birk, a solicitor, went about their business of 'rationalising' company strategy their main focus was, as it had to be, on Lew's film division. Over the ensuing weeks stringent new limits to its operation were defined, to be observed once existing commitments were fulfilled. No more than a handful, perhaps four or five, big-budget films to be produced in a year and these only with co-production partners sharing the risk. No movie to be undertaken with less than 90 per cent of its costs covered by pre-selling pledges (compared with 50 per cent previously). Most importantly, the pressure to produce international films at such breakneck speed was quietly released with the dismantling of Lew's costly Associated Film Distribution operation in the United States. Two years earlier Lew had boasted that AFDC's existence ensured that he could not be 'browbeaten by the major distributors'.[9] But from March 1981 onwards his, and Bernard's, films would be released, as before, mainly through the traditional major, Universal.

Along with the pain of having to accept restrictions on his film-making output, Lew also had to absorb a body blow as president of ATV Network, which was at the time encountering IBA-erected obstacles in its quest for a renewed franchise. Although Lew's title was an honorific, as he could have no executive function, he was keen to maintain ATV's prosperity, and not merely out of sentiment. Its credibility, not to mention its cash flow, was of enormous importance to the film enterprise. Television, more than the actual film product, still provided the power base for Lew's international wheeling and dealing. It was also true that Lew found his hands-off relationship with television hard to bear, and there were times when his fingers itched to be at the controls again.

Crossroads was a case in point. The mega crisis of 1981 in Lew's favourite soap opera was the mooted disappearance of Noele Gordon from the series. Charles Denton was reported as saying in irreverent vein of her screen character Meg, 'Concorde could fall out of the sky and hit her on the head. She could be hit by a bus or swallowed by a whale. We will just have to wait and see.'[10] Lew found himself swamped with anguished correspondence from her host of admirers. The Birmingham chapter of Hell's Angels was among the thousands pleading for their heroine's deliverance. All Lew could offer was a limp public statement to the effect that Noele was a very sweet person who had worked hard for ATV, but 'I don't know whether she has a future role in the network.'[11] It was all out of his hands. Shortly afterwards, Meg was unsentimentally written out of the show and dispatched to experience a 'new life' off screen in Australia.

At other times though, Lew may well have been thankful for the chance to avoid any direct responsibility for the television company. Only a year earlier, ATV had found itself deeply mired in a long controversy about its drama documentary *Death of a Princess*, which dealt with the execution of an actual Saudi princess for alleged adultery. Imaginatively produced and written by Anthony Thomas, the programme precipitated a huge diplomatic row. The Saudi Arabian government was outraged, and the Foreign Secretary, Lord Carrington, felt compelled to proffer an apology for the programme's content on behalf of the British government on three separate occasions. It was said that the crisis caused by *Death of a Princess* came close to losing Britain millions of pounds in export revenue and that a full trade boycott was only narrowly averted. Through it all, Lew was the absolute model of non-interference, passing on any enquiries about the matter to ATV's managing director, Lord Windlesham, without comment.

In the end, it was not any one particular programme or series that incurred the IBA's overall disfavour. The main contemporary problem for ATV was the exacerbation of an old one, which could be easily summarised: too much Elstree, not enough Birmingham. This issue had come into even sharper focus through the late 1970s as a group of Midlands MPs took up cudgels in the cause of making the franchise more reflective of their own region. In wholehearted sympathy with this idea, the IBA issued a directive to ATV to sell off 49 per cent of its shares, preferably to Midlands business interests, before its franchise could be renewed in 1982. The instruction to sell shares was perhaps not the worst possible sentence for an ACC holding company anxiously bent on replenishing its coffers, but it was damaging to the conglomerate's ongoing television and film operation.

Meanwhile, under the promptings of Gill's strategy committee, now known in Great Cumberland Place as 'the Supreme Soviet',[12] there was a lot of selling going on in many other directions: the telephone-answering business Ansaphone would go, as would substantial chunks of property, and a buyer for the recently acquired Classic cinema chain was actively sought. Most of this activity had the objective of making ACC's annual figures look bearable for investors, or as bearable as possible under the circumstances. There was no conceivable way they could actually look good.

When the figures were announced in June there was no attempt to disguise the fact that the film division had racked up a prodigious £26.4 million loss, indicating that the poor audience response to *Raise the Titanic* had indeed been less than the full extent of the problem. Still, there was no way of avoiding *Titanic*-flavoured metaphors in the shrill of the newspaper and trade magazine headlines that followed publication of the accounts. For the *Daily Mirror* it was the story of the 'Iceberg that wrecked an empire', while *Variety* ventured 'Titanic loss, other anguish, hits Lord Grade'. In his *Daily Mail* business column, Patrick Sergeant sounded, a shade prematurely as it turned out, the death knell for 'Lord Grade's magnificent but disastrous assault on Hollywood'.[13]

Nevertheless, the expert City page comment was not quite so adverse as might have been expected. ACC had, after all, managed to declare itself to be still in profit even though it was in no position to pay a dividend. The pre-tax figure was £2.6 million, down £9 million on the previous year and only a fraction of the profit levels recorded in earlier record-breaking years, but better than the anticipated loss. Its achievement had been largely due to the creative expedient, initiated by Jack Gill, of mortgaging all future profits from *The Muppet Show* and *Jesus of Nazareth* to the First National Bank of Boston. Without these forward sales of television product, it was estimated that ACC could have been obliged to reveal a group loss of £20 million on the year. For City observers the profit figure was less impressive than the fact that ACC was evidently committed to scaling down its debt mountain, with borrowings reduced in just six months from £77 million to just over £40 million. Although the accounts did nothing to alleviate the depressed value of ACC's shares, some commentators were cautiously of the opinion that they might one day be worth buying again. This had to be progress of a sort.

With most of its immediate work done in England, the Gill strategy committee took off for California to see Lew's man in Hollywood, Martin Starger, with a view to effecting further economies in the American operation. Lew himself had serious work to do at home, trying to turn around perceptions of his film output, recently described in a *Times* headline as being 'Over-priced, over-promoted, mid-Atlantic and sinking'.[14] As can sometimes happen with press coverage, there were indications that compensation was being made for being too nice in the past, by being too thoroughly nasty in the present.

There had, it's true, not been much deviation from the previous low earning pattern with Lew's more recent film releases. He had entertained great hopes for *Green Ice*, deploying Ryan O'Neal and Omar Sharif in a story about the exploits of emerald thieves in Mexico. As an adventure tale it was an advance on the earlier *Firepower*, with James Coburn and Sophia Loren; and more credible than the less star-strewn *Killer Fish*, about a burglary gang who stashed their loot in a reservoir stocked with piranha. But like the rest of the films in Lew's exotic crime genre, *Green Ice* had failed to thrill cinema audiences. However, he was now in a position to trumpet two upcoming movies of a different order: *The Great Muppet Caper*, the natural follow-up to Lew's one box office blockbuster, and *On Golden Pond*, which brought together the seasoned talents of Jane and Henry Fonda and Katharine Hepburn in a crime-free New England environment. Neither of them, Lew told all-comers, could possibly miss. And in this instance, he would, eventually, prove to be half right.

Lew had also derived an ego boost a month earlier from one of his other productions. His Western, *The Legend of the Lone Ranger*, was selected for a charity premiere screening at the Kennedy Centre in Washington. The enterprise was conceived to celebrate the fact that one of movieland's more diligent cowboys, Ronald Reagan, was now even higher in the saddle as President of the United States. Kathie was also invited to the event, which was complemented by a private dinner for selected VIPs with the President and his wife Nancy. As Lew proudly recalled, 'only 54 of the President's friends were there, and we were happy to be among them'. It all went off rather sweetly and Kathie had raised a good laugh. The President, still relatively new to the job, kissed Kathie on the cheek before any introduction could be made, and attempted a recovery with the enquiry, 'Do I know you?' To which Kathie had replied, 'You do now.'[15]

All the same, by Lew's exacting standards, it had been an outstandingly mirthless first six months of the year. Never equipped with a reliable reverse gear in matters of business, he had gone through the motions of giving his imprimatur to the various reforms and economies pressed on him by Gill's strategy committee. But the process was hurting, and hurting very badly, and clearly undermining his paternal authority as father of the corporate 'family'. Through July, the atmosphere within Cumberland House became feverish with rumours of major changes in the offing when the Gill group returned from the United States. The hot gossip revolved around Lew either taking an honorific, non-executive position, or being booted out with Gill as his most probable successor. A subsidiary rumour, that Lew's nephew Michael might be a contender, was most likely injected into the mix to confuse the chairman's opponents.

It's not likely that much of the in-house gossip escaped Lew's attention but he was not reliant on it as a source of information. The most authoritative stuff came to him first hand from California. As anticipated, the meetings between the Gill triumvirate and Martin Starger in Hollywood were not without friction. One of the prime objectives of the mission was to get Starger to take a cut in his pay and percentage perks. Starger was not best pleased. And, as ever, Starger reported directly to Lew. Initially, his telephone reports were about his offence at being quizzed by the interfering delegation from London. However, as the discussions became more ill-tempered, Starger picked up on oblique references to circumstances that might obtain when Lew was no longer around. Putting it all together, Starger reported his impression to Lew that there were plans afoot to 'take him out'[16] very soon.

This was close to the mark, though Gill personally, unlike some others in the company, was never in favour of a corporate solution that removed Lew from titular leadership of ACC. He wanted Lew's dignity, if not his power, well preserved. Ideally, he wanted a formula that allowed Lew continued scope for selling the company's wares, but that would detach him from any buying activity. However, the impact of Starger's reports, combined with some City page commentaries openly advising him to stand aside and let Gill take over, convinced Lew that he had better move fast. Suddenly, the idea of 'Jack Gill presents' was not such a big joke.

There was a brief lull in events when Gill, incautiously as it turned out, took off for a holiday after the completion of his American mission. His eventual return to Great Cumberland Place could scarcely have been more disagreeable.

On 24 August 1981, Lew made his first overt move. He called a board meeting for two days hence without specifying any agenda. In the intervening period he worked on the sympathies of all those likely to attend, apart from Gill. He was reasonably confident of a loyal response from Louis Benjamin, the head of ACC's theatre division, who had taken over presentation of the Royal Variety Performance from Lew's brother Bernard. The same applied to Lord Windlesham, the managing director of ATV Network, and to Lord Matthews, head of the Trafalgar House Group which owned Express Newspapers. Even so, they were all seen and canvassed individually. Sir Leo Pliatzky, who was a strong proponent of the need for more transparency in financial matters and felt that Gill was moving in the right direction, was more of a problem. Lew told Pliatzky that Gill's offence was to allow his ambition to be an impresario to interfere with his financial stewardship of ACC. Pliatzky did not find this convincing, and their interview terminated with Lew shouting, 'I tell you, Leo. It's him or me.'[17]

Lew was even less confident about Bill Michael, who had worked so closely with Gill on the company belt-tightening exercise. Michael was accordingly given more flattering exposure to Lew's persuasive skill, and allowed a glimpse of how the prospects of others in the company could be enhanced by Gill's moving on. Ellis Birk, the third member of the Gill triumvirate, was conveniently away on holiday, sailing the company yacht somewhere in the Mediterranean.

The crucial board meeting began with what could only be construed as the flourishing of a large olive branch. Lew announced that in future all feature films would have to have full board approval before they were undertaken. This was something he would never have countenanced before. Then it was briskly on to the real business of the occasion. Lew announced: 'The motions are firstly that Jack Gill be removed of all executive responsibility forthwith, secondly that his contract be terminated and he be paid compensation and the post of group managing director be abolished.'[18]

Given Lew's careful pre-planning there was not much that passed for debate. The only two directors who voted against the motion to fire Gill were Pliatzky, the newest man on the board, and Norman Collins, its longest-serving member, then on the verge of retirement. The rest sided, reluctantly in some cases, with Lew. He had won hands down. Gill, patently dumbfounded by the occasion, angrily left the room, followed by Lew in an apparent attempt to soften the blow. In the corridor outside, a tearful Gill took hold of Lew in a clumsy embrace and said, 'Lew, you've got six months.'[19]

The publicly stated reason for Gill's departure was that he had resigned following the decision of the board to scrap the job of group managing director. Lew was quoted as saying, by way of elucidation, 'The job of managing director of the company is too vast for anyone else to deal with. So I'll do it myself.'[20] His separation from Gill was, he said, 'entirely amicable'.[21] To a suggestion that there were problems with his board because of concerns about his age, Lew responded: 'I have nothing to fear. I'll be here until I'm 100. I'm just a boy – a good-looking boy. Although unfortunately I have no hair.'[22] But what would once have seemed like evidence of Lew's super competence and confidence, now sounded more like bombast. Nobody was fooled into believing anything other than that a ruthless boardroom coup had taken place.

Lew's ambush of Gill did find some appreciation among those inclined to prize the skill of getting your retaliation in first. The *Daily Mail*'s show business correspondent, David Lewin, wrote up the events of the ACC's power struggle under the admiring headline, 'Super-boss! If you want play the Power Game, don't take on Lord Grade'.[23] More perceptive comment on the conflict tended to detect that another serious mistake had been made by Lew.

People who had invested in ACC were among those least reassured by his triumph, particularly after it was reported that Gill seemed likely to get a record £560,000 handshake for saying his reluctant goodbye. Commentary in the City pages largely focused on the fact that ACC seemed to be splurging more of its limited cash reserves to get rid of the one man who, on the record, had seemed most capable of steering the conglomerate out of its difficulties. From this perspective, Lew's victory may not have looked totally Pyrrhic, but it did appear to have an exceptionally steep downside. The already undervalued shares slipped further in price.

Meanwhile, the man who was to become Lew's ultimate nemesis had already established a foothold in the company. And Lew was getting to rather like him.

TWENTY-FOUR

'That Australian'

IN MAY 1981 A SEEMINGLY rash investor bought a million of ACC's ailing shares on the open market. Although this represented no more than two per cent of the total number of shares issued, he made a courtesy call at Great Cumberland Place to pledge his support for the company and pay his respects to Lew Grade and to Jack Gill, who at that stage had yet to be acquainted with his marching orders.

From the outset, Gill perceived the new shareholder as a dangerous customer; but Lew was not disposed to see him as much of a threat. After their first meeting, he would refer to the company's new investor dismissively as 'that Australian'.[1]

As it happened, Robert Holmes à Court was not a man who bought shares lightly. Nor, in point of fact, was he an Australian. Born in Johannesburg, raised in Southern Rhodesia and subsequently educated in New Zealand, Holmes à Court had finally graduated, with a law degree, in Australia. He also traced back an English lineage as the grandson of the brother of the fourth Baron Heytesbury (family motto: 'increased by labour they grow large'[2]), and there was an aristocratic aspect to his urbane if, some thought, rather condescending manner. His principal leisure interest was in breeding racehorses on a large farm, the Heytesbury Stud. He had a slight acquaintance with Lord Windlesham, who ran the ATV network on Lew's behalf, but, initially at least, no great depth of knowledge about the British media.

Holmes à Court's business career had been mainly, though not exclusively, pursued in Australia, where he had earned a reputation as 'the Great Acquirer'. His Bell Group controlled a large cluster of industrial, newspaper and television interests from his skyscraper base in Perth, overlooking the Swan River. Aged forty-three, he had made himself known in Britain by bidding conspicuously, albeit unsuccessfully, for both *The Times* and Rolls-Royce. He also held minor stakes in Vickers and Portland Rugby Cement. Although his bids sometimes failed, he rarely emerged from any stock market speculation on the losing end. He was said to be a shrewd operator with a keen nose for devalued stock. And Lew's company, reckoned to have group assets worth around £150 million, but with a market valuation driven down by its film-making losses to below £30 million, must have smelled particularly fragrant.

On the other hand, Holmes à Court's chances of securing control of ACC looked, from the outside, impossibly remote. This was because out of its 54.3 million issued shares, only 156,000 had any voting power. Of this 156,000 Lew held the largest number, around 23 per cent, with most of the rest being held by his boardroom allies. This entrenched position had not come about through any high degree of cunning on Lew's part, but was a consequence of the IBA's insistence that voting shares in TV companies should be well protected against potentially undesirable predators. Essentially, Holmes à Court could make money out of speculating in ACC's ordinary shares but, because of the two-tier share structure, he could not necessarily gain control of the company even if he managed to acquire the whole lot.

Confidence in the security of his own position soon enabled Lew to look more benignly on Holmes à Court's intervention, which at least had the merit of helping to stave off a complete collapse in ACC's share price. With this in mind, Lew was even able to welcome the next manifestation of Holmes à Court's interest, which was the purchase of more ACC shares in July, bringing his holding up to nearly 17 per cent. Lew was quoted as saying, 'I don't mind anybody buying the shares. It expresses faith in the company and Mr Holmes can buy up to 50 per cent if he wants.'[3] By now Holmes à Court had ceased to be 'that Australian' in Lew's private discourse and was referred to more respectfully as 'young Robert'. Jack Gill maintained his strong original reservations about ACC's new major stockholder; but Gill, although unaware of it, was already on the way out.

In the normal course of events meetings of ACC's ordinary share-holders were not of great significance. Because of their disenfranchised status even the largest shareholders had little influence in the governance of the company. Nevertheless, they did have the potential to make life disagreeable if they were not kept reasonably happy, preferably with money but, failing that, with a genuine prospect of money to come.

This was the case at the ACC shareholders' annual general meeting of 10 September 1981, held in Great Cumberland Place shortly after Jack Gill's ejection from the company. Among those present, bulking up the numbers of the regular corporate star-gazers, were stern-faced representatives of some of ACC's largest institutional shareholders, which included the likes of Imperial Tobacco, Norwich Union, Eagle Star, and the Post Office and Greater London Council pension funds. Also present, as the personal guest of the company chairman, was Robert Holmes à Court, whose shareholding had recently risen yet another notch to 29 per cent. It was a tough audience, and Lew gave it a performance of some brio.[4]

Resplendent in red and green Muppet tie with a Kermit motif, Lew thought the investors should all know that he was 'confident, buoyant and ebullient. Lovely word ebullient. Well I am. I have faith in this company.' They were also informed that he felt younger every day. They were not, however, permitted to inquire further into the reasons for his deputy's recent exit and the convulsion in the company's leadership. Some admired his deftness at turning evasion into a virtue – 'my word is my bond and I gave my word that I would not discuss the matter of Jack Gill's departure' – but few found it satisfactory. Nor was there much satisfaction to be obtained in the way of information about current trading figures, with Lew refusing to go beyond sums that were already in the public domain (his evasion on this point would prove understandable in December when ACC divulged another £8 million film division loss in the six months up to 30 September). But Lew was able to wax lyrical about the extraordinarily strong asset base of ACC's many divisions; and about the 'great future' that lay ahead, abounding in new opportunities. They were all, he confided, sitting on 'a gold mine' of old film and TV stock which could now be shown on video. And, of course, he wanted everybody to appreciate that 'I feel that all the shareholders are part of my family.'

At the same time, it was a family in which members had to know their place. When one shareholder suggested that things could be better if all the shares carried votes, Lew came back in jocular style: 'What would happen if Colonel Gaddafi of Libya bought shares? But I don't want you to repeat that because I know him, you see. I've just sold him twenty-six episodes of *The Muppet Show*.' But when another shareholder expressed disenchantment on the same score, there was a glimpse of Lew's steel – 'We built this company,' he said, gesturing towards his fellow board members on the platform, 'you either have faith in us or you get out.'

Holmes à Court, seated in the front row, was accorded a special welcome into the fold. 'I hope,' said Lew, 'he will get some idea from this meeting of what this company is all about. I want to congratulate him on acquiring so many shares at what I think is a ridiculous and ludicrous price when you consider the asset value of the company.' Holmes à Court politely acknowledged the accolade but made no comment. He was also demurely reticent at the impromptu press conference after the meeting, referring all questions deferentially to his host. Lew was moved to describe him as 'a charming, nice young man', without being drawn on whether he could figure in ACC's future as anything other than an ordinary shareholder. For the press and shareholders alike, Lew and Holmes à Court preserved a convincing display of amity, though Lew affirmed that there was 'no chance' of his parting with any voting shares.

Much of Lew's address made for smiles and some laughter, but shareholder happiness proved rather more elusive. 'Terrific cabaret, but very low on reassurance' was the terse comment of an investment fund manager summing up his take on the proceedings for reporters on his way out of the meeting. The occasion did produce a crop of colourful headlines about the lively performance of 'Lord Muppet', but it signally failed to enhance the chairman's credibility. Lew had effectively steamrollered the meeting, but in a way that raised even more question marks about his leadership.

The City was frankly puzzled by Holmes à Court's involvement. No commentator considered it at all likely that he could be long content with supporting Lew in a passive background capacity. It did not seem to make any sense. There was speculation that Holmes à Court might be tempted to lead a coup against Lew, but given the voting share situation, nobody could quite see how it might be accomplished, at least in the short term. Even so, the impression of some City speculators, as reported in the next morning's *Daily Telegraph*, was that 'yesterday's annual general meeting was probably the last that Lord Grade would command'. This indication of Lew's new-found public vulnerability was soon further underscored by renewed manifestations of shareholder discontent, particularly among the pension fund investors, over Jack Gill's reputed £560,000 payoff. This was deemed to be excessive, and aggravation on this score led naturally on to other complaints about directors' perks and the alleged lavish lifestyle of ACC's top executive tier.

Lew's story by now had moved out of the chummy show business columns and had become the property of the City and news pages. This meant that coverage of his activities was more likely to be in the hands of reporters who had never quaffed a drop of Lew's free champagne and who, very likely, had never seen the inside of the London Palladium. And the story line they were inevitably drawn to was not that of the irrepressible Lew on the way up, but of Lew stumbling on the way down. Viewed from their unsentimental perspective, Lew was a businessman who had dug himself into a deep hole by getting rid of Jack Gill, and had gone on digging deeper with his entertaining, but less than convincing, address to his shareholders. This was not in itself unfair. Indeed, it was objectively a correct appreciation of the situation, but it did result in reporting that was sometimes less than sympathetic, and not always strictly accurate. For Lew, accustomed to many decades of playing the press like a violin, it was a hurtful new experience.

As Lew's corporate competence was deemed to be in question, nothing seemed too picayune to illustrate the facts – or the presumed facts – of the matter. Lew was particularly distressed by press stories that emerged about ACC being a spendthrift company, needlessly maintaining a fleet of sixteen Rolls-Royces and an armada of company yachts. In fact, there were only four Rolls-Royces on the company books: one for Gill, one for Louis Benjamin and one for Lew (for which he had tendered his own model in part exchange), and one lying fallow in a garage. The actual ACC flotilla boiled down to three vessels: one for company recreational purposes which cruised the Mediterranean; another, tethered at a fixed location in the Thames, providing an entertainment facility for prospective business clients; and the third, moored off Cannes, which constituted the lone surviving prop of a movie called *The French Villa*, which never got around to being made.

Lew was mystified as to why these modest ostentations should have suddenly acquired such an inflated and carpingly critical significance when, in the past, a certain amount of swank in the enterprise had been deemed almost wholly praiseworthy. At the same time, Lew's dealings with his fellow directors became much less cheering. Residual guilt over the eviction of Jack Gill and uncertainty about the company's direction made once easy relationships in the boardroom more complicated, and often fractious. Accustomed to experiencing a high degree of friendliness in his personal contacts, and to witnessing a benign reflection of himself in the press, Lew was in dire need of a friendly, uncritical face. Robert Holmes à Court adroitly provided it.

Shortly after the shareholders' AGM, Holmes à Court became a familiar visitor to Cumberland House. As Lew recalled in *Still Dancing*: 'Robert would come in to see me at the office regularly and sit with me while I conducted various business negotiations. He appeared to be fascinated with the way I operated and, just by being in the same room as me, he was, he said, learning so much about the entertainment industry.'[5]

Holmes à Court was hovering in close attendance as Lew worked his telephone selling transatlantic distribution rights for his upcoming movies, *On Golden Pond* and Jim Henson's *The Dark Crystal*. He was wonderfully impressed. And Kathie got to meet Robert's wife, Janet, and they all lunched together, and they shared business and family reminiscence, and Lew grew to like Holmes à Court, as he put it, 'immensely'.[6] Lew took his new friend with him on forays to Los Angeles and Las Vegas, introducing him to Martin Starger and to Sammy Davis Jr, who, at Lew's request, agreed to appear in a TV charity telethon in Perth. Holmes à Court could not have been more appreciative.

It is highly improbable that a younger Lew Grade would have mistaken the obvious signs of an operator giving him a 'schmooze', but at this stage of his long career the effect of Holmes à Court's flattery was deeply soothing. In the eyes of old friends and acquaintances Lew must have detected an apprehension that he was finally losing his touch, but there was no hint of doubt in Robert's admiring gaze.

It is not clear from Lew's narrative at which point he began to perceive Holmes à Court as some kind of replacement for Jack Gill. But it is not improbable, given the exceptionally fast flowering of their friendship, that

Lew might have had this in mind for some time, possibly even in advance of Gill's abrupt banishment. In any event, by November 1981 Lew had clearly decided that the man who was now his 'great friend Robert'[7] should be accorded some recognition. And Holmes à Court, who had by this time garnered 51 per cent of the ordinary shares, did not appear to be asking for any excessive recompense for his continued, valuable support and counsel – just a seat on the board.

There was some complication to this in that all ACC board members had to be equipped with 1,000 voting shares – a nominal number, but their possession had to be approved by the IBA. It would be Lew who personally gave his assurance to the IBA that Holmes à Court was a man of integrity and well fit for television purpose. On 17 December, Holmes à Court duly became a director of ACC with the main official obstacle to his ambition, possible outright veto by the IBA, now behind him.

The uncertainty about what this portended was reflected in *The Times'* report, which commented on Holmes à Court's arrival at boardroom level that it 'either amounted to the timely arrival of the United States cavalry or a telling debut appearance of Sitting Bull'.[8] There was, however, no uncertainty that December was yet another wretched month for ACC, with the pension fund investors continuing to cut up rough and threatening legal action over the company's alleged profligacy, and the board in a state of despond at having to announce further losses. The situation seemed to be justifying the comment, recently made in the columns of *Screen International*, that the Grade empire was proceeding 'from vertical integration to virtual disintegration'.[9]

The conversations between Lew and his new co-director now took a more pessimistic turn, Holmes à Court pressing the alarm button with his suggestion that bankruptcy might be imminent. Early in the New Year the two men thrashed out the perceived options during a long session in the ACC's apartment in New York. Lew figured that the solution might be for Holmes à Court to take over responsibility for the financial side of the operation, effectively as Jack Gill's replacement, leaving himself free for film-making pursuits. But Holmes à Court had what he thought was a better idea, one that could relieve his good friend of even more worry. The final words on the subject were spoken between them on Concorde flying back to London. Holmes à Court told Lew that he was in a position to make a full offer for the entire company, and that he was prepared to go ahead if Lew gave his support and sold him his voting shares. They shook hands on the deal before the plane touched down.

What ensued was not, as had been predicted in the City columns, a coup against Lew by Holmes à Court, but a coup engineered by Holmes à Court with Lew's complete blessing and support – to start with at least. Aside from the voting share transaction, said to have been written on a Concorde napkin, there was no formal written agreement between the two men. But it was clear from subsequent statements that in the event of a Holmes à Court takeover Lew fully expected that he would be assured of (a) an elevation to dignified prominence as 'Life President' of ACC, (b) a free hand on the movie-making side, and (c) job and income security. At the time, Lew saw no need to get these matters clearly defined on paper as Holmes à Court 'kept repeating that he felt that I was ACC's greatest asset and that we would make a great team together'.[10] Later on, he would reflect, 'he performed on me like the greatest actor in the world'.[11]

Two days after their return from New York, Lew delivered on his side of the bargain. At a board meeting on 8 January 1982, he told fellow directors that he was selling his voting shares to Holmes à Court and that he hoped they would do likewise. There was surprise at this development but also, given the demoralised condition of the board, something akin to relief at what seemed like a way out. Holmes à Court was appointed chairman and chief executive and it was agreed that his Bell Group should prepare a bid for the entire company as soon as possible. Holmes à Court indicated that this could not be over-generous, given the company's parlous condition.

It took a marathon series of further board meetings, with the IBA closely involved at all stages, before the details could be done and dusted. But within a week the form of the deal had emerged. Lew would receive £318,338 for his voting shares, and a majority of the rest were 'irrevocably' pledged by other board members to the Bell Group on similar terms. The offer for the ordinary shares would be based on a modest valuation of £36 million for the whole group. Though displaced from the leadership, Lew provided public evidence that he was happy with his reduced circumstance and with Holmes à Court's considerate treatment of his own interest. 'I've got a job for life,' he exuberantly told

David Lewin of the *Daily Mail*, 'and I'll keep my office . . . We'll find a cupboard for Rupert.'[12]

The ostensibly amiable smoothness of the operation, however, was disrupted by the unexpected emergence of another bidder intent on upsetting the apple cart. This was tough on Holmes à Court, and to a lesser extent on Lew, but wonderfully uplifting for the long-suffering 'family' of ACC investors. Gerald Ronson, the rough-hewn boss of Heron International, a conglomerate consisting of petrol stations and property interests, had none of Holmes à Court's silky skills, but he did have a combative nature. As did his close business associate, Jarvis Astaire, an astute entrepreneur who had made a fortune with his closed-circuit TV boxing broadcasts, bringing 'The Rumble in the Jungle' and 'The Thrilla in Manila' live to raucous late-night cinema audiences.

Ronson came in with an initial bid of £42.5 for the ordinary shares, topping Holmes à Court's offer by more than £6 million, and a battle royal was joined. The thrust of the Heron attack was that ACC was being disposed of for much less than its true worth and that a British company was, inappropriately, being surrendered into foreign hands. It led to one of the most tangled takeover struggles of the decade with the law courts, the Takeover Panel and the IBA all drawn into a bitter conflict which lasted almost three months. Ronson never did manage to detach enough voting shareholders from their 'irrevocable' allegiance, but he certainly shook ACC's boardroom resolve with his charge that Holmes à Court, as 'a proven asset stripper',[13] intended to sell off bits of the company, as and when it pleased him, to the highest bidder. Sir Leo Pliatzky and Lord Matthews both tendered their resignations while the takeover battle was in progress, after expressing disenchantment with Holmes à Court's leadership.

Of more consequence to ordinary investors was the bidding war between Holmes à Court and Ronson. Holmes à Court's superior money power eventually won the day, but it would have to be with a final bid of £60 million, £24 million more than the figure he first conjured up. Those who had hung on to their ACC stock were paid out at 110p a share instead of the less interesting 66p they had been led to expect some weeks earlier.

Throughout the epic struggle for control of his company, Lew's head remained tucked well below the public parapet. At ACC board level, his support for Holmes à Court remained undeviating, despite Ronson's determined efforts to turn him as the key to delivery of the voting shares and IBA approval. Lew had, as he almost apologetically explained later, given his word, and there was no way he could possibly go back on the pledge he had made with a shake of hands on the Concorde flight. However, it was noticeable from late January 1982 onwards that Lew's warm testimonials for his 'great friend Robert' had dried up. This was no accident. Lew recalled in *Still Dancing*:

> I'd begun to realize that there was a decidedly different atmosphere in the company and that Mr Holmes à Court wasn't the warm-hearted Mr Nice Guy I'd thought he was. As soon as he took control of the company, he started firing people who'd been there a long time and were part of the ACC 'family', so to speak. For example, he got rid of Katie the tea lady, who'd been with us for years . . .[14]

'Katie' and the others who got early notices to quit could of course still leave the company with their heads held high. But for Lew there was more humiliation in store.

TWENTY-FIVE

Humiliation

THE 'JOB FOR LIFE' THAT LEW ENVISAGED holding down as Holmes à Court's close buddy and team-mate at the helm of ACC lasted just six months. And it must have seemed far too long, probably for both parties. Photographs of the two men together showed an intriguing development, the lanky Holmes à Court appearing ever more elongated and stiff-backed, while Lew became progressively more stooped and gnome-like. Their growing apart was almost literal.

While the strenuous takeover battle with Gerald Ronson's Heron group was in progress there were some grounds for believing that Holmes à Court had too much on his plate to be able to attend to Lew's precise role in the new order of things at ACC. But with his emergence as the outright victor in early April 1982, there was a clear opportunity for Holmes à Court to implement his side of the bargain with Lew by elevating him to 'Life President', or some such dignified eminence. Instead, on 20 April, he made a clean sweep of all the remaining ACC directors, with the sole exception of Lord Windlesham who was away at the time. Among those obliged to accept the chairman's request for his resignation was Lew. Patience Wheatcroft, one of the most able journalistic Lew-watchers, wrote in the *Sunday Times*: 'Overnight he moved from film mogul to third spear carrier on the left.'[1]

Lew commented that the man who now seemed more like his usurper than his team-mate 'was obviously well aware of the company's potential from the very beginning. Certainly more than our own board of directors. But he played it so cool that he never revealed his hand.'[2]

Yet, by this stage, Lew cannot have been surprised by his demotion.

Unlike Katie the tea lady, he had not been promptly invited to leave, but he had already picked up on enough broad hints to indicate that his continued presence was regarded as being less than essential. Shortly before ceding leadership of the company, Lew had been involved in negotiations with Paul McCartney over the sale of Northern Songs, the principal asset in ACC's music division. This promised to bring the long saga over the Beatles' ownership of their own music to a sentimental conclusion, and one that could also help ACC out of its liquidity crisis. The negotiations had stalled over money, with Lew deeming the £21 million offered by McCartney short of his own valuation. There was also some impediment in the fact that Lew wanted, if possible, to sell off the whole music division, while McCartney was only interested in securing the catalogue of Beatles songs, describing those he had composed as his 'babies'.[3] Still, the gap that separated them was not wide, and seemed capable of being bridged by further discussion. But when Holmes à Court took charge, Lew was given to understand that his services as a negotiator on this front were no longer required, and McCartney would also find himself chocked off. Sometime later ACC did sell off Northern Songs, for $48 million, to an eminent pop star, but the buyer would be Michael Jackson.

Even more wearing for Lew in his newly subservient role was Holmes à Court's attitude to film-making. The early indication that there had to be a low ceiling on any budget for new movies was bad enough, but the new boss seemed to have a special talent for spoiling Lew's enjoyment of the films he had already set in motion. One of the projects Lew had been most closely involved with was Jim Henson's film, *The Dark Crystal*, a complex fairy tale in which young lovers defeat a race of evil, grotesque creatures who have taken over the world. It was an expensive undertaking, and Lew and Henson were in regular contact at every stage of the film-making process. Henson expected this relationship to continue through the film's post-production phase in the early months of 1982. Prior to his becoming chairman of ACC, Holmes à Court had met with Henson and told him how fond he was of Lew, and how keen he was to retain his services. But Henson later recalled, 'it became obvious to me that he was completely cutting Lew out. I'd have meetings with Holmes à Court on the release of *The Dark Crystal* and Lew would be left in the next room.'[4]

In March 1982, there would be what seemed like an occasion for mutual celebration of the new Holmes à Court/Lew Grade accord when the Oscars ceremony came around. Lew had experienced some disappointment with *The Legend of the Lone Ranger* and even more with the second Muppet movie, which had failed to replicate the runaway success of its predecessor, but *On Golden Pond* had proved a big money-spinner and was rated as a strong contender for high honours. But when Lew flew off to Los Angeles, Holmes à Court felt a pressing need to emplane in the opposite direction, to attend to matters in Perth. In the event, *On Golden Pond* collected three Oscars, proudly witnessed by Lew. But there was not much in the way of office celebration on his return, though Lew did have drawn to his attention a stiff new Holmes à Court directive on the need to limit overseas business expenses.

After the dumping of the old directors from ACC's board in April, the relationship between Lew and his employer moved effortlessly from cool to icy. Lew avoided addressing him by his name as much as possible, and in his conversation with others, Holmes à Court was referred to as 'that man'.[5] The division between them was also mirrored in staff relationships, with many old hands pointedly insisting on calling Lew 'Guv'nor' to differentiate themselves from the overlay of new executive talent coming in. ACC was now a deeply divided family, with evidence of its discontents being shared by sympathisers on the outside. As comedian Spike Milligan wrote, in a stern letter to the *Financial Times*,

> Sir,
> Many people from the entertainment world will be depressed at the forced resignation (for forced it was) of Lord Grade. It was Lew and Leslie Grade's agency which helped hundreds of us during the post-war Variety years. But for them it would not have existed . . . he was a big man, he still is a big man . . . Holmes à Court has got the company not because he's interested in show business, but because he's nothing more than a business magnate. I am appalled at the short memories of the world of finance.[6]

There was some humour in the situation, but not of the healing variety. Lew happened to overhear Holmes à Court, huddled with some newly arrived Bell Group executives, having a good laugh about the old boy's string of failed movies. This put Lew in mind of Holmes à Court's string of racehorses, one of which, acquired for a million Australian dollars, had recently finished a distant last in its first race. At his next encounter with Holmes à Court, Lew deftly manoeuvred the conversation around to his employer's favourite subject of the turf, and announced that he had just acquired a horse for a million dollars, 'to keep yours company at the back of the field'.[7]

With barbed witticisms of this type being honed, the relationship was clearly into its end run. The final straw for Lew was Holmes à Court's intervention in the deal to set up *Sophie's Choice*, a film project, based on William Styron's best-selling book, to which Lew had become deeply attached, though it could hardly be considered in the escapist tradition of most of his earlier film product. With Martin Starger's assistance, Lew had managed to secure the services of Meryl Streep for the leading role of a young woman haunted by her past in a concentration camp. Streep's eagerness to play the part had been reflected in her acceptance of a lower fee to accommodate the movie's tight budget. A few days before shooting was scheduled to commence, under the direction of Alan J. Pakula, Holmes à Court came into Lew's office with an extra requirement. He wanted Pakula to come up with half of the completion guarantee money, some $300,000, upfront, before the cameras started to roll. Lew recalled:

> I was appalled and extremely distressed. I told him that such behaviour was unheard of. But he was adamant. Unless Pakula came up with the money, he insisted, no production. For me, personally, this was a catastrophic blow. The completion guarantee had not been part of my deal with Pakula and, for the first time in my life, I was being forced to go back on a deal. In desperation I offered to put up the money myself.
>
> No, he said. It had to come from Pakula.[8]

Pakula did come up with the money and, as the movie was brought in within budget, it was later returned. But the episode sharpened Lew's awareness that he was operating in an environment where his word could no longer be reliably regarded as his bond. Moreover, part of him suspected that Holmes à Court had engineered the Pakula problem with the idea of deliberately undermining his reputation for fair dealing. With this disagreeable thought in mind, Lew knew for certain it was time to move on.

On 16 June 1982, Lew resigned from the company he had founded and run for twenty-seven years looking infinitely more cheerful than he had done for many months past. His carefully prepared one-liner for the press indicated the liberating nature of the occasion – 'You can say The Lone Ranger rides again.'[9]

The deepest irony of Lew's career as a movie mogul was that his greatest hits, with the exception of *The Muppet Movie*, all put in their appearance after he had been shuffled off centre stage. The critical and commercial success of *On Golden Pond* would be followed by more of the same with Jim Henson's *The Dark Crystal* and with *Sophie's Choice*, for which Meryl Streep's performance was awarded an Oscar. But by the time *Sophie's Choice* came out Lew had long since moved on from ACC. In his book *The Once and Future Film*, John Walker ventured the opinion that had *On Golden Pond* and *The Dark Crystal* been available for earlier release, 'they might have saved Grade from the loss of his company'.[10]

It is also worth noting that none of these films was in the all-action adventure style that Lew originally thought would pave his way to blockbuster success. They were also, interestingly, all conceived at a time when Lew was coming under increasing pressure to slow down. He had no choice but to be more selective about his targets. After the chastening experience of *Raise the Titanic*, the record shows that the Lew–Starger partnership did become more efficient at picking winners.

It is possible to render a harsh judgement on Lew for his last year in office at ACC, seeing it as exemplifying the obstinacy of an old man ready to put himself and his oldest friends in his company through the wringer in a desperate attempt to cling on to power. In mitigation, however, it is important to recognise that it was not the exercise of power over other people that constituted Lew's prime motivation, but the power to go on making movies, something at which, admittedly rather late in the day, he was showing a glimmer of promise.

So could Lew's grand design have ever worked out? With a little more luck, and a shade more judgement, his run at it could certainly have been extended. Had his four greatest hits come earlier in his long film parade, had he scuppered *Raise the Titanic* before its Maltese cost escalation, and had Bing Crosby not fallen into a Pasadena orchestra pit and derailed the

'Road' movie, Lew could have bought himself more time. But the effort to seize a chunk of Hollywood's home market, given the dominance of the traditional majors, was probably never destined to last for very long. In his authoritative book, *The Media in Britain*, Professor Jeremy Tunstall saw the odds as always being stacked against success for Lew's ACC and Bernard's EMI in their attempt to become major independent producers in Hollywood. Many other 'indy majors' had been that way before and the story, Tunstall records, was invariably the same – 'initial investment, some limited success, and then costly disaster'.[11]

Lew's removal from front-line mogul status could scarcely have been more public with the word 'humiliation' featuring in many of the headlines. Bernard, however, was able to beat a slightly more dignified retreat from the movie limelight. He had already become semi-detached from the production process in late 1980, when, mainly at his bidding, Thorn-EMI had decided to offload the major part of its non-cinema and film leisure interests in a £16 million deal with Trust House Forte. Bernard, who was never comfortable with the manufacturing side of the Thorn-EMI operation – 'I'm not terribly interested in fridges and cookers, frankly',[12] he once confessed – went over to Trust House Forte as part of the deal, becoming chief executive of its expanded leisure group. However, he still maintained a keen interest in the film business by serving as a non-executive director of EMI Cinema and Films, with Barry Spikings taking over his erstwhile executive role. Carefully clarifying his status for the benefit of *Screen International*, Bernard said, 'I shall be remaining close to the film side, but I emphasize that Barry Spikings is in sole control, and my capacity will be purely to offer advice to him should he feel that he wants or needs it.'[13]

Despite the eruptions and dramatic twists in EMI's financial affairs over the years, Bernard and Spikings, with the assistance of Nat Cohen, had managed to ensure a reasonable continuity of film product. There was even evidence of some progressive uplift in its domestic output, ranging as it did from *Keep It Up Downstairs*, with Diana Dors and Willie Rushton deployed in a saucy bed-hopping farce in 1976, to *The Elephant Man* (1980), which elicited a moving and compelling performance from John Hurt. But the determined quest for another international blockbuster, as a follow-up to *The Deer Hunter*, proved unavailing. *Death on the Nile*, the predictable sequel to *Murder on the Orient Express*, sustained hopes for a while, but expensive musical extravaganzas such as *The Jazz Singer* (in which Neil Diamond shared top billing with Laurence Olivier) and *Can't Stop the Music* (with the Village People) had a disappointing impact on the box office. It was felt by many people in the industry that the obsessive pursuit of international success was leading EMI to overlook potential winners that were lurking under its own nose; and there was some weighty evidence to support this contention. *Chariots of Fire* and *Gandhi*, the two main British Oscar-winning films of the early 1980s, were both projects that had been originally submitted to EMI, and turned down.

One of the last big EMI pictures with which Bernard was associated was *Honky Tonk Freeway*, a strained effort to raise laughs about a Florida town which painted itself pink in order to attract tourists, and then got more than it had bargained for. The movie's production was dogged with delays and difficulties, but it was granted no mercy on its release in 1981. In the final reckoning, it was shown to have lost almost as much money as *Raise the Titanic*.

Possibly because its title did not so readily lend itself to witty, doom-laden headlines, *Honky Tonk Freeway* managed to escape the level of derision in the popular press that had attended Lew's most disastrous movie. But, as Alexander Walker put it in *National Heroes*, 'it helped to seal the fate of the last concerted effort to "beat the Americans" at their own game of block-buster film-making by employing them to play the game for the British'.[14] By the summer of 1982, Bernard, like Lew, had effectively ceased to be part of the big Hollywood picture.

TWENTY-SIX

Lew Also Rises

L EW DEPARTED FROM Great Cumberland Place without a payoff, but with some blessings that were well worth counting. His pension had been established at an agreed £46,000 per annum, while his already healthy bank balance had recently been refreshed by close to another half a million pounds from the combined sale of his ACC voting and ordinary shares. And he kept the Rolls-Royce.

There was a minor problem with his fixed abode, the Knightsbridge penthouse that he and Kathie called home, which had been attacked as 'a director's perk' by disgruntled pension fund investors. But the storm had passed, and Lew was allowed, on leaving his employ, to exercise the discretionary option to purchase the property for a kindly £125,000 (the sum originally paid for it by his company back in the early 1970s), rather than its then current market valuation of £405,000.

All in all, Lew could be considered nicely set up for a long, comfortable and stress-free retirement, which he never appears to have contemplated for as long as one millisecond. When things were going seriously awry with Holmes à Court, Bernard had loyally made the public prediction, 'Lord Grade may be down, but he certainly isn't out. I'm sure he'll come bouncing back.'[1] But even Bernard was startled by the speed of his brother's bounce.

Less than a week after severing relations with ACC, Lew summoned the show business writers to the Inn on the Park Hotel, overlooking Hyde Park, for a 'tea party' of smoked salmon sandwiches and giant strawberries, with champagne as an optional alternative beverage. They were there to bear witness to the fact that Lew – 'aged 75 but feeling 25'[2] – was back in business, with an entirely new family. His impressive formal title was to be chief executive of Embassy Communications International, the new European offshoot of a major entertainment group in the United States with interests in television, theatre and film.

Blending sentiment with business, Lew urged the raising of cups or glasses to the fact that the day was also the fortieth anniversary of his marriage to Kathie. By way of demonstrating his physical fitness for the new post, Lew did an impromptu dance routine, repeating it on request for those photographers who had missed the shot. To a question about why he wanted to go on working, Lew responded with one of his own, 'Is it fair to ask a man who is having so much fun to stop?' And he would rise above somewhat unfeeling mention of his greatest disaster. 'Look,' said Lew, 'I said I'd raise the Titanic. I did. The trouble was, I didn't raise it high enough.'[3]

The show was indulgently observed by the two founders of Embassy, the hard-nosed tycoon Jerry Perenchio, promoter of the Muhammad Ali–Joe Frazier fights, and the writer/producer Norman Lear, whose many screen credits included the lucrative transformation of Britain's Alf Garnett into America's Archie Bunker for *All in the Family*, the US version of *Till Death Us Do Part*. Both Americans seemed delighted with the performance of the new European figurehead for their enterprise, though not in the least surprised. They already had a good idea of what they would be getting. Not long before they had evinced their belief in the Grade family brand by inducing Lew's nephew Michael to abandon his LWT career and head up the television operation in California which represented their core business.

As Michael had served longer in the company and was technically his senior, Lew was naturally asked by reporters if he was prepared in future to call his nephew 'Sir'. 'Why not,' Lew responded, 'I'm polite to everyone.'[4] When it was indicated that his elevation to prominence in an international company which included a close blood relative among its many employees was, though undoubtedly impressive, not exactly the same thing as going it alone, Lone Ranger-style, Lew made the educated point, 'even the Lone Ranger had Tonto'.[5] The consensus was that it was good to have the old, pre-Holmes à Court Lew back, dancing and freely wisecracking and seemingly unimpaired. The operation, described by one journalist as 'Raise the Grade',[6] was deemed a great success.

As it turned out, the job of being Embassy's London supremo was not overly onerous. Most of the company's investment was concentrated in its sitcom factory in California, where Michael was being run off his feet. In an echo of Lew's original film-making style, Perenchio had told Michael, 'Just remember one thing. Shows are like pancakes – you keep throwing them against the wall and eventually one of them will stick and we'll make a lot of money.'[7] Michael later described the part of his job that involved pitching Embassy's shows to the networks as being not unlike 'selling crap to assholes', though later still he severely reprimanded himself for making 'a cheap crack'.[8] As Lew's role was deemed to be more ambassadorial, flying the flag for Embassy at film festivals and movie openings and extending the company's range of European contacts, he was never under the same pressure to produce.

Lew's operation downsized neatly to a suite of rooms in Audley Square in one of the quieter reaches of Mayfair. Although his powers of hire and fire were now limited, aspects of his earlier high tycoon environment survived. The enormous old oak desk across which Lew had launched a thousand deals dominated the main room, while his calls were expertly fielded in an adjoining office by Marcia Stanton, his loyal personal assistant for the past eighteen years.

During her last years at ACC Marcia had been especially prized for her deftness in shielding Lew from an excess of unwanted callers. This skill was no longer required to anything like the same extent, but there was usually something interesting going on to keep her occupied between regular duties of maintaining Lew's stock of Montecristos and organising his overseas trips. Lew tinkered with a number of projects, ranging from a film version of the Broadway musical, *A Chorus Line*, to a series about Flashman, the imaginative creation of George MacDonald Fraser. But he would eventually put most of his energy into the promotion of a real-life tale of triumph over adversity, which understandably had become one of his favourite themes.

He persuaded Perenchio to put up the money for a British movie about jockey Bob Champion and his fight against cancer. Champion's successful battle against the disease was ultimately crowned by victory in the Grand National astride a horse called Aldaniti that was also in the process of making a heroic recovery, after breaking a leg. Lew recruited John Hurt to play the lead and the feature film *Champions*, released in 1984, was the outcome. Despite its uplifting theme, the movie was unfavourably received by the critics, one of whom cruelly dubbed it 'Galloping Cancer'.[9] However, it did make money.

Less predictably, Lew was drawn to the subject of Steve Biko, the charismatic young Black Consciousness leader who had been brutalised and beaten to death in the custody of South Africa's apartheid police. This grim incident had originally been featured in a half-hour documentary by Jon Blair, an energetic, South Africa-born Thames Television producer. Blair was later persuaded to write a more extended version to be directed by Albert Finney.[10] In the film, called *The Biko Inquest*, Finney plays Biko's lawyer, Sydney Kentridge. Lew put up the money and, at Finney's request, undertook to get the film as widely shown as possible. Lew readily sold it to Channel Four, but even the Embassy connection in California could not come up with a buyer in the United States for what seemed like an uncommercial product. Undeterred, Lew pressed the film's merits as a prestige project on the top executives in the Showtime cable system, with a result that exceeded all expectations. *The Biko Inquest* was screened for delegates to the United Nations in New York, as a VIP special invitation event, prior to its general transmission.

Lew was with Embassy for three years with some interruption from a life-threatening bout of peritonitis which afflicted him after an operation on his gall bladder. This had him hospitalised for almost a month, and caused one of the rare postponements of his time-honoured Christmas lunch for the show business writers. He never came anywhere close to rescaling Hollywood's commanding heights, but it was a period that allowed him to decelerate with some dignity. And there were undoubted fringe benefits for others that flowed from the reduced scale of Lew's business activity.

The one most appreciated by reporters was that they no longer had to get up before the crack of dawn in order to obtain a private audience. Some were allowed to make appointments for as late as 8.15 a.m. Within the Grade family, Kathie came to appreciate the fact that her husband was up for occasional dinner parties, which had not previously been among his preferred social occasions. There was also some progress, of a more complex sort, in relation to his son Paul.

As a young boy, Paul had exhibited some delicacy of feeling in relation to his father. Lew boasted that his son always thoughtfully switched off the

BBC's *Doctor Who* before he walked in the door. The rebellious stage surfaced when he went away to Millfield School, and persisted thereafter. Paul left Millfield as a good athlete, accomplished at tennis and playing close to a scratch handicap at golf, but a modest scholar. He went on to become a worse gambler. As a young man, Paul's relationship with his father was severely tested when Lew had to shell out £250,000 to pay off his son's gaming debts. At one stage Lew threatened to disown him in an attempt at a shock cure for Paul's addiction.

Rows about gambling were made worse by arguments about his son's philandering and playboy lifestyle, though Paul was not altogether workshy. He had periods of employment in the car business and the music industry, but found it hard to settle down, either in work or in relationships. An early marriage had yielded two children, David and Georgina, affording Lew and Kathie the delight of becoming grandparents, but the union did not last. However, Paul had steadied by his late twenties, assisted by his mother's late development of a business interest. Seeking creative occupation after the death of her own mother, whom she had nursed for many years, Kathie bought the Ivy, theatreland's most famous restaurant and the preferred venue for Lew's Christmas media lunches. Her intention was to be a hands-on owner, and Paul became a co-director and his mother's principal assistant in this enterprise.

He was clearly a young man who had extreme difficulty in locating his place in the world, and matters were made no easier by his involvement in a weird court case. Early in the morning of 7 July 1980 he was arrested at his Wimbledon home by three police officers and charged with theft. It was claimed that he had been identified as the man previously seen in the area stealing a Harrods handbag from a young woman's car. Paul's protestations of innocence and of being a victim of mistaken identity made no difference to the slow course of justice. It was another two years before his case was heard at the Old Bailey, where after five hours' deliberation, the jury came back to announce that it could not agree a verdict. A retrial was ordered. Two weeks later Paul was back in the dock to hear the prosecution say that it did not intend to proceed with the case. He was not guilty, awarded full costs.

The *News of the World* invited Paul to unload his feelings about the stress of this ordeal, which he duly did, with more of an embarrassing nature to his family besides. 'Black sheep of the family: the wayward life of Lord Grade's son' was the strapline over the first in a series of articles published in January 1983. There was a sad confusion about their content, but the rawness of the emotion expressed by the young man about his upbringing and background seemed genuine. Paul's portrait of a father 'so busy making millions that he's never had any time left for family life' was not unaffectionate, but it was certainly harsh. Under the heading, 'If only dad loved me more', he was quoted directly as saying:

> If only Dad had stuck me in an office, made me work, probably I'd be a raving success by now. Instead I mess about. Wheel and deal. Dad will give me anything – except what I really want. His time, love and attention. Instead it's presents, gifts, a load of shares for my birthday. Sod the shares. I'd give the world to spend a normal family evening together, just the three of us, chatting, laughing, being close.

On the other hand, Paul never seemed to have developed an appetite for being force-fed his father's way of life. 'No way do I want to be a tycoon,' he says at another point, 'No room for fun. No hobbies, no holidays, nothing but work, work, work.'[11]

Lew's philosophy of work being in itself the best fun of all was evidently not one he had been able to pass on. There was however some indication of paternal influence at the conclusion of the series, with the editor's comment: 'Mr Paul Grade has declined any payment in respect of this series. Instead, at his request, donation is being made to his favourite charity, Dr. Barnardo's.' The fact that Paul was not prepared to profit from being so publicly wounding may have softened the blow, but it cannot have made easy reading for Lew or Kathie. However, it did appear to have something resembling a catalytic effect. Relations between Lew, with more time available for family matters, and Paul, with some powerful resentments declared and off his chest, did markedly improve. A few years later Paul was quoted in *Variety* describing Lew as 'a real special guy' and 'a really great, great father'.[12]

The most substantial improvement in Lew's family relationships was in that with his brother Bernard, which moved from the competitive to the mutually supportive. The days when they had only communicated, often a shade edgily, at family gatherings were long gone. They were now often on the phone to one another swapping anecdotes and ideas. There had already been some easing of the tension between them after Leslie's illness had brought them closer together, but this process had subsequently been disturbed by the problems relating to the American film distribution project and the unfortunate case of the two *Titanics*. With these frictions well behind them, there was a flowering of brotherly affection.

Time had rendered them, if anything, more dissimilar in appearance. Lew, becoming more round-shouldered with advancing years, closely resembled a diminutive reincarnation of Winston Churchill, though his cigar seemed to be a shade longer than the one sported by the war leader. Bernard, contrastingly, still held himself erect and was blessed with a full thatch of hair which, expertly shampooed and blow-dried by Carole every morning, rose dramatically from his forehead in an impressive bouffant style. People said that Bernard looked like a man in his fifties; while Lew did look his age, even if he was never inclined to act it. However, in most other respects, the two brothers were coming to a recognition of their more and more basic similarities.

Both had made bold late career moves in order not to be sidelined and rendered redundant. Lew, as we have seen, went into films, while Bernard's prime motivation in steering his leisure group out of Thorn-EMI and into the arms of Trust House Forte had been to avoid a company regulation requiring senior executives to retire at the age of seventy. Thereafter, Bernard had gone on, in late 1982, to maximise his insulation against any threat of compulsory retirement by negotiating a management buyout of the leisure group from Trust House Forte, raising an impressive £38.5 million in the City to facilitate the arrangement.

As chief executive, aged seventy-three, of his new creation, the First Leisure Corporation, Bernard's range was slightly more limited than it had been in his earlier days at EMI. There was no film division, for example. Bernard saw it as being 'too volatile'[13] for First Leisure. But there were West End theatre interests with the Prince Edward, doing just fine with *Evita*, and the Prince of Wales, profitably revisiting *Underneath the Arches*; along with a constellation of ten-pin bowling alleys, snooker halls, discotheques, restaurants, squash courts, seaside piers, yacht marinas, holiday parks and, the jewel in the corporate crown, a magnificent complex of leisure interests in Blackpool, including its Tower and the Winter Gardens. With the arrival of bargain basement air fares for British holidaymakers, there would come a time when it was said that the donkeys on Blackpool beach were reduced to giving each other rides. Bernard was fortunate enough to surf the last commercial wave before that dire development. In his day Blackpool could still count on getting in excess of fifteen million holidaying visitors a year, many of whom were intent on being lightly entertained in one or other of his facilities.

There were some ironies in the situation for Lew and Bernard as two go-getting septuagenarians, but they were of the kind that naturally brought them into a closer understanding of each other. For most of their lives, Lew had perceived himself as the organisation man in the family, while Bernard had seemed keener to hang loose and preserve a freelance status, at least until Leslie's illness had dictated a change of direction. Now their roles were close to being reversed, with Bernard immersed in the day-to-day running of a large organisation, and Lew operating with a high degree of independence on the fringe of someone else's outfit.

Similarly, Bernard as the gambler in the family had always been regarded as its greatest risk-taker, sailing closest to the business wind. However, this estimate had to be seriously revised after Lew's incursion into film-making, which represented gambling on a scale that appeared reckless even by Bernard's advanced standards. The consciousness that they were more alike than even they themselves had perceived contributed to their intimacy as senior citizens. But there was another important element. For the first time in their adult lives, they could relate to one another without any prospect of being in competition: Lew being resolved never again to expose himself to the harrowing rigours of big-time boardroom politics, while Bernard was equally determined never to get seduced into making another movie.

Lew's Embassy connection ended in August 1985 when Jerry Perenchio sold off the whole enterprise to the Coca-Cola Company, which in turn sold on the film side of the operation to Dino De Laurentiis. Michael had already taken off from the Embassy payroll some time earlier to become, at the age of forty-two, a youthful Controller of BBC1. He was already trailing clouds of glory in this new role, as the man who introduced *EastEnders* into the BBC schedule (though it was originally conceived prior to his watch), and making a distinctive contribution to the Grade brand image by always exhibiting himself in shirtsleeves, with brilliantly red braces as a complement to the trademark cigar. His uncle, meanwhile, still under doctor's orders to take it easy after his encounter with peritonitis, was confronted with the need for another 'Raise the Grade' operation. Lew was technically out of work for six weeks before resurfacing in October with a new film production company, his own, which he called simply The Grade Company.

He now conformed much more closely to his self-description as the Lone Ranger, with Marcia Stanton, still securely in post, as his faithful Tonto. He was nonetheless a lone rider, with several irons warming in the campfire. Coca-Cola had decided to have a piece of him as its 'entertainment consultant'. Jerry Perenchio maintained his connection by appointing him as a vice-chairman of Loews, the prestigious American cinema chain. And Lew was still doing interesting business with his film-making buddy, Martin Starger, their most profitable new venture being a co-production of Andrew Lloyd Webber's musical *Starlight Express* on Broadway. However, it was the old business with Starger that caused Lew's next most flagrant exposure in the headlines.

For the sake of public appearances, Lew maintained the fiction that he and Robert Holmes à Court had separated on good terms, affirming a readiness to do more business with him in future if a suitable project presented itself. This pretence failed to survive 1986, when Starger took Holmes à Court's Bell Group to the High Court, claiming non-payment of $5 million (about £3.3 million) in fees and royalties for his film-making efforts.

The action arose out of the 1977 agreement under which Starger had been taken on by Lew as his creative consultant in Hollywood. The major part of the claim related to *On Golden Pond* and *Sophie's Choice*, which yielded the bulk of the profits after Lew had handed over the reins of power at ACC. Holmes à Court, feeling himself not bound to honour what was termed an 'over-generous, sweetheart deal'[14] between Lew and Starger, was not paying up. And Starger was not inclined to go whistle for his money. Unlike Lew, he had never enjoyed a honeymoon period with Holmes à Court, distrusting him from the beginning of their acquaintance. After every meeting with ACC's new boss, he had made careful notes of what had been said, a precaution which later made him an excellent witness in court. When the case came up for hearing in October 1986 Starger's counsel, Sydney Kentridge, the QC who had previously represented Steve Biko's family at his inquest, opened aggressively, asserting that Holmes à Court had 'a mean and unscrupulous attitude towards the payment of the company's obligations'.[15]

But Holmes à Court could be a lot meaner than even Starger had suspected. His affidavit, which was read out in court on the second day, affirmed a suspicion that Starger and Lew had a secret deal which involved Starger paying half the money he received for his share in any movie profits back to Lew in the form of 'kickbacks';[16] in essence, a fraudulent arrangement that deprived ACC's shareholders of legitimate funds. This sensational allegation was immediately denied by Starger but his testimony manifestly required corroboration by Lew to be effective. A date for Lew's appearance in court was set, though he never made it into the witness box.

In the ensuing proceedings, the detailed evidence and documentation in the case clearly moved strongly in favour of Starger, and on 17 November, Holmes à Court's representatives threw in their hand. There had been a settlement. Kentridge rose to tell the court that the 'serious allegations of fraud' had been formally withdrawn and that Starger's action had been settled for 'a considerable sum – considerable even by the standards of the film industry',[17] though he could not disclose the exact amount. It was in fact for the full extent of Starger's claim, plus interest, making a final figure of close to $8 million. The costs of the action, estimated at £700,000, were allocated for payment by the Bell Group.

Lew was outside the High Court, waiting to give his own evidence, when the climbdown by Holmes à Court's company was announced. Magnanimous in what was, in terms of reputation, even more of a victory for him than it was for Starger, he told reporters, 'I bear no grudges against Mr Holmes à Court, but whether I would do business with him is another matter.'[18]

Lew always insisted that the Starger case had never presented him with any personal worries, but his evident jubilation at its conclusion did suggest that his vindication ranked as an especially welcome early eightieth birthday present. The best actual birthday present was the 24 December

1986 issue of *Variety*, which ran an immense twenty-page 'Lord Lew Grade 80th Birthday Salute' headlined, 'From Vaud Boards to House of Lords'. Among the tributes from Hollywood's finest, there were many paid-for advertisements extolling Lew's virtues, placed by the showbiz outfits and personalities he had come into contact with over his long career. Organisations on both sides of the Atlantic were well represented, with the notable absence of anything from the old ACC companies taken over by Holmes à Court. It emerged that ITC and the costumiers Bermans and Nathans, another subsidiary, had reserved space when first approached by *Variety*, but later pulled out after receiving guidance from on high.

The business between Lew and Holmes à Court was still not quite finished. In April 1987 Lew's quarterly pension cheque failed to put in an appearance. This time it was Lew's turn to seek the assistance of the High Court and the threat of proceedings proved to be enough. His pension was restored three days before the case was due to be heard. When, later in the year, Holmes à Court's international empire took a battering on the occasion of the Stock Exchange crash of Black Wednesday, Lew was understandably unmoved. Nor could he muster any great show of grief when the news came through that Holmes à Court, aged fifty-three, had died from a sudden heart attack in Perth on 2 September 1990, though, when asked to comment, Lew did impassively observe, 'he died quite a young man for all his millions'.[19]

On arriving in his eighties, Lew made a slight adjustment to his retirement programme. Attracted by the prospect of going out on a round number, he indicated that he was advancing the date when he would 'consider'[20] giving up work by a full twelve months, to the year 2000 (when he would be ninety-four). His brother was of much the same mind. Bernard did not entirely rule out an earlier retirement, almost certainly as a way of keeping the peace with Carole, but said that he did not want to spend an excessive amount of time 'sitting in God's waiting room'.[21] And, like Lew, he always claimed that, whatever people might say, he worked on for the fun of it, not the money.

For the many who spent a large portion of their working lives keenly looking forward to the ease of retirement such an assurance fell on sceptical ears. There had to be a presumption that Lew and Bernard, probably the most highly publicised businessmen of their era, could not abandon a reverence for Mammon which compelled them to go on amassing ever greater personal wealth when they could have been cultivating their gardens in the manner deemed appropriate to their age. For a while at least, *Private Eye*'s characterisation of Lew as 'Low Greed' did not seem to be entirely misplaced. In this regard, the credibility of both brothers was well served by the *Sunday Times Book of the Rich*, first published in 1990. This was because neither of them was in it.

The bar was set relatively high. To qualify as being among the four hundred richest people in Britain, there had to be evidence of personal wealth of £20 million or above. Even so, the list featured a large number of people in the world of entertainment who were reckoned to have the wherewithal to merit inclusion. Although it was not the central point of the enterprise, the information assembled by Philip Beresford and his two able researchers, Patrick 'Paddy' Masters and Kevin Cahill, did provide for the first time a relatively accurate comparative portrait of the people who made major fortunes out of the entertainment business. And it was evidently not Lew Grade and Bernard Delfont.

Among those who dwarfed them in terms of wealth were the pop stars, with Paul McCartney way out front on £380 million, and with, in descending order from £100 million down to £20 million, Elton John, Mick Jagger, George Michael, Cliff Richard, Sting, George Harrison, Sheena Easton, Rod Stewart, Phil Collins and David Bowie. Next to being a pop star, the clearest avenue to great wealth was the ability to compose popular songs or promote their singers. This helped to explain Andrew Lloyd Webber at £80 million, along with Mickie Most, the pop Svengali who blazed a trail for Simon Cowell, and Peter Waterman, the pop promoter, both in the £55 million region.

There were also manifestly large rewards possible for impresarios more adept than Bernard at actually holding on to their gains. Thus Cameron Mackintosh, the man who introduced *Cats* to the West End and the rest of the world, at £75 million, and Paul Raymond, whose Revuebar raised the profile of sex in Soho to a new level, at £60 million. Among those who managed to creep into the bottom of the list were Britain's top male movie stars, Michael Caine and Sean Connery, respectively at £25 million and

£20 million. The sisters Joan and Jackie Collins, who regarded Lew as their surrogate 'Uncle',[22] were listed as being jointly worth £30 million.

None of the above named, of course, came anywhere near to Lew and Bernard in terms of job creation in show business and influence on its overall output. But all the evidence indicates that they were not that much interested in maximising their own personal wealth, and were content with the modest status of being single-digit multi-millionaires, giving away almost as much as they earned. Lew claimed that his wealth was better measured in terms of the quantity of friendly relationships rather than money. On that yardstick, he did place himself close to the top.

Although Lew and Bernard were not in the super-rich elite, and did not aspire to be, they were on excellent hobnobbing terms with some of those who were. The property developer and philanthropist, Lord (Max) Rayne (£75 million), had as chairman of the National Theatre been one of Lew's greatest cheerleaders during his Shakespearean period at ATV, and had subsequently headed the consortium of City interests that enabled Bernard to effect the buyout whereby the First Leisure Corporation was created. The hotelier Lord (Charles) Forte (£167 million) could also be counted as a good friend. He and Bernard had experienced some disappointment when their main joint venture, the Talk of the Town supper and cabaret enterprise, had finally been obliged to cease trading for want of enough customers, but they remained close during Bernard's association with Trust House Forte. And Lew and Bernard could rightfully claim to be on warmer terms than most with the richest person in the first *Book of the Rich* – Queen Elizabeth II, listed with £7,000 million as head of state.

Despite the opportunities for improving his acquaintance with the country's great and good in the House of Lords, Lew never made much of them. He delivered one speech in the Lords, about the television franchise, and took advantage of its excellent catering arrangements to celebrate his and Kathie's fiftieth wedding anniversary there, but was rarely seen inside its precincts at other times. He maintained that he served his country better by sitting behind his desk helping its export trade. Bernard, similarly, stated a preference for 'the coal-face'[23] over the debating chamber. As both men were effective public speakers and eminently intelligent, it was possible to regard this as some loss to the national debate. However, neither brother lost his diffidence in relation to politics. As first-generation immigrants, they seem to have had inculcated in them the notion that it was unwise to be too freely opinionated in their country of adoption. Sensitivity on this point may have declined after Olga's death, but the habit of reticence outside their area of competence remained.

Both brothers produced ghost-assisted memoirs, though at an interval that precluded their being in direct competition. Lew's *Still Dancing*, crediting assistance by Kathie, Marcia and veteran *Sunday Express* theatre critic Clive Hirschhorn, was published in 1987, while Bernard's *East End, West End*, written with Barry Turner, a young ex-*Observer* journalist, came out three years later. Lew's book launch, at which he paraded around flourishing a custom-built 24-inch cigar, was more spectacular than anything that could be mustered on Bernard's behalf. But Bernard delivered much the better book.

Neither publication set the Thames alight, but Bernard's urbane and mildly ironic style conveyed the highs and lows, along with the affections, animosities and some of the ambiguities, experienced in a long and complicated career. Lew's effort, however, did him few favours. His book had most charm when describing his dancing years as Jack the Lad, hopefully lugging his oval table round Europe. But it soon dissolved into a relentlessly sunny-side-up appreciation of the many real and wonderful people he met on his business travels who became such staunch and loyally abiding friends. All this was undoubtedly true, but a bit cloying when serious problems encountered along the way tended to be rapidly surfed over, minimised or simply not mentioned. Another unfortunate consequence of the high tide of *schmaltz* was that it came close to drowning the author's natural wit.

The overall effect was to produce an impression that a life story was being sold, rather than told; no great surprise perhaps, given that selling was Lew's forte. But in this specialised case, the talent was misplaced. *Still Dancing* was politely reviewed by Lew's chums in the showbiz press, but for most general readers there must have been a huge element of relief when a character called Holmes à Court puts in an appearance, and Lew finally grants himself permission to say something nasty about somebody for a change.

TWENTY-SEVEN

Grindstone

L EW'S FIRST STRATEGIC MOVE ON behalf of his fledgling Grade production company was to acquire the rights to Barbara Cartland's romantic novels, most noteworthy for having heroines who seldom went voluntarily to bed with a man without having a ring firmly affixed on the relevant digit. Cartland had speed-written no fewer than 416 of them, though Lew, more mercifully, only made television films of four.

'A victory for purity over pornography'[1] was Cartland's view of the project, and Lew evidently saw it in much the same light. He certainly gave the enterprise his best shot after obtaining an expression of interest from the CBS television network in America. The first two-hour film off the production line was *Hazard of Hearts*, a swashbuckling Regency romance with Edward Fox, Stewart Granger and Christopher Plummer as the dashingly handsome male leads, Diana Rigg as the scheming, black-hearted villainess, and Helena Bonham Carter as the essential endangered virgin.

Perceiving it as a product capable of turning the permissive tide, Lew was quoted in the press as saying: 'What's exciting in these times is to come up with a movie without sex and violence. We had a couple of duels, that's all. We don't go around murdering everybody like they do in *Miami Vice*. And there's no bad language either.'[2]

As it turned out, *Hazard of Hearts* failed to excite its home audience when it was shown on BBC Television. But the Americans and the Germans rather took to the genre, and would come back for *Dangerous Love* and a couple more that sold well on video. This comfortably extended Lew's career into the 1990s, by which time he had added to his consultancy chores by accepting an invitation to serve on the supervisory board of Euro Disneyland, then in the process of building its £1 billion theme park near Paris. Lew's sagacious counsel was much appreciated, though he caused mild disappointment to the Disney publicity department by declining an opportunity to test-drive the Space Mountain roller coaster for promotional purposes.

At this stage of his life Lew may have felt that the roller-coaster aspect of his favourite nephew's career was providing more than adequate exhilaration. Having found his view of the route to the top of the BBC obscured by the bulk of John Birt, an executive who had been his junior at LWT, Michael had taken a sideways option by becoming chief executive of Channel Four, as the successor to the opera-loving Jeremy Isaacs. Intent on making the channel more popular and more appealing to minorities, a difficult combination, Michael introduced a string of programmes that caused mingled admiration and outrage. His support of talented playwrights such as Dennis Potter and Alan Bleasdale won applause, as did the *Film on Four* series, which provided a valuable prop for the British film industry and brought *The Madness of King George*, among other treats, to the attention of a wider public. Michael always had fans who regarded him as a welcome harbinger of the future in television, but his critics tended to be more vociferous.

Particularly heavy fire was directed at anarchic late-night programmes, like *The Word* and *Eurotrash*, which were geared to a youth audiences, and were undeniably rich in scatological and profane content. *The Word* brought to viewers' attention the impressive feat of a man who could lift two stone of sausages attached, in suspension, to a ring through his penis. But the level of skill involved in such manifestations failed to win over Middle England. It was said that they lowered the tone of the whole medium. Paul Johnson, the *Daily Mail's* irascible right-wing columnist, famously asserted that in Michael Grade British television had found its 'Pornographer-in-Chief'.[3]

In interviews with newspapermen, Lew regularly found himself obliged to comment on his nephew's controversial progress, which on the face of it seemed to be proceeding along radically different lines to the one envisaged by Lew during his Barbara Cartland period. Yet nobody could ever get Lew to utter a remotely disloyal word. 'He's brilliant,' Lew told the man from the *Daily Telegraph* in 1996, 'I'm very proud of Michael. He's the only person in the British entertainment industry with great creative ability and business ability. Very rarely do the two go together.'[4]

No doubt endorsements of this type were heartfelt, but mortality was also dictating some closing of ranks by the surviving Grades. Lew's sister, Rita, died in 1992 and Bernard died two years later, aged eighty-four, after spending a bare minimum of time sitting in 'God's waiting room'. Bernard's last public engagement as president of the First Leisure Corporation and uncrowned 'King of Blackpool' was to act as host to the Queen of England on the occasion of the 100th anniversary of the Blackpool Tower. A week later, on 28 July 1994, he experienced his fatal heart attack at his country home in Angmering, West Sussex. With his elevation to the presidency of First Leisure, two years earlier, he had cut his working days down to four a week, but he never did get around to devising a retirement plan.

Under Bernard's leadership the company he had originally assembled for less than £40 million had expanded rapidly and, a few years after going public, was valued at £450 million on the Stock Exchange. It was always handsomely in profit. As a company boss, Bernard had exhibited a more relaxed style than Lew, more like a shrewdly benign uncle than a hard-driving father figure. He was good at delegating responsibility while maintaining a firm grip on the organisation's general direction, and excelled as a spotter of possible future trends, capacities which had arguably deserted Lew in the last days of his stewardship at ACC. During his own final period at First Leisure, Bernard had demonstrated his prescience by forging an alliance on the theatre front with Cameron Mackintosh, the coming impresario of the day. He had also appointed his nephew as a non-executive director, and as a potential future leader of the company. Some years later, after Michael grew weary of Channel Four, he did become chief executive of First Leisure.

Bernard's astonishing record of staging more than two hundred West End shows, which is unlikely to be surpassed, ensured a magnificent turnout for his memorial service at the Liberal Jewish Synagogue in St John's Wood. Music provided its theme with Sir Harry Secombe contributing a resonant 'My Heart and I', Frankie Vaughan singing 'Raisins and Almonds' and Dame Vera Lynn rendering an elegiac 'September Song'. Lord Rayne and Cameron Mackintosh gave readings from the Psalms.

Formal tributes to 'the Great Showman' were paid by Laurie Mansfield, chairman of the Entertainment Artistes' Benevolent Fund, and by Michael, speaking on behalf of the family.

Bernard's will, unlike his brother Leslie's, did not provide any significant margin for public speculation. In the final accounting of his estate, £40,000 was allocated in bequests for his chauffeur and secretary, with Carole inheriting the balance, valued at £3,868,157. Bernard's solicitor, Michael Rose, said of his late client, by way of explaining the comparative modesty of his fortune on demise, 'He was an enormously generous man. He gave away many gifts while he was alive.'[5]

Lew was moved by the loss of his brother but, as was the case after Leslie's death, he did not see it as being any major impediment to the conduct of business as usual, which very soon became business even better than usual. Within six months of Bernard's death, Lew received a life-enhancing offer. Polygram, the Dutch music and entertainment group, which counted *Four Weddings and a Funeral* among its most recent film successes, had as part of its expansion programme taken over ITC, the company Lew had founded almost forty years earlier to guarantee a flow of film product for ATV. This provided the Dutch company with a comprehensive backlog of material totalling more than 10,000 hours, most of which was produced during Lew's long television reign. Polygram's boss, Michael Kuhn, accordingly invited Lew to become the new model ITC's new top man with the imposing title, 'Chairman for Life – Active'. Kuhn insisted that this was not simply an honorific appointment, but one that required Lew's special competence as a man with Hollywood contacts that 'remained second to none'.[6]

'This is a very joyous day for me,'[7] said Lew, when publicly accepting the post at a celebration luncheon at the Hyde Park Hotel on 10 January 1995. To his other consultative chores, he could now add the pleasant responsibility of ensuring that his old favourite series, among them *The Prisoner*, *The Persuaders!*, *Thunderbirds* and even ATV's original *The Adventures of Robin Hood*, were seen all round the planet again, but this time on cable or satellite. He also assisted with Polygram's current movie deal-making in a way that led Kuhn to say later, 'far from being a name on the notepaper, Lew repaid me many times over'.[8] For an 88-year-old man, this did appear to be quite enough to be going on with, but Lew, though happy, was not entirely content. He still hankered after making another feature film, but was stuck for the right idea.

Lew's public image by this stage hovered between that of a national treasure and an environmental delinquent. No smoker fought more valiantly against the dying of lighting up. A regular by-product of Lew's frequent trips abroad would be gossip items about the stratagems he used in an effort to outflank the smoking prohibitions which were then being introduced by most of the major airlines. Not all of them were successful, but the Iberia airline and Qantas did, for a brief while, create an informal authorised smoking class consisting of one seat, Lew's. By the mid-1990s, with smoking bans edging into the world of television, Lew was conscious of having to wage his war on many more fronts. Visiting Michael at Channel Four, Lew had been forewarned of the company's new strict no-smoking policy which was also apologetically explained to him by the receptionist when he arrived there, wreathed in the usual nimbus. Lew responded by producing a hand-made sign which he hung round his neck. 'No Smoking Allowed', it read, 'for Anyone Under 87'.[9]

Under the combined pressure of the 'smoking police' and doctor's orders Lew managed to cut his intake of Montecristos down from sixteen to eight a day, which made such pantomimes less essential. But he remained a passionately evangelical advocate of a good smoke, on psychological and health grounds. Journalists too delicate to share the joys of an early-morning puff with Lew in his Mayfair office invariably left with a top pocket distended by one of his cigars 'for later'.

Although he had less actual news to impart, Lew's relationship with the press entered what was probably its most felicitous phase. As Britain's favourite tycoon emeritus, he could still be relied upon to come up with a few fresh one-liners to brighten up any features page on a slow day. And what Lew had to say, without the need to keep his merchandising reflexes in perfect working order, was often genuinely intriguing. He still could not acknowledge that he was actually growing older, but he did allow himself to exhibit symptoms of growing up. The once doughty opponent of ITN's *News at Ten* now confessed that his favourite programme on television was in fact the news, and there was even a partial apology for his launching so many quiz shows, which, to Lew's mature way of thinking, had become over-prominent in the schedules.

Lew's main strictures on the contemporary television scene, however, were reserved for its drama – 'too much kitchen sink'.[10] *Coronation Street* and *EastEnders* were both 'past their sell-by dates'.[11] Most of the other stuff was also disfigured by an excess of explicit sex and violence. Drama producers had lost the ability to distinguish between a violent series and an action adventure series, though Lew exempted *Murder She Wrote*, along with its motherly star, Angela Lansbury, from this blanket criticism. He and Kathie always watched it.

It was not difficult to see why. Lansbury's showcase vehicle exhibited many of the qualities apparent in Lew's old best-selling serials – a wholesome central character, predictably happy endings with Good invariably getting a decisive edge over Evil, glossy settings, rapid scene shifts, and a nicely calculated level of implausibility that made it possible to have a generous leavening of sanitised homicides and other types of mayhem without causing serious offence. Lew claimed to be convinced that the public was close to becoming heartily sick of realistic sex-and-violence, and that demand for a return to the more relaxing escapist formulas of yesteryear would soon manifest itself on a much broader front.

This was not among Lew's soundest predictions, and very possibly he did not entirely believe in it himself. The dawning era in which multiple television channels would become the norm effectively delivered a knockout blow to entertainment fare whose central ethos was to give the least offence to the largest possible number. It could be argued that the medium was not hugely improved by these developments, but it certainly had to be different in its approach. Michael at Channel Four was among the first to grasp the implications and Lew, given that he was in regular supportive contact with his nephew, may well have done so too, privately. But, as the truest of true believers in his own style of productions, Lew was not about to provide any public hint of a feeling that their day might be done.

A similar consistency would apply to Lew's attitude to royalty. With Rita and Bernard both gone, he had a heightened consciousness of his being the most conspicuous surviving royalist in the family, though he liked to think of himself as a discriminating one. 'Royalty does a fantastic job,' he told the *Guardian*'s Tom Hutchinson. 'Diana I don't know . . . but Charles is terrific.'[12] On the issue of bad language, Lew did make some adjustment to be more in tune with the spirit of the times. John

Edwards of the *Daily Mail* recalled being with Lew as he ploughed through a script for a prospective movie, briskly deleting every mention of the word 'fuck'. But he paused, pen raised, at one stage, with the thoughtful observation – 'This is where the guy comes back to find his car has been wrecked and I don't honestly think he'd say "oh bother". This one I will allow.'[13]

Lew's Christmas lunch for writers covering the entertainment beat remained, despite its diminishing news significance, one of the most pleasurably anticipated events in the calendar. In the absence of a large flock of employees to provide exercise for his paternal instincts, Lew intimated to the newspapermen and women that they were now very much an integral part of his 'family'. Most gave evidence of being charmed by this inclusion, regardless of what their opinion might be of Lew's overall cultural contribution. The BBC's Barry Norman and the *Guardian*'s Nancy Banks-Smith were anything but undiscriminating in their appreciation of Lew's media efforts, but they were flat-out fans of Lew personally. On the occasion of the Christmas lunch coinciding with Lew's ninetieth birthday, the writers went to the sentimental extreme of picking up the tab.

Members of the 'family' also qualified for Lew's free health and longevity advice service, which usually ran along the lines: put family and friends first, money nowhere, provided you have enough, find an occupation that you love, and avoid retirement at all costs. Lew of course was able to avoid it in more gratifying style than most, but it was an entirely genuine conviction. Joan Collins recalled an encounter with her 'Uncle Lew' when movieland's glitterati assembled for the Golden Globes awards in 1995. After the ceremony she took off for the Polygram party at the Four Seasons, 'where Lew Grade was still going strong and holding court at midnight, chattering to everybody and puffing on his cigar. Most of us could barely stand up, but Lew was so full of life it was almost contagious.' Walking back to their cars together after the party, they fell into reminiscence about Joe, Joan's father and Lew's first partner in the agency business, who had died some years earlier. From their different perspectives, both agreed that Joe's fatal decision had been to stop working. 'Goodbye, dear,' said Lew, as they went their separate ways into the night. 'Don't forget to keep your nose to the grindstone.'[14]

Lew set an example a few months later when he let it be known that, with Marcia Stanton's assistance, he was on course to produce his first full-length feature film since *Champions*. News of this development was not received with enormous enthusiasm by his closest friends, especially after it became apparent that Lew intended to finance the project with his own money. Although, like Mr Cohen in his long-time favourite anecdote, it was assumed that Lew had more than one bag of money stashed under his metaphorical floorboards, the ability of a movie to wreak havoc with an individual fortune could not be underestimated. It was also impossible, on the evidence of Lew's record, to underrate his ability to exceed a film budget. And, at the end of it all, disappointment might well be the reward. But Lew was resolved, and soon on his best hyperbolic form with pre-publicity in the press. It was a venture into which he was putting his 'heart and soul'[15] and it would be, without qualification, 'the best film I've ever made'.[16] He believed in it, he said, not least because of its title, which was conveniently *Something to Believe In*.

The story line was one that unashamedly tugged at the heartstrings, tracing the course of a romance between two young Americans whose paths cross in Italy – Maggie, a Las Vegas croupier, stricken with cancer and given two months to live, and Mike, a gifted but seriously troubled pianist. It also featured a statue of the Virgin Mary blessed with an apparent ability to weep at deeply moving moments. Despite the narrative's harrowing content there was a happy ending of the type designed to have an audience leave the cinema smiling through its tears. This genre of movie story, known in the trade as the 'twelve-hankie' variety, ran a clear risk of being viewed dry-eyed by those unable to enter into its spirit, but Lew's instinct told him the time for *Something to Believe In* was right. And so, it appeared, did Kathie's. When Lew confided to his wife that he had some concerns about money for the movie, he was enchanted by her response. 'Would you like some out of my trust?'[17] she asked.

In his capacity as executive producer, Lew appointed an experienced British director, John Hough, to shoot a film making the most of the story's international dimension, with Las Vegas, Paris and Italy as the principal locations. But Lew did economise to an extent on the casting, by allocating the leading roles to two relative newcomers, Maria Pitillo and

William McNamara. His notion was that they could efficiently be escorted to superstardom by an impressive supporting cast which he was able to assemble on the basis of friendly old relationships. This furnished the movie with a sparkling contingent of cameo role players that included Tom Conti, Robert Wagner, Maria Schneider, Ian Bannen and Jill St John. Lew later recruited Tim Rice to write the lyric for the title song. Placido Domingo accepted his invitation to sing it.

'The best deal I ever made . . .' Lew was fond of saying, pausing for dramatic effect before making the revelation, '. . . was to marry my wife.'[18] Next best came the deals that led to the making of *Jesus of Nazareth*, *The Muppet Show* and *On Golden Pond*, though not invariably in that ranking order. Kathie was never in any danger of being displaced from pole position, but, as is the case with most long-lasting partnerships, it had to undergo some degree of change. And there was a small but clearly detectable tilt in the balance of power in Lew's marriage as he progressed through his eighties.

The couple's fiftieth anniversary party at the House of Lords, though limited to a hundred close friends, had led to a rash of reciprocal social invitations well beyond the norm. And there was a renewed surge in Lord and Lady Grade's popularity as dinner-table guests in August 1994 after BBC2 aired *The Persuader: The TV Times of Lord Lew Grade*, in which Lew himself made a rare appearance. It became evident that some rationing of their social life was essential, especially given Lew's tendency to shift into overdrive as a raconteur late into the night.

It was accepted that Kathie should be arbiter of the degree of entertainment up with which they could jointly put. Thus Woodrow Wyatt, in his diary entry of 3 November 1994, records of a dinner party in the Pimlico home of former Tory minister Kenneth Baker, where he sat next to Lew and Kathie: 'She is a sweet little woman . . . not a doormat by any means. He left at once when she said she had to go though he wanted to stay.'[19] Kathie was not in any sense a killjoy. Indeed, if the social circumstance was right and Lew could persuade the band to strike up his favourite number, 'Yes, Sir, That's My Baby', Kathie readily danced along with him. But she did assume much more of a management function in Lew's way of life than had previously been the case. They could still nonetheless operate as a great team in time of crisis.

In the summer of 1997, as ninety-year-old Lord Grade was taking a shower before lunch, residents in his Knightsbridge apartment block were ordered to evacuate because of fire in a nearby restaurant. With smoke already billowing into the building there was no time for niceties like getting properly dressed, much less lunch. Pausing only to throw on a white towelling robe and to scoop up the two dogs, Tiffany and Charleston, Lew headed on down the stairs with Kathie. On reaching the pavement, Kathie picked up that something, aside from the conflagration, was amiss. Lew, in his bathroom gear, was a natural object of curiosity to passers-by and other displaced residents, but this alone was not enough to explain his obvious fretfulness. Kathie, however, was quickly on to the problem. Accompanied by an understanding fireman, she raced back through the smoke and up into the penthouse and retrieved the cigars. Within seconds of lighting up the first stogie Lew was his commanding self again, busy directing the rescue operation.

It would be a great pleasure to be able to relate that the efforts of this resourceful couple were crowned with the success of *Something to Believe In* and that Lew's film-making career, like his earlier television career, ended on a high note of public approbation. Unfortunately, it would not be true. As biography does not allow the same flexibility for happy endings as is permissible in a film script, there is no alternative to reporting that, in total defiance of Lew's instinct, the world of film entertainment had resolutely moved on.

On its British release in May 1998, *Something to Believe In* garnered some of the worst reviews ever written. 'As ludicrous as it is dull',[20] opined the *Observer*. The *Express*, picking up the Madonna element, playfully called it 'virgin on the worst film ever',[21] while the *Guardian*'s critic wrote: 'As one ludicrous scene follows another, it becomes clear that the Virgin is, in fact, weeping with helpless mirth.'[22] The *Sunday Times* reviewer reported having 'wept with tears of laughter'.[23] The *Independent* cryptically asserted, 'A movie this stupid could change your life forever.'[24]

Against this cruel tide, there was a comforting review in Glasgow's *Herald* – 'not only unforgettable, it is unmissable'[25] – along with favourable mentions in *Woman* magazine and the *Daily Mail*. Alexander Walker thought, possibly tongue in cheek, that the film might qualify for a papal blessing, while his colleague on the *Evening Standard*, Andrew Billen, wrote a compassionate piece commending the film's 'watchability', and awarded it merit marks despite detecting a dated quality in its style of address. '*Something to Believe In*', wrote Billen, 'belongs to the never-never land called Sixties prime time, where stories had beginnings, middles and happy endings. A rather good place actually.'[26]

Audiences were slightly more clement than most of the critics, but there was no way *Something to Believe In* could qualify as anything resembling a winner. Lew was able to absorb the financial loss on the movie with relative ease, but it must have been hard to digest the spectacle of his 'best film', in which his 'heart and soul' had been invested, occupying a position way down among the distant also-rans. Not that anyone was allowed to notice. Lew's most charming characteristic of being able to treat triumph and disaster both alike, while sensibly not viewing either as impostors, remained intact.

Journalists were reminded that there were still eighteen months to go to the millennium, when he might just conceivably retire. Plenty of time to make another couple of movies, both sure to be outstanding hits. But Lew was running out of puff. Alertness to this fact spread through his media 'family' when word was passed to them that the 1998 Christmas lunch might have to be held a little later than usual. Sensing that some cheering up might be required, Nancy Banks-Smith spotted a cushion embroidered with Mark Twain's devout observation 'If I can't smoke in heaven then I simply won't go',[27] and made a mental note to get it for Lew before the lunch. Sadly, the opportunity to present it never arrived.

Lew was admitted to the London Clinic in early December with a cardiac condition that failed to respond to surgery. He died there of heart failure at 12.45 a.m. on 13 December; Kathie and his son Paul were with him at the time. His death prompted an avalanche of press tributes by media bigwigs. The film-maker Lord Puttnam said, 'I've never known and will never know anyone quite like him. I loved him and that is not an exaggeration. He was ebullient, incredibly generous with his time, and over the years, with his money. He was a great man, always ahead of you.' For Sir Christopher Bland, the chairman of the BBC, 'Lew was the last of the great entertainers, a man who realised that TV and life should be fun – the most powerful force in TV of his day.' The government's Culture

Secretary, Chris Smith, lauded him as 'a giant in the world of popular entertainment'.[28] Even so, the accolade that would have enchanted Lew most was the one implicit in an *Evening Standard* news report. Lord Grade died, it said, 'at the tragically young age of ninety-one'.[29]

Four days later Lew was reunited with Bernard and Leslie when he was buried close to his brothers at the Liberal Jewish Cemetery in Willesden, north London. Michael's funeral oration, delivered on the verge of tears, blended sentiment and wit in the characteristic Grade style. 'We will', he said, 'have to learn to live without the twinkle, the phone calls, the superlatives, the sweep of his handshake and the lingering whiff of Havana tobacco. The only good thing to come out of this is the thought that the world shortage in Cuban cigars may now be close to an end.' His beloved uncle, Michael said, was not driven by mere personal gain – 'What interested him was the game – the idea, the pitch, the sale – and on to the next deal and the next.'[30]

Lew died well shy of qualification for the *Book of the Rich* but in eminently comfortable circumstances. The value of his estate, which was inherited by Kathie and Paul, aside from a £25,000 bequest for Marcia, came out at £8,423,342. Given the amount of good cheer his life had engendered, you could say that he came relatively cheap at the price.

Lew also obliged by considerately bequeathing his own best epitaph. An American newspaperman once suggested to him that in an age when accountants and lawyers had come to dominate decision-making in the world of entertainment, Lew's old-style hunch-and-handshake way of doing business qualified him supremely well for the title of being 'Britain's last mogul'.

'No,' said Lew, horrified at the idea, 'I'm the last Charleston dancer.'[31]

Acknowledgements

A s LEW GRADE DIED BEFORE THE beginning of this century at the ripe age of 91, the number of old acquaintances able to remember him in his prime is now, inevitably, somewhat limited. Even so, in researching this biography I was fortunate enough to find some of his oldest and closest friends alive and well and brimming with cheerful and intelligent reminiscence. Two in particular – Martin Starger, Lew's American ally during his epic assault on Hollywood, and Maria Stanton, who worked as the tycoon's personal assistant for almost forty years – stood out from the rest. But I was also generously furnished with lively insights into his life and times by, among others, Bruce Forsyth, Sir Roger Moore, Barry Norman, Denis Norden, John Pilger, Peter Plouviez, Tommy Steele and Michael Winner.

The account of Lew's impact on commercial television, which he pioneered in Britain and dominated for almost a quarter of a century, was influenced by conversations with many people experienced in that medium. They included Michael Archer, Jon Blair, Barry Cox, Ed Harriman, Roger Law and John Shirley. For assessment of Lew's subsequent foray into big-time movie-making, I am obliged to Quentin Falk, Dominic Prince, Peter Lennon and Professor Jemery Tunstall for sharing their thoughts with me.

Of the authors who wrote cogently about Lew during his lifetime, I am most grateful to Hunter Davies, who graciously allowed me to risk my neck in the attic of his Highgate home in a stumbling, though ultimately successful, search for the 'Olga tapes', the record of his original conversations with Lew's redoubtable mother, Olga Winogradsky. Other authors, who readily ransacked their memories and/or old filing cabinets on my behalf for further information about the Grade family, were Stephen Aris, Charles Raw and Barry Turner.

Lew wrote precious few memoranda and, as a telephone addict, even fewer letters. Original written sources are therefore rare. However, he did helpfully produce his own volume of memoirs, *Still Dancing*, as did his impresario brother Bernard, his sister Rita and his nephew Michael. Though of varying literary quality, these were all excellent sources, particularly in relation to the family's rise from impoverished immigrant status in London's East End.

For the sequence of events in later periods, when Lew and Bernard and to a lesser degree their younger brother, Leslie, were rarely out of the headlines, I was most appreciative of the record that lingers in the archives of some parts of the national press. This store of information has sadly been diminished by the relentless march of digital technology in most newspaper libraries, but not quite obliterated. I am very grateful to Helen Martin, former chief librarian at the *Guardian*, for guiding me to the few caches of old cuttings that survive from Lew's great days, preserving, for a while at least, his unique style of utterance. My thanks for being allowed access to them are extended to Richard Nelsson at the *Guardian* library; to Steve Torrington at the *Daily Mail*; and to Gertrud Erbach and Lynda Iley at News International.

Staff at the British Library in Bloomsbury were immensely helpful in tracking down the many memoirs across the show business spectrum, ranging from Harry Secombe and Max Bygaves to Dame Joan Plowright and Sir Peter Hall, in which Lew makes vivid cameo appearances.

Others who helped with specific information or by pointing me in the direction of fresh avenues of inquiry included Margaret Allen, Emma-Louise Burke, Michael Deeley, Nicholas Faith, Stephen Fay, Danielle Fluer, Terry Jones, Paul King, Phillip Knightley, Michael Leapman, Cal McCrystal, Patrick Masters, Dr Neela Malviya, Pralim Malviya, Gareth Owen, Anne Page, Bruce Page, Janet Shutt, Ros Sloboda and Sue Summers. Special thanks are due to those who read and advised on parts of the manuscript during its preparation. They are Judith Chester, Barry Cox, Alex Finer, Denis Herbstein, Philip Norman and Elizabeth Welsh. Responsibility for any errors that have survived is all mine.

For the solution of IT problems encountered at various times, I must thank my son, Cal Chester, Fiona and Rory Mulderrig and Richard Payne.

For encouragement and support along the way, I am beholden to my agent, Carol Heaton; to Piers Burnett and Graham Coster at Aurum Press; and to the Author's Foundation, which came through with a life-enhancing grant for this project when funds were running low.

Sources

Prologue

1. Lew Grade, *Still Dancing* (London: Collins, 1987), p. 262.
2. Nigel Horne, 'Meet the new Coca-Cola Kid', *Sunday Times*, 27 October 1985.
3. *Time*, 4 October 1971.
4. Nicholas Tomalin, 'Christmas's Mr Showbiz', *Sunday Times*, 22 December 1968.
5. Hunter Davies, *The Grades: The First Family of British Entertainment* (London: Weidenfeld and Nicolson, 1981), p. 254.
6. Jane Ennis, 'Lord of the Light Fantastic', *TV Times*, 1 January 1988.
7. 'From Vaude boards to House of Lords', birthday tribute to Lord Grade, *Variety*, 24 December 1986.
8. Eric Clark, 'Britain's showbiz Mr Big', *Observer* magazine, 9 December 1973.
9. Rita Grade Freeman, *My Fabulous Brothers* (London: W.H. Allen, 1982), pp. 119–20.
10. James Green, 'The funny stories they tell about Lew Grade', *Evening News*, 14 July 1959.
11. Mark Chadbourn, 'Great things Lew Grade said – or didn't say', *Sun*, 22 December 1987.
12. Davies, *The Grades*, p. 253
13. *Sunday Times*, 22 December 1968.
14. Jack Tinker, 'The last tycoon', *Daily Mail*, 15 January 1982.
15. Ned Sherrin, *Ned Sherrin: The Autobiography* (London: Little, Brown, 2005), p. 56.
16. Jane Ennis, 'Mixed blessings', *TV Times*, 2–8 January 1988.
17. John Heilpern, 'And now a word from the Bard's sponsor . . .', *Observer* magazine, 8 May 1977.
18. *Daily Express*, 10 September 1981.
19. Davies, *The Grades*, p. 254.
20. Sam Goldwyn quotes from Philip French, *The Movie Moguls* (London: Weidenfeld and Nicolson, 1969), pp. 46, 135.
21. Brian Viner, 'The Old Man and the Sea', *Night and Day*, 18 January 1998.
22. Davies, *The Grades*, p. 253.
23. Viner, 'The Old Man and the Sea'.
24. Ian Holm, *Acting My Life* (London: Bantam Press, 2004), p. 116.

1 Odessa

1. Reuben Ainsztein, *Jewish Resistance in Nazi-Occupied Eastern Europe* (London: Paul Elek, 1974), pp. 161–2.
2. Ibid., pp. 151–2.
3. Ibid., p. 150.
4. Lew Grade, *Still Dancing*, p. 17.
5. Ibid., p. 18.
6. Ibid., p. 19.

2 Whitechapel

1. James Green, 'From Tsardom to stardom: via Stepney', *Evening News*, 22 November 1976.
2. Lew Grade, *Still Dancing*, p. 20.
3. Bernard Delfont, *East End, West End* (London: Macmillan, 1990), p. 2.

4. Ibid., p. 6.
5. Hunter Davies, *The Grades*, p. 17.
6. Grade, *Still Dancing*, p. 20.
7. Davies, *The Grades*, p. 16.
8. Charles Booth, *Labour and Life of the People*, Vol. 1: East London (London: Williams and Norgate, 1889), pp. 546–7.
9. Davies, *The Grades*, p. 24.
10. Delfont, *East End, West End*, p. 15.
11. Ibid.
12. Grade, *Still Dancing*, p. 24.
13. David Lewin, 'The tale of the two Titanics', *Daily Mail*, 12 March 1979.
14. Davies, *The Grades*, p. 25.
15. Delfont, *East End, West End*, p. 12.
16. Grade, *Still Dancing*, p. 25.
17. Davies, *The Grades*, p. 30.
18. Ibid., pp. 29–30.
19. Grade, *Still Dancing*, p. 29.
20. Delfont, *East End, West End*, p. 13.
21. Davies, *The Grades*, p. 31

3 Charleston

1. Lew Grade, *Still Dancing*, p. 35.
2. Ibid., p. 33.
3. Hunter Davies, *The Grades*, p. 47.
4. Ibid., p. 39.
5. Grade, *Still Dancing*, p. 38.
6. Patience Wheatcroft, 'The golden calculator with a showbusiness heart', *Sunday Times*, 27 November 1977.

4 Dancing Years

1. Lew Grade, *Still Dancing*, p. 41.
2. Ibid., p. 44.
3. Hunter Davies, *The Grades*, p. 63.
4. Grade, *Still Dancing*, p. 51.
5. Bernard Delfont, *East End, West End*, p. 45.
6. Joan Collins, *Second Act* (London: Boxtree, 1996), p. 25.
7. Grade, *Still Dancing*, p. 53.
8. Ibid., p. 65.
9. Delfont, *East End, West End*, p. 47.
10. Grade, *Still Dancing*, p. 61.
11. Ibid., p. 66.
12. Delfont, *East End, West End*, p. 46.
13 Ibid., p. 53.

14. Ibid., p. 39.
15. Davies, *The Grades*, p. 61.
16. Ibid., p. 50.
17. Ibid.
18. Ibid. p. 65.
19. Rita Grade Freeman, *My Fabulous Brothers*, p. 31.

5 Offstage

1. Tom Hutchinson, interview with Lord Grade, *Guardian*, 13 December 1996.
2. Rita Grade Freeman, *My Fabulous Brothers*, p. 31.
3. Lew Grade, *Still Dancing*, p. 82.
4. Hunter Davies, *The Grades*, p. 75.
5. Grade, *Still Dancing*, p. 81.
6. Jack Tinker, *The Television Barons* (London: Quartet Books, 1980), p. 64.
7. Grade, *Still Dancing*, p. 86.
8. Bernard Delfont, *East End, West End*, p. 102.
9. Ibid., p. 68.
10. Freeman, *My Fabulous Brothers*, p. 35.
11. Ibid., p. 32.
12. Conversation with Denis Norden, 20 October 2008.
13. Grade, *My Fabulous Brothers*, p. 40.
14. Celeste Mitchell, 'Things I wish I'd known at the altar', *Daily Express*, 11 April 1991.
15. Jean Rook, interview with Lady Grade, *Daily Express*, 26 January 1982.
16. Grade, *Still Dancing*, p. 90.
17. Rook, interview with Lady Grade.

6 Wartime

1. Michael Grade, *It Seemed Like a Good Idea at the Time* (London: Macmillan, 1999), p. 4.
2. Lew Grade, *Still Dancing*, p. 96.
3. Ibid., pp. 96–7.
4. Ibid., p. 100.
5. Ibid., p. 101.
6. Hunter Davies, *The Grades*, p. 183.
7. Grade, *Still Dancing*, p. 106.
8. Ibid., p. 106.
9. Ibid., p. 108.
10. Nigel Horne, 'Meet the new Coca-Cola Kid'.

11. Bernard Delfont, *East End, West End,* p. 77.
12. Ibid., p. 135.
13. Ibid., p. 77.
14. Rita Grade Freeman, *My Fabulous Brothers,* p. 57.
15. *Evening Standard,* 14 June 1945.
16. Grade, *It Seemed Like a Good Idea at the Time,* p. 25.

7 Taking Planes

1. Barry Took, *Laughter in the Air* (London: Robson Books, 1976), p. 57.
2. Denis Norden, *Clips from a Life* (London: HarperCollins, 2008), p. 248.
3. Ibid., p. 355.
4. Hunter Davies, *The Grades,* p. 101.
5. Ibid., p. 102.
6. Lew Grade, *Still Dancing,* p. 118.
7. Ibid., p. 119.
8. Ibid., p. 134.
9. Bernard Delfont, *East End, West End,* p. 103.
10. Ibid., p. 102.
11. Ibid.
12. Ibid., pp. 102–3.
13. James Green, 'The showbiz Tsar goes into battle', *Evening News,* 25 November 1976.
14. Rita Grade Freeman, *My Fabulous Brothers,* p. 74.
15. Ibid.

8 Up with the Stars

1. Andrew Duncan, 'Arise Sir Lew', *Daily Telegraph,* 2 May 1975.
2. Hunter Davies, *The Grades,* p. 139.
3. Michael Grade, *It Seemed Like a Good Idea at the Time,* p. 22.
4. *Daily Telegraph,* 2 May 1975.
5. Stephen Aris, 'The hoofer who made the Grade', *Sunday Times,* 6 April 1980.
6. Davies, *The Grades,* p. 122.
7. Lew Grade, *Still Dancing,* p. 141.
8. Ibid., p. 142.
9. Davies, *The Grades,* p. 125.
10. Grade, *Still Dancing,* p. 139
11. John Edwards, 'A class act in a world of excess', *Daily Mail,* 30 September 1998.

12. Davies, *The Grades,* pp. 122–3.
13. Ibid., pp. 125–6.
14. Ibid.
15. Grade, *Still Dancing,* p. 145.
16. Bernard Delfont, *East End, West End,* p. 115.
17. Davies, *The Grades,* p. 136.
18. Delfont, *East End, West End,* p. 122.
19. Ibid., p. 16.

9 Television

1. Hunter Davies, *The Grades,* p. 139
2. Lew Grade, *Still Dancing,* p. 93.
3. Francis Wheen, *Television* (London: Century, 1985), p. 193.
4. Ibid.
5. H.H. Wilson, *Pressure Group: The campaign for commercial TV* (London: Secker and Warburg, 1961), p. 107.
6. Andrew Crisell, *An Introductory History of British Broadcasting* (London: Routledge, 1997), p. 78.
7. Wilson, *Pressure Group,* p. 215.
8. Clifford Davis, *How I Made Lew Grade a Millionaire . . . and other fables* (London: Mirror Books, 1981), p. 69.
9. Grade, *Still Dancing,* pp. 155–6.
10. Ibid., p. 156.
11. Ibid., p. 157.
12. Clifford Davis, 'Top stars in TV sensation', *Daily Mirror,* 27 September 1954.
13. Kenneth Clark, *The Other Half* (London: John Murray, 1977), p. 142.
14. Wheen, *Television,* p. 193.
15. Ibid., p. 195.

10 Showtime

1. Hunter Davies, *The Grades,* p. 101.
2. Bernard Delfont, *East End, West End,* p. 151.
3. Bernard Sendall, *Independent Television in Britain,* Vol. 1 (London: Macmillan, 1982), p. 150.
4. Ibid., p. 317.
5. Ned Sherrin, *Ned Sherrin: The Autobiography,* pp. 48–9.
6. Sendall, *Independent Television in Britain,* Vol. 1, p. 309.

7. Howard Thomas, *With an Independent Air* (London: Weidenfeld and Nicolson, 1977), p. 198.
8. Ibid., p. 164.
9. Peter Black, *The Mirror in the Corner* (London: Hutchinson, 1972), p. 96.
10. Victor Davies, 'Count of Monte Cristo', *Mail on Sunday*, 4 June 1995.
11. Rita Grade Freeman, *My Fabulous Brothers*, p. 116.
12. Full text of the 'Green Book' reproduced in Barry Took, *Laughter in the Air*, pp. 86–91.
13. Alexander Walker, 'Legend of the small screen who was larger than life', *Evening Standard*, 14 December 1998.
14. Kenneth Clark, *The Other Half*, p. 207.
15. Kathleen Burk, *Troublemaker: The life and history of A.J.P. Taylor* (Yale University Press, 2000), p. 391.
16. Black, *The Mirror in the Corner*, p. 111.
17. Ibid., p. 98.

11 'Mr ATV'

1. David Lewin, 'The man I back to win the West End', *Daily Mail*, 3 November 1960.
2. Bernard Delfont, 'Winners both!', *People*, 1 August 1954.
3. Bernard Delfont, 'I saved Winnie's grand piano from the pawnshop', *People*, 22 August 1954.
4. Jack Tinker, *The Television Barons*, p. 50.
5. Nancy Banks-Smith, 'Fancy footwork and dazzling spiel made him into Mr Entertainment', *Guardian*, 14 December 1998.
6. Martyn Harris, 'The power behind the big cigar', *Daily Telegraph*, 24 August 1994.
7. Clifford Davis, *How I made Lew Grade a Millionaire*, p. 94.
8. James Green, 'The funny stories they tell about Lew Grade'.
9. Michael Grade, *It Seemed Like a Good Idea at the Time*, p. 18.
10. Hunter Davies, *The Grades*, p. 151.
11. Ibid., p. 152.

12. *Daily Mail*, 10 March 1960.
13. Tinker, *The Television Barons*, p. 57.
14. *Financial Times*, 2 November 1960.
15. Tinker, *The Television Barons*, p. 56.
16. Anthony Davis, *Television: The first forty years* (London: Independent Television Publications, 1976), p. 90.
17. Tinker, *The Television Barons*, p. 59.
18. Bernard Delfont, *East End, West End*, p. 155.

12 Pilkington

1. Jeremy Potter, *Independent Television in Britain*, Vol. 4 (London: Macmillan, 1990), p. 34.
2. Asa Briggs, *The History of Broadcasting in the United Kingdom: Competition 1955–1974*, Vol. 5 (Oxford University Press, 1995), pp. 13–14.
3. John Boorman, *Adventures of a Suburban Boy* (London: Faber and Faber, 2003), p. 88.
4. Bernard Sendall, *Independent Television in Britain*, Vol. 1, p. 317.
5. Pikington Committee, *Report of the Committee on Broadcasting* (HMSO Cmnd. 1753, London, 1962), pp. 17–19.
6. Ibid. p. 68.
7. Briggs, *The History of Broadcasting in the United Kingdom*, Vol. 5, p. 301.
8. Denis Forman, *Persona Granada* (London: Andre Deutsch, 1997), p. 265.
9. Lord Hill of Luton, *Behind the Screen* (London: Sidgwick and Jackson), p. 16.
10. Ibid., p. 28.
11. Lew Grade, *Still Dancing*, pp. 187–8.
12. Denis Norden, Sybil Harper and Norman Gilbert, *Coming to you Live!* (London: Methuen, 1985), p. 142.
13. Francis Wheen, *Television*, p. 71.
14. *Daily Mail*, 12 February 1963.
15. David Nathan, *The Laughtermakers* (London: Peter Owen, 1971), p. 126.
16. Gary Morecambe and Martin Sterling, *Morecambe and Wise: Behind the Sunshine* (London: Robson Books, 2001), p. 79.
17. Nathan, *The Laughtermakers*, p. 149.

18. Peter Black, *The Mirror in the Corner*, p. 166.
19. Potter, *Independent Television in Britain*, Vol. 4, p. 34.
20. Hunter Davies, *The Grades*, p. 174.
21. Bernard Sendall, *Independent Television in Britain*, Vol. 2 (London: Macmillan, 1983), p. 237.
22. Mary Whitehouse, *Whatever Happened to Sex?* (Hove: Wayland, 1977), p. 17.
23. Ivor Herbert, 'The money comes automatically . . .', *Evening News*, 10 April 1968.
24. Dorothy Hobson, *Crossroads: The Drama of a Soap Opera* (London: Methuen, 1982), p. 36.
25. Philip Purser, *Halliwell's Television Companion*, Second edition (London: Paladin, 1985), p. 136.
26. Noele Gordon, *My Life at Crossroads* (London: W.H. Allen, 1975), p. 69.
27. Alexander Walker, *National Heroes* (London: Harrap, 1985), p. 93.
28. Milton Shulman, *The Least Worst Television in the World* (London: Barrie and Jenkins, 1973), p. 23.
29. *TV Times*, 1 January 1988.
30. Steve Turner, *Cliff Richard: The Biography* (Oxford: Lion Hudson, 2005), p. 185.
31. Davies, *The Grades*, p. 154
32. *The Times*, 10 October 1968.
33. *Daily Sketch*, 17 December 1965.

13 Monopoly

1. Eric Sykes, *If I Don't Write It, Nobody Else Will* (London: Harper Perennial, 2006), p. 326.
2. Ibid., p. 374.
3. Ibid.
4. Harry Secombe, *An Entertaining Life* (London: Robson Books, 2004), pp. 180–1.
5. Quoted on the cover sleeve of Pat Kirkwood's autobiography, *The Time of My Life* (London: Robert Hale, 1999).
6. Max Bygraves, *Max Bygraves in His Own Words* (Derby: Breedon Books, 1997), p.118.

7. Conversation with Bruce Forsyth, 1 December 2009.
8. Conversation with Tommy Steele, 12 November 2008.
9. Conversation with Sir Roger Moore, 9 April 2009.
10. Jeremy Thorpe, MP, 'An unchallenged family monopoly', *News of the World*, 24 July 1960.
11. Insight team, 'The show business octopus', *Sunday Times*, 8 May 1966.
12. *Financial Times*, 1 April 1965.
13. Insight, 'The show business octopus'.
14. *Daily Telegraph*, 22 February 1968.

14 Cashing In

1. *Daily Mirror*, 12 June 1968.
2. Barry Took, 'Saluting a mogul who made the Grade in TV's golden age', *Daily Express*, 27 August 1994.
3. James Thomas, 'How I pick my winners', *Daily Express*, 12 October 1966.
4. *Sun*, 22 December 1987.
5. Conversation with Martin Starger, 15 January 2009.
6. Martin Starger, 'Send in the Clouds', part of an 80th birthday salute to Lord Grade under the general heading, 'From Vaude boards to House of Lords', *Variety*, 24 December 1986.
7. Patrick McGoohan in an interview with Warner Troyer, conducted on behalf of the Ontario Educational Communications Authority. Broadcast on TV Ontario, March 1977.
8. Marshall Pugh, 'What I would do if I ran the BBC', article based on an interview with Lew Grade, *Daily Mail*, 16 March 1965.
9. Peter Black, 'Want to sell a TV series – right?', *Daily Mail*, 19 December 1968.
10. *New Statesman*, 28 April 1967.
11. *Sun*, 16 June 1967.
12. Lord Hill of Luton, *Behind the Screen*, pp. 46–7.
13. Michael Grade, *It Seemed Like a Good Idea at the Time*, p. 57.
14. Ibid., p. 22.

15. Ibid., p. 25.
16. Ibid., p. 7.
17. Ibid., p. 1.
18. Bruce Forsyth, *Bruce: The Autobiography* (London: Pan Books, 2002), p. 204.
19. Grade, *It Seemed Like a Good Idea at the Time*, p. 81.
20. Hunter Davies, *The Grades*, p. 164.
21. Howard Thomas, *With an Independent Air*, p. 224.

15 Knighthood
1. 'The day that Mrs Winogradsky made the Grade', *News of the World*, 28 November 1966.
2. Oliver Pritchett, 'Loveable Lew', *Guardian*, 1 January 1969.
3. Jeremy Potter, *Independent Television in Britain*, Vol. 4, p. 68.
4. David Frost, *From Congregations to Audiences* (London: HarperCollins, 1993), p. 363.
5. Jack Tinker, *The Television Barons*, p. 73.
6. Andrew Crisell, *British Broadcasting*, p. 127
7. Nicholas Tomalin, 'Christmas's Mr Showbiz', *Sunday Times*.
8. Bruce Page, 'Palladium counter-attack', *Sunday Times*, 15 September 1968.
9. *Financial Times*, 28 February 1969.
10. *The Times*, 19 September 1969.
11. Jeremy Potter, *Independent Television in Britain*, Vol. 3 (London: Macmillan, 1989), pp. 44–5.
12. Ibid., p. 47.
13. *Sunday Times*, 7 March 1971.

16 The Beatles
1. Richard Hill, 'Sir Lew bids for Beatle song firm', *Sun*, 29 March 1969.
2. Conversation with Philip Norman, 31 August 2008.
3. Bernard Delfont, 'My biggest mistake', *Independent on Sunday*, 1 April 1991.
4. Philip Norman, *Shout!* (London: Pan Books, 2004), p. 198.
5. Brian Southall with Rupert Perry, *Northern Songs* (London: Omnibus Press, 2007), p. 13.
6. Ibid., p. 50.
7. Ibid., pp. 57–8.
8. Norman, *Shout!*, p. 381.
9. Stephen James, son of Dick James, on the BBC2 programme, *Northern Songs*, broadcast 24 July 2007.
10. Norman, *Shout!*, p. 381.
11. Southall and Perry, *Northern Songs*, p. 76.
12. Norman, *Shout!*, p. 382.
13. Southall and Perry, *Northern Songs*, p. 79.
14. Lew Grade, *Still Dancing*, p. 193.

17 Family Matters
1. Graham Bridgstock, 'Vision built on splendid Folies', *Evening Standard*, 25 September 1991.
2. Michael Grade, *It Seemed Like a Good Idea at the Time*, p. 26.
3. Bernard Delfont, *East End, West End*, pp. 200–1.
4. Michael Grade, *It Seemed Like a Good Idea at the Time*, p. 29.
5. Lew Grade, *Still Dancing*, p. 185.
6. Alex Harvey, 'Czar behind the big cigar', *Sun*, 8 January 1982.
7. Grade, *Still Dancing*, p. 217
8. Angela Levin, 'At home with Lord Grade', *Mail on Sunday* magazine, 25 October 1987.
9. Hunter Davies, *The Grades*, p. 213.
10. Conversation with Marcia Stanton, 9 October 2008.
11. Stephen Aris, 'Enter the mogul and his Muppets', *Sunday Times*, 20 April 1980.
12. Sheridan Morley, 'That was Entertainment', *Times*, 10 July 1994.
13. *Sunday Express*, 19 January 1969.
14. Stephen Aris, *The Jews in Business* (London: Jonathan Cape, 1970), p. 207.
15. Davies, *The Grades*, p. 100.
16. Nicholas Tomalin, 'Christmas's Mr Showbiz'.
17. Alix Palmer, 'Far, far along the Rainbow', *Daily Express*, 22 March 1967.

18. David Lewin, 'The greatest showman', *Daily Mail*, 29 July 1994.
19. Delfont, *East End, West End*, p. 170.
20. Rita Grade Freeman, *My Fabulous Brothers*, p. 185.
21. *Daily Mail*, 15 June 1974.
22. Morley, 'That was Entertainment'.
23. Ibid.
24. *Campaign*, 18 February 1972.
25. Hunter Davies, 'The mogul of mass taste', *Sunday Times*, 5 December 1971.
26. John Heilpern, 'And now a word from the Bard's sponsor . . .'
27. Paul Dacre, 'When it's a question of taste in TV . . . meet Mr. Universe', *Daily Express*, 20 October 1973.
28. Nicholas Tomalin, 'Christmas's Mr Showbiz'.
29. Jack Tinker, *The Television Barons*, p. 107.
30. George Brock and Tony Lyons, 'Why no one can pass this grade', *Observer*, 6 September 1981.
31. Grade, *Still Dancing*, p. 175.
32. Conversation with Stephen Aris, 25 April 2007.

18 Changing Times

1. Joan Plowright, *And That's Not All: The memoirs of Joan Plowright* (London: Orion, 2002), p. 188.
2. Peter Hall, *Peter Hall's Diaries*, ed. John Goodwin (London: Hamish Hamilton, 1984), p. 97.
3. Jeremy Potter, *Independent Television in Britain*, Vol. 4, p. 34.
4. Ibid., p. 215.
5. Ibid., p. 39.
6. Potter, *Independent Television in Britain*, Vol 3, p. 65.
7. Peter Fiddick, *Guardian*, 10 December 1973.
8. Potter, *Independent Television in Britain*, Vol. 4, p. 112.
9. Conversation with John Pilger, 8 October 2008.
10. Alan Road, 'Grade bans Michael Collins film', *Observer*, 4 February 1973.
11. Ibid.
12. Potter, *Independent Television in Britain*, Vol. 4, p. 210.
13. Howard Thomas, *With an Independent Air*, pp. 214–15.
14. Jeremy Isaacs, *Look Me in the Eye: A Life in Television* (London: Little, Brown, 2006), p. 205.
15. Philip French, *The Movie Moguls*, p. 13.
16. Shirley MacLaine, *You Can Get There from Here* (London: Bodley Head, 1975), pp. 27–31.
17. Ibid., p. 40.
18. Ibid.
19. Shaun Usher, 'Why the eyes of America are watching Britain', *Daily Mail*, 5 October 1972.

19 Moses, Jesus and The Muppets

1. Catherine Olsen, 'The Pope told me to make "Jesus"', *Evening News*, 7 April 1977.
2. Lew Grade, *Still Dancing*, pp. 197–8.
3. Ibid., p. 198.
4. *Evening News*, 7 April 1977.
5. William Hickey gossip column, *Daily Express*, 31 July 1974.
6. *Times*, 2 August 1974.
7. *Daily Mail*, 31 July 1974.
8. Ian Holm, *Acting My Life*, p. 117.
9. John Miller, *Peter Ustinov: The Gift of Laughter* (London: Weidenfeld and Nicolson, 2002), p. 151.
10. Holm, *Acting My Life*, p. 116.
11. Ibid., p. 117.
12. *Sun*, 22 December 1987.
13. Nigel Dempster column, *Daily Mail*, 1 July 1975.
14. Conversation with Peter Plouviez, 30 September 2008.
15. Bernard Delfont, *East End, West End*, pp. 198–9.
16. Gordon Leak, 'No. 10 chief in Marcia clash rejects peerage', *News of the World*, 30 May 1976.
17. Ziegler, *Wilson: Authorized Life* (London: HarperCollins, 1995), p. 496.
18. James Green, 'I'm so proud my sons have made the grade', *Evening News*, 27 May 1976.

19. Hunter Davies, *The Grades*, p. 187.
20. John Heilpern: 'And now a word from the Bard's sponsor . . .'
21. Davies, *The Grades*, p. 185.
22. 'Lord Grade rides storm over Jesus film', *Daily Mail*, 16 March 1977.
23. *Evening News*, 7 April 1977.
24. Miller, *Peter Ustinov: The Gift of Laughter*, p. 152.
25. Philip Jordan and Nicholas de Jongh, 'How faceless financiers could fill the ITV screens', *Forbes* magazine. Quoted in *Guardian*, 12 November 1980.
26. *Evening Standard*, 6 April 1977.
27. Ibid., 30 July 1980.
28. Jeremy Potter, *Independent Television in Britain*, Vol. 4, p. 78.

20 Movie Mogul

1. Stephen Aris, 'Enter the mogul and his Muppets'.
2. John Walker, *The Once and Future Film* (London: Methuen, 1985), p. 40.
3. David Hewson, 'Over-priced, over-promoted, mid-Atlantic and sinking', *Times*, 2 July 1981.
4. *Time*, 4 October 1971.
5. *Evening Standard*, 19 January 1972.
6. Conversation with Quentin Falk, 9 September 2008, and Dominic Prince, 19 September 2008, and their book, *Last of a Kind: the sinking of Lew Grade* (London: Quartet Books, 1987), pp. 34–5.
7. Alexander Walker, *National Heroes*, p. 114.
8. Howard Thomas, *With an Independent Air*, p. 199.
9. Walker, *National Heroes*, p. 111.
10. Conversation with Michael Winner, 27 February 2009.
11. John Bartholomew, 'Lord Grade: More than a fat cigar', *Financial Times*, 21 August 1978.
12. John Boorman, *Money into Light* (London: Faber and Faber, 1985), p. 34.
13. *The Times*, 21 December 1977.
14. Falk and Prince, *Last of a Kind*, p. 43.

15. Joan Collins, *Second Act*, p. 215.
16. *Evening News*, 16 August 1978.
17. *Daily Telegraph*, 17 August 1978.
18. *Evening News*, 16 August 1978.
19. Paul Dacre, 'When it's a question of taste in TV . . . Meet Mr. Universe'.
20. Angela Levin, 'At home with Lord Grade'.

21 Two Titanics

1. *The Times*, 28 October 1978.
2. Bernard Delfont, *East End, West End*, p. 194.
3. Lew Grade, *Still Dancing*, p. 251.
4. *Daily Mail*, 29 November 1976.
5. Brian Viner, 'the Old Man and the Sea'.
6. David Lewin, 'The tale of the two Titanics'.
7. Alexander Walker, *National Heroes*, p. 204.
8. Ibid., p. 196.
9. Conversation with Terry Jones, 22 April 2008.
10. Delfont, *East End, West End*, p. 191.
11. *Evening Standard*, 18 January 1979.
12. Ivan Rowan, 'The man behind the big cigar', *Sunday Telegraph*, 4 March 1979.
13. *Evening Standard*, 18 January 1979.
14. Walker, *National Heroes*, pp. 203–4.
15. *Daily Telegraph*, 15 August 1979.
16. Sheridan Morley, 'That Was Entertainment'.
17. Order of service for the memorial to Leslie Grade at the Liberal Jewish Synagogue, St John's Wood, 2 December 1979.
18. *Daily Telegraph*, 15 August 1979.
19. *Daily Mirror*, 6 January 1980.
20. Grade, *Still Dancing*, p. 106.

22 Chutzpah

1. *Evening News*, 16 May 1980.
2. John Walker, *The Once and Future Film*, p. 45.
3. Michael Pye, 'Would you believe an industry could die', *Sunday Times*, 15 June 1980.

4. Conversation with Barry Norman, 27 October 2008.
5. Alexander Walker, 'For whom the gong tolled', *Evening Standard*, 10 June 1980.
6. Alexander Walker, *National Heroes*, p. 94.
7. Brian Viner, 'The Old Man and the Sea'.
8. Lew Grade, *Still Dancing*, p. 262.
9. *Daily Mail*, 21 December 1977.

23 Power Game
1. Bernard Delfont, *East End, West End*, p. 201.
2. Lew Grade, *Still Dancing*, p. 182.
3. Ibid.
4. *The Times*, 17 January 1981.
5. Brian Viner, 'The Old Man and the Sea'.
6. *Daily Mail*, 22 December 1980.
7. Chairman's Statement in the 1980 Annual Report of Associated Communications Corporation Limited.
8. Quentin Falk and Dominic Prince, *Last of a Kind*, p. 110.
9. Ibid., p. 79.
10. Dorothy Hobson, *Crossroads: The Drama of a Soap Opera*, p. 18.
11. Ibid.
12. *Daily Mail*, 26 January 1981.
13. Patrick Sergeant City column, *Daily Mail*, 26 June 1981.
14. *Times*, 2 July 1981.
15. Grade, *Still Dancing*, pp. 258–9.
16. Falk and Prince, *Last of a Kind*, p. 114.
17. Ibid., p. 117.
18. Ibid., p. 116.
19. Ibid.
20. *Daily Mail*, 3 September 1981.
21. Philip Robinson, 'Why Lord Grade must look over his shoulder', *The Times*, 3 September 1981.
22. Baz Bamigboye, 'I'm just a boy', *Sun*, 3 September 1981.
23. *Daily Mail*, 3 September 1981.

24 'That Australian'
1. Patience Wheatcroft, 'The humiliation of Lew Grade', *Sunday Times*, 25 April 1982.

2. John Moore, 'Lord Grade at bay', *Financial Times*, 15 January 1982.
3. *The Times*, 7 July 1981.
4. Account of ACC's 1981 AGM based on Falk and Prince, *Last of a Kind*, pp. 125–6 and reports in *The Times*, *Daily Telegraph*, *Daily Express* and *Daily Mail*, 11 September 1981.
5. Lew Grade, *Still Dancing*, p. 278.
6. Ibid., p. 275.
7. Falk and Prince, *Last of a Kind*, p. 129.
8. *The Times*, 18 December 1981.
9. *Screen International*, 5–12 December 1981.
10. Grade, *Still Dancing*, p. 277.
11. Brian Viner, 'The Old Man and the Sea'.
12. *Daily Mail*, 16 January 1982.
13. Falk and Prince, *Last of a Kind*, p. 146.
14. Grade, *Still Dancing*, p. 279.

25 Humiliation
1. Patience Wheatcroft, 'The humiliation of Lew Grade'.
2. Lew Grade, *Still Dancing*, pp. 280–1.
3. Brian Southall with Rupert Perry, *Northern Songs*, p. 130.
4. Quentin Falk and Dominic Prince, *Last of a Kind*, pp. 85–6.
5. Ibid., p. 153.
6. *Financial Times*, 20 January 1982.
7. Southall and Perry, *Northern Songs*, p. 143.
8. Grade, *Still Dancing*, p. 281.
9. *Times*, 17 June 1982.
10. John Walker, *The Once and Future Film*, pp. 46–7.
11. Jeremy Tunstall, *The Media in Britain* (London: Constable, 1983), p. 58.
12. *Daily Express*, 6 November 1982.
13. *Screen International*, 8–15 November 1980.
14. Alexander Walker, *National Heroes*, p. 164.

26 Lew Also Rises
1. *Daily Mail*, 21 April 1982.
2. *Daily Mirror*, 17 June 1982.
3. Alexander Walker, *National Heroes*, p. 215.

4. *Daily Mail,* 24 June 1982.
5. *Sunday Telegraph,* 27 June 1982.
6. Ibid.
7. Michael Grade, *It Seemed Like a Good Idea at the Time,* p. 127.
8. Ibid., p.145.
9. *Guardian,* 5 March 1984.
10. Conversation with Jon Blair, 9 October 2008.
11. *News of the World,* 2 and 9 January 1983.
12. *Variety,* 24 December 1986.
13. Prufrock column, 'No end to the Peer show', *Sunday Times,* 12 February 1984.
14. *The Times,* 18 November 1986.
15. *Independent,* 1 November 1986.
16. Ibid.
17. *The Times,* 18 November 1986.
18. Ibid.
19. *Guardian,* 14 December 1998.
20. Lew Grade, *Still Dancing,* p. 299.
21. *The Times,* 21 January 1988.
22. Joan Collins, *Past Imperfect* (London: Coronet, 1979), p. 11.
23. Bernard Delfont, *East End, West End,* p. 199.

27 Grindstone

1. *Sun,* 29 December 1985.
2. Baz Bamigboye, 'Lord of romance', *Daily Mail,* 14 October 1987.
3. Michael Grade, *It Seemed Like a Good Idea at the Time,* p. 356.
4. *Daily Telegraph,* 30 October 1996.
5. *Evening Standard,* 29 November 1994.
6. *Guardian,* 11 January 1995.
7. *The Times,* 11 January 1995.
8. Michael Kuhn, *One Hundred Films and a Funeral* (London: Thorogood, 2002), p. 107.

9. *Guardian,* 8 September 1995.
10. *Mail on Sunday,* 22 October 1989.
11. *Daily Mail,* 14 December 1998.
12. *Guardian,* 13 December 1996.
13. John Edwards, 'Foul films won't ever make the grade', *Daily Mail,* 17 October 1995.
14. Joan Collins, *Second Act,* p. 419.
15. *Daily Telegraph,* 30 October 1996.
16. *Independent,* 1 May 1998.
17. Andrew Billen, 'Ninety-one, still dancing . . . Come on, someone is looking after me'. Article based on an interview with Lord Grade, *Evening Standard,* 13 May 1998.
18. *Daily Mail,* 19 August 1994.
19. *The Journals of Woodrow Wyatt,* Vol. 3, ed. Sarah Curtis (London: Macmillan, 2000), p. 432.
20. *Observer,* 10 May 1998.
21. *Daily Express,* 8 May 1998.
22. *Guardian,* 8 May 1998.
23. *Sunday Times,* 10 May 1998.
24. *Independent,* 8 May 1998.
25. *Herald,* 7 May 1998.
26. Andrew Billen interview, *Evening Standard,* 13 May 1998.
27. Nancy Banks-Smith, 'Fancy footwork and dazzling spiel made him Mr Entertainment'.
28. Janine Gibson, 'Lord Grade, showbiz colossus, dies at 91', *Guardian,* 14 December 1998.
29. *Evening Standard,* 15 December 1998.
30. *Independent,* 17 December 1998.
31. Howard Raikes, 'A Lord of hunch and handshake', *International Herald Tribune,* 19 April 1988.

Bibliography

Adie, Kate, *The Kindness of Strangers*, London: Headline, 2002

Ainsztein, Reuben, *The Jewish Resistance in Nazi-Occupied Eastern Europe*, London: Paul Elek, 1974

Annan Committee, *The Report of the Committee on the Future of Broadcasting*, H.M. Stationery Office, Cmnd 6793, London, 1977

Aris, Stephen, *The Jews in Business*, London: Jonathan Cape, 1970

Attenborough, David, *Life on Air*, London: BBC Books, 2003

Attenborough, Richard, *Entirely Up to You, Darling*, London: Hutchinson, 2008

Behan, Dominic, *Milligan: The Life and Times of Spike Milligan*, London: Methuen, 1988

Bennett, Alan, *Untold Stories*, London: Faber and Faber, 2005

Bermant, Chaim, *Troubled Eden: Anatomy of British Jewry*, London: Valentine, Mitchell, 1969

Beresford, Philip, *The Sunday Times Book of the Rich*, London: Penguin, 1991

Bessborough, Lord, *Return to the Forest*, London: Weidenfeld and Nicolson, 1962

Bevan, Ian, *Top of the Bill (The Story of the Palladium)*, London: Frederick Muller, 1952

Beveridge Committee, *The Report of the Broadcasting Committee*, H.M. Stationery Office, Cmnd 8116, London, 1951

Bevins, Reginald, *The Greasy Pole*, London: Hodder and Stoughton, 1965

Black, Peter, *The Mirror in the Corner*, London: Hutchinson, 1972

—— *The Biggest Aspidistra in the World*, London: BBC, 1972

Blond, Anthony, *Jew Made in England*, London: Timewell Press, 2004

Booker, Christopher, *The Neophiliacs*, London: Fontana, 1970

—— *The Seventies*, London: Allen Lane, 1980

Boorman, John, *Money into Light: The 'Emerald Forest' Diary*, London: Faber and Faber, 1985

—— *Adventures of a Suburban Boy*, London: Faber and Faber, 2003

Booth, Charles, *Labour and Life of the People*, Vol. 1: East London, London: Williams and Norgate, 1889

Bose, Mihir, *Michael Grade: Screening the Image*, London: Virgin Books, 1992

Brandreth, Gyles, *Breaking the Code: Westminster Diaries*, London: Weidenfeld and Nicolson, 1999

Briggs, Asa, *The History of Broadcasting in the United Kingdom: Competition 1955–1974*, Oxford: Oxford University Press, 1995

Burk, Kathleen, *Troublemaker: The Life and History of A.J.P. Taylor*, London: Yale University Press, 2000

Bygraves, Max, *Max Bygraves in his Own Words*, Derby: Breedon Books, 1997

Carpenter, Humphrey, *Dennis Potter: The Authorized Biography*, London: Faber and Faber, 1998

Clark, Kenneth, *Another Part of the Wood*, London: Book Club, 1974
—— *The Other Half*, London: J. Murray, 1977
Coleman, Ray, *Lennon: The Definitive Biography*, London: Pan, 1995
Collins, Joan, *Past Imperfect*, London: Coronet, 1979
—— *Second Act*, London: Boxtree, 1996
Corner, John, *Popular Television in Britain*, London: BFI Publishing, 1991
Cotton, Bill, *Double Bill*, London: Fourth Estate, 2000
Crisell, Andrew, *An Introductory History of British Broadcasting*, London: Routledge, 1997
Curran, Charles, *A Seamless Robe*, London: Collins, 1979
Curtis, Sarah (ed.), *The Journals of Woodrow Wyatt: Volume Three*, London: Macmillan, 2000
Curran, James and Seaton, Jean, *Power Without Responsibility* (fifth edition), London: Routledge, 1997
Davies, Christie, *Permissive Britain: Social Change in the 60s and 70s*, London: Pitman, 1975
Davies, Hunter, *The Beatles: the Illustrated updated Edition*, London: Cassell Illustrated, 2004
—— *The Grades: The First Family of British Entertainment*, London: Weidenfeld and Nicolson, 1981
Davies, Russell (ed.), *The Kenneth Williams Diaries*, London: HarperCollins, 1993
—— *The Kenneth Williams Letters*, London: HarperCollins, 1994
Davis, Anthony, *Television: The First Forty Years*, London: Severn House, 1976
—— *TV's Greatest Hits*, London: Boxtree, 1988
Davis, Clifford, *How I Made Lew Grade a Millionaire . . . and Other Fables*, London: Mirror Books, 1981
Deeley, Michael, *Blade Runners, Deer Hunters and Blowing the Bloody Doors Off*, London: Faber and Faber, 2008.
Delfont, Bernard (with Barry Turner), *East End, West End*, London: Macmillan, 1990

Dench, Geoff (with Kate Graham, Michael Young), *The New East End: Kinship, Race and Conflict*, London: Profile, 2006
Eberts, Jake and Illot, Terry, *My Indecision is Final: The Rise and Fall of Goldcrest Films*, London: Faber and Faber, 1990
Elson, John and Tomalin, Nicholas, *The History of the National Theatre*, London: Jonathan Cape, 1978
Emden, Paul H., *Jews of Britain*, London: Sampson Low Marston, 1943
Falk, Quentin and Prince, Dominic, *Last of a Kind: The Sinking of Lew Grade*, London: Quartet Books, 1987
Esslin, *The Age of Television*, San Francisco: W.H. Freeman, 1982
Evans, Jeff, *The Penguin TV Companion*, London: Penguin, 2003
Farnes, Norma, *Spike: An Intimate Memoir*, London: Fourth Estate, 2003
Fisher, John, *Tommy Cooper: Always Leave them Laughing*, London: HarperCollins, 2006
Fishman, William J., *East End Jewish Radicals*, London: Duckworth, 1975
Forbes, Bryan, *Notes for a Life*, London: Collins, 1974
—— *A Divided Life: Memoirs*, London: Heinemann, 1992
Fore, W.F., *Television and Religion*, Minneapolis: Augsburg Publishing House, 1987
Forman, Denis, *Persona Granada*, London: Andre Deutsch, 1997
Forsyth, Bruce, *Bruce: The Autobiography*, London: Sidgwick and Jackson, 2001
Freeman, Rita Grade, *My Fabulous Brothers*, London: W.H. Allen, London, 1982
French, Philip, *The Movie Moguls*, London: Weidenfeld and Nicolson, 1969
Fried, Albert and Elman, Richard, *Charles Booth's London*, London: Pelican Books, 1971
Frischauer, Willi, *David Frost*, London: Michael Joseph, 1971
Frost, David, *David Frost: An Autobiography. Part One: From Congregations to Audiences*, London: HarperCollins, 1993

Gans, Herbert, *Popular Culture and High Culture*, New York: Perseus, 1999

Gartner, Lloyd, *The Jewish Immigrant in England, 1874–1914*, Detroit: Wayne State University Press, 1960

Glinert, Ed, *East End Chronicles*, London: Allen Lane, 2005

Godwin, Cliff, *When the Wind Changed: The Life and Death of Tony Hancock*, London: Century, 1999

Goodwin, John (ed.), *Peter Hall's Diaries: The Story of a Dramatic Battle*, London: Hamish Hamilton, 1983

Gordon, Noele, *My Life at Crossroads*, London: W.H. Allen, 1975

Grade, Lew, *Still Dancing*, London: Collins, 1987

Grade, Michael, *It Seemed Like a Good Idea at the Time*, London: Macmillan, 1999

Green, Timothy, *The Universal Eye*, New York: Stein and Day, 1972

Griffin, Stephen, *Ken Dodd*, London: Michael O'Mara Books, 2005

Hall, Peter, *Making an Exhibition of Myself*, London: Oberon, 2000

Halliwell, Leslie with Purser, Philip, *Halliwell's Television Companion*, London: Granada, 1982

Henry, Brian, *British Television Advertising: the first 30 years*, London: Century Benham, 1986

Hill, Lord (Charles) of Luton, *Behind the Screen*, London: Sidgwick and Jackson, 1974

Hobson, Dorothy, *Crossroads: The Drama of a Soap Opera*, London: Methuen, 1982

Holm, Ian, *Acting My Life*, London: Bantam, 2004

Isaacs, Jeremy, *Look Me in the Eye: A Life in Television*, London: Little, Brown, 2006

ITV: Evidence to the Annan Committee, London: ITV Books, 1975

Kirkwood, Pat, *The Time of My Life*, London: Robert Hale, 1999

Kuhn, Michael, *One Hundred Films and a Funeral*, London: Thorogood, 2002

Lahr, John (ed.), *The Diaries of Kenneth Tynan*, London: Bloomsbury, 2001

Lealand, Geoffrey, *American Television Programmes on British Screens*, Broadcasting Research Unit Paper, London, 1986

Leapman, Michael, *The Last Days of the Beeb*, Coronet, London, 1987

——— *Treachery? The Power Struggle at TV-AM*, London: Allen and Unwin, 1984

Levin, Bernard, *The Pendulum Years*, London: Jonathan Cape, 1970

Lewis, Roger, *The Life and Death of Peter Sellers*, London: Century, 1994

Lewisohn, Mark, *The Complete Beatles Chronicle*, London: Hamlyn, 1992

Lipman, D.V., *Social History of the Jews in England 1850–1950*, London: Watts, 1954

Lord, Graham, *John Mortimer: The Devil's Advocate*, London: Orion, 2005

MacLaine, Shirley, *You Can Get There From Here*, London: Bodley Head, 1975

Martin, George with Hornsby, Jeremy, *All You Need Is Ears*, New York: St Martin's, 1979

Marx, Arthur, *The Secret Life of Bob Hope*, London: Robson Books, 1994

Miller, John, *Peter Ustinov: The Gift of Laughter*, London: Weidenfeld and Nicolson, 2002

Mills, John, *Up In The Clouds, Gentlemen Please*, London: Orion, 1980

Moore, Roger, *My Word is My Bond*, London: Michael O'Mara, 2008

Moorehead, Caroline, *Sidney Bernstein*, London: Jonathan Cape, 1984

Morecambe, Eric and Wise, Ernie, *There's No Answer to That*, London: Arthur Barker, 1981

Morecambe, Gary and Sterling, Martin, *Morecambe and Wise: Behind the Sunshine*, London: Robson Books, 1994

Morecambe, Gary, *Life's Not Hollywood, It's Cricklewood*, London: BBC Books, 2003

Nathan, David, *The Laughtermakers*, London: Peter Owen, 1971

Norden, Denis with Harper, Sybil and Gilbert, Norman, *Coming to You Live!*, London: Methuen, 1985

Norden, Denis, *Clips from a Life*, London: Fourth Estate, 2008

Norman, Barry, *And Why Not? Memoirs of a Film Lover*, London: Simon and Schuster, 2002

Norman, Philip, *Shout!: The True Story of the Beatles*, London: Sidgwick and Jackson, 2003

Palin, Michael, *Michael Palin Diaries 1969–1979, The Python Years*, London: Weidenfeld and Nicolson, 2006

Paskin, Barbara, *Dudley Moore: The Authorized Biography*, London: Pan, 1998

Perry, George, *Life of Python*, London: Pavilion, 1983

Phillips, Sian, *Public Places: The Autobiography*, London: Hodder and Stoughton, 2001

Pilger, John, *Heroes*, London: Jonathan Cape, 1986

Pilkington Committee, *The Report of the Committee on Broadcasting*, H.M. Stationery Office, Cmnd 1753, London, 1962

Potter, Jeremy, *Independent Television in Britain*, Vol. III, *Politics and Control (1968–1980)*, London: Macmillan, 1989

—— *Independent Television in Britain*, Vol. IV, *Companies and Programmes (1968–1980)*, London: Macmillan, 1990

Plowright, Joan, *And That's Not All: The Memoirs of Joan Plowright*, London: Orion, 2002

Roth, Cecil, *History of the Jews in England* (third edition), Oxford: Oxford University Press, 1964

Sandford, Christopher, *McQueen*, London: HarperCollins, 2002

—— *McCartney*, London: Century,, 2006

Secombe, Harry, *Strawberries and Cheam*, London: Robson Books, 1996

—— *An Entertaining Life*, London: Robson Books, 2004

Sendall, Bernard, *Independent Television in Britain*, Vol. I, *Origins and Foundation (1946–1962)*, London: Macmillan, 1982

—— *Independent Television in Britain*, Vol. II, *Expansion and Change (1958–1968)*, London: Macmillan, 1983

Seymour-Ure, Colin, *The British Press and Broadcasting since 1945*, Oxford: Basil Blackwell, 1991

Shepherd, Don and Slatzer, Robert F., *Bing Crosby: The Hollow Man*, London: W.H. Allen, 1981

Sherrin, Ned, *Ned Sherrin: The Autobiography*, London: Little, Brown, 2005

Shulman, Milton, *The Least Worst Television in the World*, London: Barrie and Jenkins, 1973

Southall, Brian with Perry, Rupert, *Northern Songs*, London: Omnibus, 2006

Spitz, Bob, *The Beatles: The Biography*, London: Aurum Press, 2006

Teller, Judd, *The Jews: Biography of a People*, New York: Bantam Books, 1966

Tinker, Jack, *The Television Barons*, London: Quartet Books, 1980

Thomas, Howard, *With an Independent Air*, London: Weidenfeld and Nicolson, 1977

Took, Barry, *Laughter in the Air*, London: Robson Books, 1976

Tracey, Michael, *A Variety of Lives: A Biography of Sir Hugh Greene*, London: Bodley Head, 1983

Tunstall, Jeremy, *The Media in Britain*, London: Constable, 1983

Turner, Steve, *Cliff Richard: The Biography*, London: Lion Hudson, 2005

Walker, Alexander, *Hollywood, England*, Michael Joseph, London, 1974

—— *National Heroes: British Cinema in the Seventies and Eighties*, London: Harrap, 1985

Walker, John, *The Once and Future Film*, London: Methuen, 1985

—— *Halliwell's Film and Video Guide*, London: HarperCollins, 2006

Whale, John, *The Politics of the Media*, Glasgow: Fontana, 1977

Wheen, Francis, *Television: A History*, London: Century, 1985

White, Jerry, *Rothschild Buildings; Life in an East End Tenement Block, 1887–1920*, London: Routledge and Kegan Paul,1980

Whitehouse, Mary, *Whatever Happened to Sex?* Hove: Wayland, 1977

—— *A Most Dangerous Woman?* London: Lion, 1982

Williams, Raymond, *Communications*,
London: Chatto and Windus, 1966
Williams, Raymond and O'Connor, Alan,
Raymond Williams on Television, London:
Routledge, 1989
Wilson, A.E., *East End Entertainment*,
London: Arthur Barker, 1954
Wilson, H.H., *Pressure Group: The
Campaign for Commercial TV*, London:
Secker and Warburg, 1961
Winder, Robert, *Bloody Foreigners*, London:
Abacus, 2006

Wisdom, Norman (and Bernard Bale) *'Cos
I'm a Fool*, Derby: Breedon Books, 1996
Wyatt, Will, *The Fun Factory*, London:
Aurum Press, 2003
Young, Hugo with Silcock, Brian and
Dunn, Peter, *Journey to Tranquillity: A
History of Man's Assault on the Moon*,
London: Jonathan Cape, 1969
Ziegler, Philip, *Wilson: The Authorized Life*,
London: HarperCollins, 1995

Index